Out at Work

Cultural Politics

A series from the Social Text Collective

Kitty Krupat

Patrick McCreery

editors

A Cultural

Politics Book

for the Social

Text Collective

Out at Work

Building a

Gay–Labor

Alliance

Cultural Politics / Volume 17

University of Minnesota Press

Minneapolis ► London

Published by the University of Minnesota Press
111 Third Avenue South, Suite 290
Minneapolis, MN 55401-2520
http://www.upress.umn.edu

Library of Congress Cataloging-in-Publication Data

Out at work : building a gay-labor alliance / Kitty Krupat and Patrick McCreery, editors.
   p.   cm.—(Cultural politics ; v. 17)
   ISBN 0-8166-3740-7 (hc : acid-free paper)—ISBN 0-8166-3741-5 (pbk. : acid-free paper)
   1. Gays—Employment—United States. 2. Gay labor union members—United States—Political activity. 3. Gay liberation movement—United States. 4. Gay rights—United States. 5. Civil rights—United States. 6. Coming out (Sexual orientation)—United States. I. Krupat, Kitty. II. McCreery, Patrick. III. Cultural politics (Minneapolis, Minn.) ; v. 17.
   HD6285.5.U6 O878 2001
   331.88'086'640973—dc21
                                                                              00-010634
Printed in the United States of America on acid-free paper

The University of Minnesota is an equal-opportunity educator and employer.

11 10 09 08 07 06 05 04 03 02 01   10 9 8 7 6 5 4 3 2 1

Contents

Acknowledgments

We are in the habit of referring to *Out at Work* as a *project* because it developed from a series of events. The first occurred in 1997, when we saw the documentary film *Out at Work: Lesbians and Gay Men on the Job*. The film inspired us to think more about matters of class and social identity, especially how sexual identity translates into working-class struggle when rights are at stake. Our ideas about this evolved over time, and we have many people to thank for thinking, arguing, and working with us. The first of these are Kelly Anderson and Tami Gold, the producers of that first version of *Out at Work* and a sequel made later for HBO television. In their hands, the stories of five courageous individuals became a political story of power and beauty. Nat Keitt, Cheryl Summerville, Sandy Reily, Ron Woods, and Mark Anderson have been in our minds and hearts since we began the project. We are also grateful to the *Out at Work* audiences. The reception these films received made us realize that people are eager for honest and provocative discussions about sexual identity in the workplace. With that in mind, we organized a screening and symposium at New York University in November 1997. We would probably have stopped there were it not for Andrew Ross, director of NYU's American Studies program and someone we feel privileged to call a friend. He saw the potential for a book and pushed us to take up the political and intellectual debates that were implicit in the films. It is our good fortune to be students in a program that encourages projects like this one and our good luck, as well, to have the administrative support of Alyssa Hepburn. She has always been there for us.

It goes without saying that our contributors are the bedrock of this book. We cannot thank them enough. Sadly, one *Out at Work* contributor will not see the fruits of his labor. Van Alan Sheets, a devoted trade unionist and Pride at Work activist, died on October 21, 1999, after a long battle with AIDS. We hope this book is a fitting tribute to his memory.

Earlier versions of seven articles in this anthology—those by Kitty Krupat, Patrick McCreery, John J. Sweeney, Tami Gold, Amber Hollibaugh and Nikhil Pal Singh, Cathy J. Cohen, and the roundtable of labor leaders—first appeared in the winter 1999 issue of *Social Text*. We were enormously gratified by the interest and unstinting support of the entire *Social Text* collective. Toby Miller and Bruce Robbins, the editors when we began writing, always believed we could turn the project into a book. Monica Marcickiewicz was a great copy editor. Then, at Duke University Press, Kay Alexander and

Rachel Caref guided us through the mysteries of journal production. When we were ready to move on, Andrew, Bruce, and Toby opened the door for us at the University of Minnesota Press. Doug Armato, director of the press, has been a pleasure to work with, and we are immensely grateful to his associates for the assistance they provided. We owe special thanks to Gretchen Asmussen, Pieter Martin, and Linda Lincoln, our meticulous copy editor.

We presented early versions of our own essays at the 1998 Lavender Languages and Linguistics conference in Washington, D.C. We thank Professor William Leap of American University for that opportunity and for his very enthusiastic response to our final text. Faculty members and students from NYU and other universities have given us invaluable counsel. Lisa Duggan, one of our most thoughtful critics, was extraordinarily generous with her contacts. Several of the essayists in this anthology came to us through her. Phillip Brian Harper and Nikhil Pal Singh were two of our biggest boosters. George Yúdice, our program's director of graduate studies at the time we began this project, was the most patient of advisors, helping us fit the project into our academic lives. Carlos Ulises Decena, Lisa Duggan, Licia Fiol-Matta, Phillip Brian Harper, Paul Kariouk, Robin D. G. Kelley, William Leap, Steven Maynard, Nikhil Pal Singh, Danny Walkowitz, and the graduate students in Robin's research seminar read essays in this anthology and made valuable suggestions. Miriam Frank was among the first scholars to document the growth of gay activism in the labor movement. She has shared her research with us unsparingly, as well as her remarkable collection of buttons.

We could not have gotten off the ground without support from many colleagues in the labor movement. At the AFL-CIO, we thank Denise Mitchell, Joyce Moscato, Nadra Floyd, Mark Splain, and—above all—Bill Fletcher, who was a good friend and advisor throughout. The office of Linda Chavez-Thompson was our first port of call at the AFL-CIO, and staff writer Paul Gordon deserves thanks for his efforts. Among our colleagues in several unions, we thank in particular Michael Funke, a reporter for UAW's *Solidarity* magazine, and UNITE staffers Carrie Kim, Elba Liz, and former research director Desma Holcomb. Our comrades in GSOC-UAW (the Graduate Student Organizing Committee of NYU) have cheered us on. Of these we owe most to Julie Kushner—as dear to Kitty as any sister could be—and to our organizer, Lisa Jessup, who turned the other cheek when we missed a union meeting or two.

Many friends supported our efforts even when they didn't know it. Much of what we *feel* about our subject comes from treasured personal relationships. For Kitty, these include lifelong friendships with John Corigliano, Richard Pearlman, Bill Hoffman, and a newer one with Mark Adamo. Likewise, Robert Larew and Michael Lentz gave Pat not only their love and encouragement, but also a comfortable crash pad during many trips to Washington, D.C. Karen Ackerman, Bob Muehlenkamp, and their son, David, made their Takoma Park home a welcome oasis for Kitty. Mona Kreaden provided much-needed computer assistance and lots of encouragement, and Andrea McArdle went beyond the call of duty to help us with some legal research. We enjoyed hours of good conversation and wise advice from Bridget Brown, Erin Clune, Carlos Ulises Decena, Donette Francis, Paul Kariouk, Richard Koseff, David Paskin, Jerry Philogene, Milton Reverby, Ralph Rivera, and Mabel Wilson. And we should not forget the Dodgers—Jackie Robinson and Roy Campanella—whose affectionate ways and silly antics have given us so much pleasure.

The friendship we have found most important to this project is our own. We have learned a great deal from one another. In the process we have developed mutual respect and the basis for a lasting relationship—the sort that grows when two people struggle together over questions of principle and then work like hell to make them useful.

Our final and deepest debt is to our families. They have given us enduring love and support, both emotional and material. Kitty dedicates this book to the memory of her father, Paul Weiss, whose prodigious energy and passionate opinions were both irritating and inspiring, and to her mother, Magda, whose intelligence and grace continue to amaze. Pat dedicates this book to his father, Mel, who knows hard work from a lifetime of it, and to his mother, Mary, who understands that work and love take many forms.

Introduction

Patrick McCreery and Kitty Krupat

Those who came of age in the 1960s remember the street fighting in Chicago, when New Left radicals and counter-cultural hippies descended upon the 1968 Democratic convention. It was a moment of political passion that would not be seen again in the United States until December 1999, when protesters of every political stripe, from liberal to radical, effectively derailed the World Trade Organization summit on global trade. In Chicago, organized labor was safe and sound inside the Democratic Party convention hall. Thirty years later, in Seattle, labor was in the street, thirty thousand strong. Though uncounted, lesbian and gay union members were there, as they are everywhere.

In the name of workers and the environment—in the name of democracy, diversity, and inclusion—demonstrators in Seattle used tactics ranging from nonviolent protest and "town hall" meetings to trashing shops and banks. Public disagreements over these maneuvers were rare, and for one chaotic week, a disparate movement for social change seemed to find common ground. Activists longing for some political passion on the left and those imagining new movements for social change saw the uprising in Seattle as a triumph and a cause for hope.

The editors of *Out at Work* were working feverishly to meet publication deadlines just as all hell was breaking loose in Seattle. Wishing we were there, we took solace in the fact that Seattle might be something of an omen for the workers and movements who lie at the heart of this book. *Out at Work* is about advancing the workplace rights of lesbians, gay men, and other sexual minorities. We start from the belief that sexual rights can be pursued most effectively through a radical coalition between the labor and LGBT movements. Though we cannot know what will come in the aftermath of Seattle, the militance of trade unionists and the blending of political cultures that we saw there suggests the time for a gay–labor alliance is now. That said, we believe a lasting alliance can come about only if both movements reexamine priorities and practices and only if both movements consciously strive toward strategies of organizing that are bold, imaginative, and fully inclusive.

There have been signs for some time that activism is taking a turn in this direction. In the mid-1990s, organized labor began a comeback. Between 1997 and 1999, 1.5 million workers came into unions of the AFL-CIO through new organizing efforts.[1] Students in the antisweatshop movement have been staging sit-ins at numerous college campuses, winning agreements on fair labor standards not only for workers in Central America and Asia but, in some cases, also for workers on their own campuses. The impulse for direct action has been felt in the LGBT movement, as well.

Nowhere was this more apparent to us than at the New York City rally in October 1998 to protest the murder of Wyoming college student Matthew Shepard. Having announced the event just a few days before it occurred, the rally's ad hoc group of organizers expected only a few hundred protesters. When we arrived at the Plaza Hotel assembly point, there were more than five thousand people preparing to march. Police on foot and on motorcycles lined the streets, clearly agitated by the swelling crowd. Demonstrators were both angry and excited: angry at Shepard's murder and the NYPD's characteristically heavy-handed approach to "unlawful" gatherings; excited by the power in our numbers. Spontaneously, the crowd spilled into the middle of Fifth Avenue, stopping rush-hour traffic and frustrating police efforts to keep us on the crowded sidewalks. We were not among the ninety or so people who got arrested that night; instead we trudged home, weary but satisfied that we had helped make a big mess—a mini Seattle.

The Gay–Labor Alliance

Out at Work has been in the making for more than two years. Our ideas for the book evolved over a period of time, starting from the night we saw *Out at Work: Lesbians and Gay Men on the Job*, a film coproduced by Kelly Anderson and Tami Gold.[2] This film and its sequel, made for HBO television, follow a lesbian and three gay men who came out on their jobs and—in two cases—in their unions. When we conceived this book, we imagined it would be filled with coming-out stories, like those in the film. It has turned out very differently, however. While the issue of coming out is implicit in virtually every essay in this anthology, there is actually very little in the book that speaks directly to the topic. And while the anthology contains some deeply personal accounts, ultimately it focuses on a broad political issue: how to bring movements for gay and labor rights closer and into a long-lasting coalition.

The men and women in *Out at Work*—Nat Keitt, Cheryl Summerville (and her partner, Sandy Reily), Ron Woods, and Mark Anderson—are mentioned only occasionally in the essays that make up this volume. Yet they were the inspiration for our book. They represent a spectrum of the American workforce—a municipal librarian, a short-order cook, an autoworker, and a financial analyst. Their lives were profoundly changed by what they encountered in a homophobic society and a homophobic workplace—first the indignities and injustices they endured, then the struggles they embraced and sustained. Despite their differences, each one made us literally see that coming out is not just a declaration of personal freedom, but a class-conscious, political act. If that seems obvious in retrospect, at the time it was a discovery for us. It reinforced our belief that class and identity are not separate categories of human experience, but integrated in the ways we understand our economic and social positions in life.

Out at Work challenges political and intellectual debates that treat class and identity separately or argue their merits as opposing modes of social and political action. Our interest in these debates is more practical than theoretical, however. By exploring the connections between class and social identity, we hope to stimulate strategic thinking about how LGBT workers can participate effectively within and through a coalition of political movements and, more broadly, how these movements can make progress together.

Any collaboration between movements dedicated to advancing specific rights for specific groups faces practical difficulties. *Out at Work* brings LGBT and labor activists together with cultural analysts to consider how these difficulties might be overcome. We have asked them to address some basic questions: How would an effective gay–labor collaboration work? What would its goals be? What strategies would it employ to reach them? Is there a history from which both movements can learn? Our contributors uncover many of the obstacles and points of resistance to such a coalition. At the same time, they disarm many of the arguments for maintaining single-issue politics. As our contributors argue quite forcefully, the barriers to a gay–labor alliance are lowered significantly when we recognize that LGBT workers are represented in and by both movements. This plain fact makes a coalition not only possible, but essential to the development of both movements. Before a long-term and stable alliance can be envisioned, however, each movement will have to take stock.

For the LGBT movement, taking stock may require a profound transformation. Much younger and more fractured than organized labor, the LGBT movement is beginning to engage in a necessary project of self-criticism. Progressives in the movement rightly denounced the Human Rights Campaign (HRC), the nation's largest gay rights organization, when it endorsed Senator Alfonse D'Amato's 1998 bid for reelection. Conservatism and opportunism of this sort have alienated many activists and encouraged them to form alternative networks and coalitions. Activists are asking who owns their movement and whom it serves.

With the demise of Queer Nation and ACT-UP, the LGBT movement has been left without a recognizably radical wing. Its mainstream organizations have long imagined a monolithic gay community that is invariably white, educated, monogamous, gender normative, and middle-class. In *Out at Work*, several LGBT activists expose this vision for the fantasy it is. They remind us of what should be obvious: the majority of gays and lesbians are working-class people. Thus, the LGBT movement needs to rethink its constituency before it can effectively address the concerns of most LGBT communities.

For its part, the labor movement will also profit from a reassessment of its present and future membership. In the United States, where the right to organize is curtailed by antiunion legislation and corporate power, most workers—and thus most gays and lesbians—remain unorganized. Energized by new and progressive leadership, however, the labor movement is beginning to pick up lost ground. Inherently democratic in principle, unions are obliged to represent the rights and demands of all employees in a workplace. That makes unionization a powerful vehicle for gay rights.

If it is to grow, the labor movement must organize immigrant workers in low-paid, low-skill jobs. It must also reach out to service and professional workers and to women and people of color, who are close to a majority in the workforce. LGBT workers cut across all these lines. They are out there, unorganized, in the millions. The labor movement will find many organizers and leaders if it looks to the LGBT community. Pride at Work, a national coalition of LGBT union members and an AFL-CIO "constituency" group, can be revisioned as an organizing group.

We do not want to suggest that labor's interactions with gay members or gay organizations are always easy. Pride at Work, for example, was fully incorporated into the AFL-CIO in 1998, when it received a budget allocation, office space, and full-time staff. But as John Sweeney and other contributors to this book are quick to point out, LGBT union activists won these allocations only after years of lobbying and at least two resolutions recommending affiliation. Nor are gay–labor relations always constructive. Indeed, the trade unionists who appear in *Out at Work* are forthright in acknowledging that some unions routinely ignore the rights of gay and lesbian members and that many gay and lesbian workers are subject to blatant homophobia inside their own unions. Nevertheless, gay union members are making gains. Increasingly, they are winning domestic-partnership benefits. The most far-reaching agreement on this was announced on June 8, 2000, when the United Automobile Workers (UAW) won an agreement on same-sex partnership benefits in contracts covering 466,000 workers at DaimlerChrysler, Ford, and GM. At a minimum, sexual orientation is included in many union antidiscrimination clauses. But the term "sexual orientation" elides a diversity of identities and sexual practices that many unions and most workplaces neither acknowledge nor protect.

In *Out at Work*, Amber Hollibaugh argues for a vision of class struggle that recognizes difference as an enhancement of power. The labor movement will grow, she says, but only if it is a "home," where no one has to check her private life at the door. In such a place, Hollibaugh believes, coming out as gay or as a sex worker or as someone who is HIV-positive would not be a trial by fire, but an opportunity for new and creative forms of organizing.

If unions should organize LGBT workers, LGBT workers should make more determined efforts to unionize. Without institutional support, however, such efforts will remain limited. Unfortunately, many LGBT activists and organizations remain aloof from the union movement, distrustful and sometimes even disdainful, choosing instead a politics of assimilation that inhibits any radical analysis of class. For example, the two largest LGBT rights groups in the United States, HRC and the National Gay and Lesbian Task Force, have focused primarily on two issues: the rights of gays to marry and to serve in the military. In articulating what they suggest are the imperatives of gay and lesbian rights, they have conceded opportunities to examine the diverse ways that gay people make sense of their everyday lives.

To be effective in the long term, an LGBT–labor collaboration has to enlarge the ground for common struggle. The beginnings of a coalition already exist, but its parameters may be too confining. For the most part, LGBT organizations and the labor movement have forged alliances around one-shot legislative campaigns. While an alliance must pursue legislation, such efforts will continue to be limited unless both movements also envision broad and creative strategies for organizing. For both movements, this means welcoming workers in every public *and* private aspect of their lives. That includes sex in all its messy arrangements.

Out at Work and How It Grew

Before we say more about the contents of this book, it might be useful to backtrack a bit. We did not arrive at our purposes or conclusions easily. We offer some history of this book not to be indulgent, but because we think this history—which is at times quite personal—encapsulates some of the political questions and problems set forth in this anthology.

We met in 1995, as first-year graduate students in the American Studies program at New York University. Our backgrounds were very different. Kitty was a veteran of New Left social movements who went from there to the labor movement in the mid-1970s. She was returning to school after a twenty-two-year career as an organizer and union educator. Patrick was younger and interested in gay activism, but he had no labor experience at all. Our interests came together in 1997, when NYU graduate assistants formed a union and affiliated with the United Automobile Workers (UAW). We were among the first students active in the organizing campaign.

In January 1997, as the union drive at NYU was gathering steam, the film *Out at Work* premiered. We attended a screening at the Public Theater in New York City. We found ourselves in a large audience of activists, many of whom were both trade unionists and gay rights advocates. Producers Kelly Anderson and Tami Gold were detained for a good hour after the screening, answering questions and participating in debates about the issues raised in their film. Here, it seemed, was a rare public opportunity for dialogue between workers, labor leaders, and advocates for gay rights. There should be more of this, we thought, so we organized a symposium and screening of *Out at Work* at NYU. We invited three workers who appeared in the film: Cheryl Summerville, a lesbian who had been fired from a Cracker Barrel restaurant in Georgia, her partner, Sandy Reily, and Nat Keitt, a municipal librarian active in his union's gay and lesbian caucus.

The day before the symposium, Cheryl, Sandy, and their three-year-old daughter, Devon, piled into a minivan and started the long drive from Georgia. They made it to New Jersey by nightfall and set out early the next morning for Manhattan. Somewhere between the Holland Tunnel and Greenwich Village, they called to say they were hopelessly lost. So we went ahead without them. As the final film credits were rolling and the lights came up, they appeared in the doorway. Nat had never met any of the others featured in the film, and he rushed to embrace Cheryl and Sandy. The audience went wild. Cheering and crying, they gave these workers a ten-minute ovation.

At that precise moment, we were emotionally caught up. Later, we began to think about the meanings of this exchange between two working-class lesbians and an audience in a university hall. This was more than a rousing cheer for bewildered out-of-towners. It was an act of solidarity—of respect and recognition. For labor and gay rights activists in the audience, Cheryl and Sandy (and Nat, too) were frontline heroes. For academics who might engage in debates about identity politics and class, here were people in whose lives identity and class were virtually one and the same. From that point on, our ideas about class and social identity began to unravel and reform.

```
┌──────────────────────────────────────────────────────────────────────────────────┐
│                          State of Georgia                    FORM # 144            │
│   (seal)      Department of Labor — Employment Security Agency                      │
│                                                                                    │
│                           SEPARATION NOTICE                                        │
│                                                                                    │
│  1. Employee's Name   CheryL SummeRville        2. S.S. No. 259-19-3377            │
│     a. State any other name(s) under which employee worked.   Above                │
│  3. Period of Last Employment: From   6-18-90           To   2-16-91               │
│  4. REASON FOR SEPARATION:                                                         │
│     a. LACK OF WORK  ☐                                                             │
│     b. If for other than lack of work, state fully and clearly the circumstances   │
│        of the separation:  This employee                                           │
│        is being terminated due to Violation of Company Policy. The                 │
│        employee is Gay.                                                            │
│                                                                                    │
│  5. Employee received:  ☐ Wages in Lieu of Notice  ☐ Separation Pay  ☐ Vacation Pay│
│     In the amount of $_____ for period from _____ to _____          │
└──────────────────────────────────────────────────────────────────────────────────┘
```

5. Employee received: ☐ Wages in Lieu of Notice ☐ Separation Pay ☐ Vacation Pay

In the amount of $_____ for period from _____ to _____

Employer's Name CRACKER BARREL OLD COUNTRY STORE

Address HARTMANN DRIVE, P. O. BOX 787
(Street or RFD)

City LEBANON State TN ZIP Code 37087

Employer's Telephone No. 615 444-5533
(Area Code) (Number)

Ga. E.S.A. Account Number 083772-0
(Number shown on State Quarterly Tax and Wage Report, Form ESA-4.)

I CERTIFY that the above worker has been separated from work and the information furnished hereon is true and correct. This report has been handed to or mailed to the worker.

Maurice Watson / Maurice Watson
Signature of Official or Employee of the Employer who has first-hand knowledge of the separation

General Manager
Title of Person Signing

2-16-91
Date Completed and Released to Employee

NOTICE TO EMPLOYER
At the time of separation, you are required by the Employment Security Law, OCGA Section 34-8-170, to provide the employee with this document, properly executed, giving the reasons for separation. If you subsequently receive a request for the same information on an ESA-403FF or an ESA-419, you may attach a copy of this form (ESA-800) as a part of your response.

NOTICE TO EMPLOYEE
OCGA SECTION 34-8-170, OF THE EMPLOYMENT SECURITY LAW REQUIRES THAT YOU TAKE THIS NOTICE TO THE EMPLOYMENT SECURITY CLAIMS CENTER IF YOU FILE A CLAIM FOR UNEMPLOYMENT INSURANCE BENEFITS.

SEE REVERSE SIDE FOR ADDITIONAL INFORMATION.

ESA-800 (R-11/82)

The State of Georgia makes it official: Cheryl Summerville's notice of termination by Cracker Barrel, February 16, 1991. This document is reprinted as it appeared in *Out at Work: America Undercover*, a documentary produced for HBO TV by ANDERSONGOLD Films. Reprinted with permission from ANDERSONGOLD Films.

It seemed possible, for example, to conceive of a gay doctor and a lesbian police officer bound by a common class interest. In the thirty-nine states where employers may legally fire workers simply because they are known or thought to be gay, these workers would be equally vulnerable, despite traditional class distinctions such as disparities in income and education. In this instance, the workplace itself represents a common ground for struggle, a place where working people can translate traditional notions of class solidarity into new struggles for rights and recognition. So, we stopped talking about the *intersections* between class and social identity and started thinking about social identity as *fundamental* to class, and we began to think about the potential of an alliance between the labor and LGBT movements.

Believing we were clear on the class-identity connection, we felt ready to outline a book on lesbian and gay rights in the workplace. Very soon, however, our own intellectual practices betrayed our best intentions. Here's how we decided to work: Krupat, the trade unionist, would deal with the labor side; McCreery, the gay activist, would handle the sex part. Over dinner one evening, we got into a heated discussion about the question of sexual deviance. Krupat reeled off the union line: "The principle of equal rights for all is a class bond between workers. It applies, whatever your sexual orientation. What on earth does 'deviance' have to do with it?" Everything, McCreery insisted. "Does 'equal rights for all' include sex workers, fetishists, or men who have sex in parks? 'Deviance' is not so much about sexual orientation as it is about sexual practices that 'normal' people don't like."

For days thereafter, we argued about how heteronormativity operates in the workplace to create and divide class alliances. It soon became apparent that we were arguing from opposite perspectives on class and identity politics. We had come of age in different political and intellectual movements, and we were stuck in the orthodoxies of our own traditions—exactly what we wished to avoid. Quite consciously, we abandoned the lines of authority in our original work plan and parceled out the jobs almost randomly. As we crossed the great divide between trade unionist and gay activist, we first began to understand the issues and problems we were trying to explore.

This discussion about deviance was not our only moment of ambivalence or anxiety. Both of us are dedicated unionists now, and we are both advocates for gay rights. It has not been easy to subject our own beloved movements to scrutiny and criticism. A necessary job has been made easier by a group of contributors whose objectives are uniformly and wholly constructive. Where there seemed to be a synergy between essays, we have grouped them together. Otherwise, we have tried to provide a little variety in content and style.

Out at Work begins with a historical essay by Kitty Krupat that provides a context within which the gay–labor coalition can be conceived. Krupat traces the continuities between New Left social movements and the contemporary labor movement. Identity-based organizing has not only sustained the labor movement but transformed it in dramatic ways. First women and people of color, then lesbians and gays, put social identity on the bargaining table in the form of demands that reflected private as well as public concerns. While they were winning rights, these workers were also transforming the culture of organizing.

Following Krupat's essay, John Sweeney, president of the AFL-CIO, outlines an organizing agenda that defines gay rights as fundamental workers' rights. We are immensely proud that this agenda appeared for the first time in a collection of essays we edited for the winter 1999 issue of *Social Text*. It is reprinted here.

Patrick McCreery examines the proposed federal Employment Non-Discrimination Act (ENDA). In its latest formulation, ENDA would protect workers from discrimination on the basis of sexual orientation, but it would not necessarily protect workers whom heteronormative culture considers deviant in gender or sexual terms. In his essay, McCreery argues that ENDA would do little to challenge heteronormative mores or conservative family values that dominate the workplace, many unions, and most mainstream LGBT organizations.

Cathy Cohen calls out the LGBT movement for making unholy alliances with corporations like Coors and Nike, who infamously exploit workers. She challenges the movement to confront elitism and inequalities, to acknowledge common cause with other social movements, and to wage its struggles at the intersections of class, race, and gender. Nikhil Singh and Amber Hollibaugh suggest that the labor movement can profit from an examination of queer political strategies, looking to the margins of our society to find the roots of common oppression and the issues around which marginalized people—particularly sexual minorities—can organize.

Andrew Ross describes one instance in which queer organizing strategies have inflected traditional union practices. Workers at Barneys department store, who are members of UNITE (the garment workers' union), staged a drag fashion show outside the chic emporium. A crowd of UNITE members—toilers in the decidedly unglamorous garment factories of Chinatown and Seventh Avenue—stood in the street, cheering the queers on.

Gender-bending does not always get applause, however. Riki Anne Wilchins makes clear that gender queers typically receive little support in the workplace. Discrimination on the basis of gender occurs everywhere, she argues, not least within the agendas of many mainstream gay rights organizations.

Heidi Kooy chronicles a union campaign among strippers in San Francisco's Lusty Lady Theater. These workers won their campaign but say the labor movement remains skeptical about using queer organizing tactics to invigorate other, more traditional union drives. Teresa Conrow says that both the labor and LGBT movements have to make conscious efforts to understand the full extent of relationships between the various identities workers themselves assume or privilege at different times and in different settings.

Tami Gold offers a history of the *Out at Work* films, weaving into the narrative memories of her own experiences in and out on the job. In her essay, Tamara Jones shows how a gay and lesbian caucus has flourished even in the heart of a union bureaucracy. In "Homophobia, Labor's Last Frontier?" a group of union leaders discusses daily observations of class contradictions: worker solidarity in the midst of rampant homophobia. They make concrete suggestions for organizing initiatives, education programs, and community alliances that would call attention to the needs and concerns of gay and lesbian workers.

Jeff Truesdell examines the corporate side, showing how Walt Disney's historically antiunion company has evolved over time into the contemporary benefactor of Gay Days at its Florida theme park. This volume concludes with a forum: "Imagining the Gay–Labor Alliance." Each of four essayists—Urvashi Vaid, Kent Wong, Desma Holcomb, and Representative Barney Frank—offers his or her vision for the labor–LGBT alliance. In the afterword, Lisa Duggan sums it all up and manages to provide the reader with some well-earned comic relief.

A Postscript

Not long ago, we had a conversation with a colleague in the antisweatshop movement. He was describing a meeting between American students and workers in a Central American garment factory. "One kid asks them if gays and lesbians are harassed in these sweatshops. How can you ask that question when workers don't even have a living wage?" Three years ago, Pat would have written this guy off. Today, he would answer the question and engage in a friendly argument. On the other hand, Kitty would have agreed with our colleague three years ago. Today it is hard for her to imagine how more money might compensate a worker for the loss of personhood. We end on this redemptive note, hoping it will carry the message of *Out at Work*.

Notes

1. The figures on new union members were supplied by Mark Splain of the AFL-CIO organizing department. He noted the unfortunate fact that new organization has not

meant a net growth in union membership, which continues to be offset by plant shutdowns, layoffs, and retirements.

2. A second version of this film, *Out at Work: America Undercover,* was made for HBO television and premiered in January 1999. Mark Anderson appeared only in this second version; Nat Keitt appeared only in the first.

Out of Labor's Dark Age:
Sexual Politics Comes to the Workplace

Kitty Krupat

In October 1995, John Sweeney was elected to head the nation's labor federation. He had come to office in a coup d'état of sorts, engineered from within the AFL-CIO by an oppositionist cadre bent on ousting the administration of Lane Kirkland.[1] His victory was widely regarded as a repudiation of forty years of conservative leadership under Kirkland and his predecessor, George Meany. To mark the first anniversary of this event, a group of historians organized a labor teach-in at Columbia University in October 1996. It drew nearly two thousand participants, a mixed crowd of leftist intellectuals and progressive trade unionists, coming together in a spirit of celebration and rapprochement. The teach-in was explicitly future-oriented, but implicitly it was also an homage to an earlier moment in labor history, when factory workers and intellectual workers might meet at a union hall or on a picket line.

This is the period Michael Denning has called the "Age of the CIO." Breaking away from the American Federation of Labor, the Congress of Industrial Organizations undertook mass industrial organizing campaigns in the 1930s and 1940s that brought many thousands of immigrant workers, people of color, and women into unions. Along with auto workers and meat packers came professionals and semiprofessionals in the burgeoning communications industries, such as film and radio. This intellectual and social mix was stirred not only by an activist cadre of socialists and communists within the CIO, but also by an alliance of intellectuals and cultural workers Denning defines as a cultural front.[2] In this atmosphere, a concept of social unionism developed that was still an ideal for many who joined the labor teach-in at Columbia. Distanced from labor in the Meany-Kirkland era, they now wished to reassert an alliance between labor and intellectuals. Timely as well as visionary, the Columbia Teach-In gave voice to these ambitions.

The teach-in has justly earned its referential status. That said, it was not without its contradictions or its moments of historical amnesia. On opening night, an array of labor luminaries and academic celebrities sat front and center on the stage. Behind them, a group of clerical workers from Barnard College sat mutely, like so many actors in a *tableau vivant*. Members of the

1

KITTY KRUPAT

United Automobile Workers union, they had just won a bitter six-month strike against the college, a Columbia University affiliate. Midway through the proceedings, the philosopher Richard Rorty rose to deliver a stinging critique of New Left movements in the 1960s and 1970s. The failures of identity politics in this period, he maintained, were largely responsible for a vitiated left in the following decades.[3] Rorty's remarks drew an audible hiss from some members of the audience. Silently, I took offense myself. In the presence of these Barnard workers, Rorty's remarks seemed incongruous, even rude.

In 1974, fresh from the antiwar movement, I had joined the organizing staff of District 65.[4] The Barnard workers—a markedly diverse group, with women and people of color in the majority and a significant number of openly gay members—were already there. They had organized into District 65 in 1973, at the height of New Left social activism. They were not an anomaly but among thousands of office and professional workers in both public and private sectors—mainly women and people of color—who were unionizing on the heels of identity-based political movements. Many new union leaders, who emerged from these organizing campaigns, had been through basic training in New Left political movements. Though we didn't theorize it this way, we apprehended class as a category that had been reconfigured by identity politics of the '60s and '70s. From our shop-floor perspective, class appeared much as labor historian Daniel Walkowitz has argued that it is: an amalgam of identities, including race and gender along with economic position.[5]

I have begun with recollections of the Columbia Teach-In because it was among the first public forums for a discussion about American labor in the millennium. Since then, public intellectuals—both inside and outside the labor movement—have continued the discussion.[6] In the process, a new discourse of pro-unionism has emerged and settled around a narrative whose historical analogues are the Dark Ages and the Renaissance. The narrative usually goes something like this:

> Organized labor, awakening from its quarter-century "era of stagnation" finds itself, Rip Van Winkle–like, in a world transformed. While labor slept. . . .[7]

This example is taken from "Labor's Day: The Challenge Ahead," an important essay by Jeremy Brecher and Tim Costello, published—along with seven responses—in a September 1998 issue of *Nation*. For good reasons, Brecher and Costello chose to discuss the industrial sector and the challenges John Sweeney will face as labor struggles to rebuild its traditional base in the

2

new century. In that circumstance, the deep-sleep metaphor works. However, the service sector, with its very diverse workforce, falls outside the scope of their essay. Yet that is where most Americans are employed and where unions have organized, even in the doldrums of a quarter century. Unintentionally perhaps, service workers in all their identities are left out when the authors talk about a "reconfigured working class." They map this new working class along geographical and economic lines. Race is factored in tangentially; gender and sexuality are virtually absent from their argument.[8]

Social identity is present to some extent in most public debate about the future of organized labor, but it is easily sidelined, or muted. This can happen in the most progressive analysis. I couldn't help noticing it, for example, in a collection of essays I otherwise admire. In the introduction to *A New Labor Movement for a New Century*, editor Gregory Mantsios asks the big question: "Why did a labor movement that was so vibrant, massive and capable of bringing about fundamental change in the 1930s and 1940s become virtually moribund in the 1980s and 1990s?"[9] Twenty-one commentators in this very excellent volume provide thoughtful answers to that question and offer prescriptions for a healthy labor movement in the twenty-first century. Four essays, focusing specifically on women and people of color, are grouped under the heading, "Diversity and Inclusion." The numbers are okay, but the articles are segregated in a way that suggests "diversity and inclusion" are distinct from the larger discussion of organizing strategies, union democracy, and political action. More to the point, of the four essays on diversity, only one—"Getting Serious about Inclusion," by José La Luz and Paula Finn—suggests that social identity is a component of class.[10] And, despite a generous sprinkling of comments on racism and sexism throughout the anthology, not one essay even refers to homophobia or to sexual orientation as a factor in workplace struggle.

Current labor critique is generous in spirit, compared to the relentless negativity of most labor reporting in previous decades. However, to the extent this critique glosses over questions of social identity, it tends to distort both the history and the meaning of John Sweeney's victory. It obscures the steady development of an identity-based class formation that I believe *created* the political space for labor reform in the first place. My argument rests on two interrelated points. First, while the institutional labor movement was moving rightward in the 1950s—and while it was in a period of drastic decline—workers themselves were laying the basis for progressive change in the 1990s. Seen in this light, the ouster of an old-guard leadership was not a mutiny engineered by a few union presidents at an AFL-CIO convention, but an inevitable response to pressures from below. Second, identity-driven campaigns beginning in the late 1960s and continuing through the next two decades of labor's "dark age" were reshaping our conception of class struggle.[11] I hope to add something by a third claim: the beginnings of a gay and lesbian workers' movement can be traced through emerging forms of class struggle in this period.

If sexual identity is rarely defined as a component of class, it is brought into clear view by the documentary, *Out at Work: Lesbians and Gay Men on the Job*.[12] This film, by Tami Gold and Kelly Anderson, follows three workers—two of them union members—who come out on their jobs and become leaders in the struggle for sexual rights and representation in the workplace. The class consciousness of their position is underscored by the nature of their demands: not simply issues of principle, but economic rights as well—rights to job security and equality of benefits, among other things. Here, then, is a clear case in point, not just for the constitutive relationship between class and social identity, but also for the argument that social identity can be, and often is, the axis of class struggle. In this sense, it provides the inspiration for a revisionist history of working-class formation.

In his book, *The Origins of Postmodernity*, Perry Anderson makes an almost offhand remark that sums up the context for a decline-and-fall narrative of labor since the 1950s. With the onset of cold war, Anderson observes, "the labour movement was neutered and the left hounded."[13] His use of the term *neutered* is of some interest, suggesting, as it does, that "big labor" was emasculated. As I hope to show later in this essay, the masculinity of labor *was* compromised, but to more productive purposes than Anderson envisions. His point, here, is that conservative political forces and growing corporate power in the cold war years conspired to undermine organized labor. Of that there is no doubt, and this idea is the bedrock upon which most accounts of recent labor history rest.

My attempt to reframe conventional accounts is not intended to dispute fundamental verities. Nor do I wish to downplay the importance of a change in institutional leadership. That cannot be underestimated. This essay was completed in December 1999, just days after John Sweeney led 30,000 trade unionists through the streets of Seattle to protest antiworker policies of the World Trade Organization. In the old AFL-CIO, this thrilling act of political defiance would have been unthinkable. The Sweeney administration has defined a progressive agenda for labor that has already borne fruit in some legislative gains, including an increase in the federal minimum wage. New organizing campaigns, which increasingly involve students and youth groups, have brought 1.5 million new members to the AFL-CIO in the three-year period between 1997 and 1999.[14] In full recognition of all that has been accomplished, I nevertheless offer a ground-floor perspective on the new labor order, ushered in by John Sweeney and his administration. Mine is a counternarrative, or revisionist history, that foregrounds a wave of organizing and new class formation. Looking at our history this way suggests two things: that the "dark ages" of labor's decline were not so dark and that the "renaissance," heralded in 1995, was in the making decades earlier.

The Narrative of Decline

Labor's right to organize, guaranteed under the National Labor Relations Act (NLRA) of 1937, was sharply curtailed by restrictive provisions of the Taft-Hartley Act, passed in 1947. Bitterly opposed by organized labor from its inception, Taft-Hartley has never been overturned, nor has labor achieved ameliorating labor law reform. Throughout the Reagan-Bush era, new organizing was stymied by a series of probusiness changes in the NLRA, virtually transforming pro-union legislation into an instrument of corporate power. This combination of factors—coupled with deindustrialization and the flight of jobs to global markets—accounts for labor's sharp decline in the past forty years. In some respects, however, labor contributed to its own undoing. The decline-and-fall view of recent labor history relies heavily upon labor's "sins," starting with its turn from social to business unionism.

Class was the matrix of solidarity in CIO social unionism, the rubric that united working men and women of all races and social positions. At its most visionary, social unionism can be described as a culture of organizing: militant in its class-consciousness; "holistic" in its attention to education and leisure activities;[15] ideological in its stance on a range of social justice issues, from civil rights to war and peace. One of social unionism's more utopian aims was the development of rank-and-file democracy and leadership. Ideally, rank-and-file democracy would lead to full representation on the basis of race, ethnicity, and gender. But this principle was honored in the breach more often than not. Though African Americans and women made strides during the Age of the CIO, they continued to be underrepresented in the union movement, both in membership numbers and leadership positions.[16]

By the end of World War II, social unionism was badly compromised. Organized labor had made its greatest gains during the New Deal administration of Franklin Roosevelt, but in this period it had also set a precedent for compromise. Linked to the Popular Front alliance by strong antifascist sentiment,[17] the CIO joined forces with the administration, entering into a wartime compact with government and business. Labor had a seat on the tripartite War Labor Board (WLB), for example. Often a reluctant partner, labor nevertheless helped to establish WLB policies that were adamantly opposed by its own constituency. These included wage restrictions and a "no-strike" pledge, fiercely resisted by wildcat strikers in auto, steel, and other industries.[18] If the cause of antifascism could be served by this form of cooperation—and if, in the bargain, labor might achieve favorable conditions for organizing—it would also lay the basis for concession bargaining and for a long-term marriage of convenience between labor and the Democratic Party.

The anti-red crusade that crippled the labor left also had its origins in the New Deal period. The House Committee on Un-American Activities (HUAC), headed by Martin Dies, held its first hearings in 1938, an ominous beginning to the witch hunt that would culminate in anticommunist affidavits, required of union leaders under provisions of Taft-Hartley. Persecuted from the outside, CIO unions battled internally. Communists and fellow travelers were purged. Between 1948 and 1950, eleven unions and a million members were drummed out of the CIO.[19] When the AFL and CIO merged in 1955, the labor movement had already begun its rightward turn.[20]

Despite the ravages of red-baiting—despite the increasing power of corporations—labor was still in a relatively strong position when George Meany was elected to head the new federation in 1955. The AFL-CIO had good reason to be confident: America's postwar industrial economy was booming. With basic industry virtually organized by the late 1940s, total union membership reached an all-time high of 37 percent in 1953.[21] Attention shifted away from organizing the unorganized toward increasing benefits for an already established membership and strengthening the existing base of labor power. Not in all unions, but on a fairly general scale, business unionism—a top-down, corporate-style of union practice—replaced social unionism. The hallmark of business unionism was bureaucratization and professionalism, with attorneys and administrators negotiating contracts and managing sophisticated benefit plans. In this model of unionism, members became, in effect, clients. Vital energies of rank-and-file activism were sapped in the process.

Following the lead of successive administrations from Eisenhower onward, the AFL-CIO assimilated into the cold war apparatus. After the Cuban revolution of 1959, for example, the federation established the American Institute for Free Labor Development (AIFLD). An affiliate of the AFL-CIO International Affairs Department, AIFLD was created to train and support anticommunist unions in Latin America. Though by 1980 AIFLD's board was composed entirely of union officials, its founding board had included executives of United Fruit, Pan American Airlines, and the W. R. Grace Company.[22] Though many unions within the federation and thousands of individual union members were playing an exceptional role in the advancement of civil rights—and later in the antiwar and feminist movements—the federation itself was drifting into the middle ground, opting for neutrality on controversial domestic issues, such as abortion rights, and toeing the administration line on foreign policy, supporting the war in Vietnam even when the nation as a whole was divided on the question.

All along the way of this history, the industrial base of America was shrinking. Often the last hired, women and people of color were among the first factory workers to lose their jobs. Unprepared for this eventuality, the labor movement was slow to react. Continuing to place its faith in the Democratic Party, the federation spent millions on electoral campaigns. But in 1980, some member unions—including the Teamsters and the air traffic controllers union (PATCO)—were staunch supporters of Ronald Reagan. In 1981, less than a year after his election, Reagan betrayed his labor allies and fired more than 11,000 striking air traffic controllers. The labor movement suffered a particularly humiliating defeat. To complicate matters, unions were coming under ideological attack from both the right and the left. If the reactionary right measured unionism on a scale of socialist evils, the left took organized labor to task for accommodationist party politics, its support of U.S. foreign policy and neoliberal economics, as well as for concession bargaining at home. Within the ranks of organized labor itself, many union members and leaders shared this left critique.

Throughout the 1980s and 1990s, union membership continued its steady decline. In an increasingly right-wing political environment, corporations had had the upper hand for quite some time and seemed to be running roughshod over unions. The percentage of organized workers had dropped to about 10 percent of the private sector when John Sweeney was elected to head the labor federation in 1995.[23] In these circumstances, the ouster of an old-guard leadership was celebrated by union members and labor advocates across the country. The renaissance was at hand.

The boilerplate of many popular accounts, this truncated history is true enough. But it is a flat account. Reading between the lines, we get a fuller picture. Something was actually going on during the putative "dark age" of labor's decline. Indeed, a renaissance of sorts was in the making. To offer but one stunning example: in 1987, home health-care workers in Los Angeles began an eleven-year struggle to gain representation through the Service Employees International Union. That struggle came to victory in February 1999, when 74,000 workers achieved what *The New York Times* described as labor's biggest win since 1937.[24] No doubt, victory in this long union struggle was facilitated in its final phase by the emergence of a new and progressive labor leadership in the mid-1990s. But the important point here is that this victory was the fruit of pioneering efforts in the service sector that had begun more than two decades before.

Rethinking the Renaissance

In the 1960s, women and people of color—office workers, professionals, and paraprofessionals in both the public and private sectors—began to unionize in significant numbers for the first time.[25] As Stanley Aronowitz points out, in the public sector alone, four million workers organized between 1959 and 1980.[26] Cultural workers were organizing alongside service employees and professionals. Writers and editors, journalists, graphic designers and museum workers, teachers and graduate students were adding their voices to an emergent class struggle, in some ways reminiscent of the Age of the CIO.[27] Though it is tempting to emphasize the grassroots nature of this groundswell in unionization, the truth is some unions spent huge sums to support white-collar organizing efforts. If a drive failed—and many did—these unions would never recoup a cent in dues income.[28]

Growth in white-collar sectors was never enough to offset losses in the industrial sector. Nevertheless it brought new issues and new forms of organization into view. The language of class had already changed. No longer the fundamental distinction between workers and owners, class was also defined by education and skill, workplace hierarchies, taste, and lifestyle. If many white-collar and professional workers had been raised in working-class families and neighborhoods, they now identified themselves as middle-class.[29] Yet, to the extent they shared workplace conditions and concerns, to the extent they occupied a common position in the power relations between labor and management, they were also working-class. While workplace inequities fueled their ambitions, the source of their solidarity often lay in the particularities of social identity rather than economic position. What emerges from these contradictions is a picture of class as a multiple identity, both complex and ambiguous. I maintain that the ambiguities inherent in this class conception are productive, for they allow workers to struggle for rights and representation on many fronts simultaneously and to recognize profound connections between the politics of identity and the universality of class.

Affinities of race, gender, and sexuality have always been points of solidarity among workers. What distinguishes this period, however, is how these affinities were articulated as fundamental trade union principles. New union members put their particular concerns on the bargaining table for the first time. These concerns had everything to do with identity politics: gender-based pay equity, comparable worth, child care, affirmative action, domestic-partner benefits, and expanded protections against discrimination. Workers introduced challenging ideas about democratic trade unionism, demanding representation at every level of union structure for women, people of color, differing age groups, and eventually sexual orientations. Negotiating for labor-management committees on issues such as health and safety, affirmative action, and child care, union members began to formulate a notion of worker involvement in policy making at a higher level than traditional collective bargaining frameworks had allowed. For example, the Harvard Union of Clerical and Technical Workers (HUCTW)—a union led by women—established an unorthodox (and still controversial) form of collective bargaining. Rather than assuming an adversarial position in bargaining, HUCTW emphasized consciousness-raising through discussions between university administrators and clerical workers. The first union contract between HUCTW and Harvard included recognition in principle of the role support staff should play in University governance.[30]

This drive toward empowerment was a significant factor in bringing sexual identity into the workplace. Nevertheless, in the early years of white-collar organizing, questions of race and gender were paramount and sexuality was low on the order of priorities. Homophobia remained largely unexplored, despite preoccupations with other forms of social injustice. But in a disciplined union movement—by which I mean, quite simply, a movement schooled in the dialectic of right and wrong—homophobia could be presented and examined as a social injustice along with racism and sexism. If only grudgingly, most committed unionists would at least stand by the old maxim: "An injury to one is an injury to all."[31] In an identity-conscious milieu, gay workers could begin to test this principle. If nothing else, the atmosphere was conducive to a new struggle for representation. Even if they were not "out" in the political sense, many gay workers in the culture industries were more comfortably assimilated in their workplaces than gay workers in other industries. If straight, unmarried couples and single parents could demand equality of union benefits, gay and lesbian workers might risk coming out of the closet to demand the same, starting with explicit protections against discrimination.

At first blush, the *Village Voice* is not a typical example of the unionized workplace. But in fact, the *Voice* is representative of an influential sector of organized professionals and cultural workers who have helped to define the current culture of organizing.[32] The *Voice* was founded in 1955 by a trio of "Beat Generation" devotees, including Norman Mailer. They conceived of the *Voice* as a neighborhood newspaper, a venue for writers and artists who

Employees of the *Village Voice* picket outside the shop for recognition of their union in 1977. Photograph courtesy of Robert F. Wagner Labor Archives, New York University, District 65/UAW collection.

congregated in Greenwich Village. In the next twenty-one years, the paper would go through several changes of ownership and management. Through it all, the *Voice* retained something of its "alternative" flavor. In the mid-1970s, it was still a polymorphous workplace, where a nine-to-five ad-taker one day could be a reporter the next; where a former *New York Times* book reviewer, Eliot Fremont-Smith, wrote stately literary prose while Jill Johnston, an open lesbian, talked about the ups and downs of her love life in a weekly column on dance.

Though faithful in some ways to its Bohemian traditions, the *Voice* was nevertheless moving perceptibly toward the commercial mainstream and was a very profitable national enterprise by the time Rupert Murdoch bought it in 1977.[33] When the sale was announced, the *Voice* workers went into a panic. Fearing that Murdoch would sweep the place clean in an effort to turn their paper into another of his commercial tabloids, they formed a wall-to-wall union over the weekend and presented themselves to District 65 on Sunday evening. I was assigned by the union to be their organizer. After an election in the spring of '77, their union was certified by the National Labor Relations Board, and several months later, they began negotiations for a first contract. Early on, *Voice* publisher William Ryan committed to affirmative action goals, mandating 10 percent minority representation in every department of the newspaper. Employees sought and won an affirmative action committee to monitor progress. In many other ways, the first *Voice* contract was revolutionary. Besides providing benefits for freelance writers—unheard of in standard newspaper contracts—the first agreement also contained a broad "Equal Rights" provision that laid the basis for redefining family to include same-sex relationships. At the time of these first negotiations, District 65's health plan was already covering unmarried straight couples as a matter of practice. Gay and lesbian couples were formally included through contract-renewal talks at the *Voice* in 1982. Jeff Weinstein, an openly gay staff writer, was a member of the negotiating committee. Backed by his straight colleagues, he bargained hard and won, despite the employer's determined defense: "We will not go beyond what the law requires." In the end, they did, and it was management's attorney, Bertrand Pogrebin, who coined the phrase "spousal equivalents" to include gay and lesbian couples for the first time in the District 65 Security Plan, as well as in the union's bereavement clause.[34]

The *Village Voice* example leads to an interesting comparison. Through a merger of District 65 and the UAW, *Voice* employees were represented by

Rupert Murdoch, owner of the *New York Post*, was the target of demonstrations during negotiations for a first contract at *Village Voice*. Leading the pack, Jack Newfield (left) and Nat Hentoff (right). Organizer Kitty Krupat is out front at the barricades. Photograph courtesy of Robert F. Wagner Labor Archives, New York University, District 65/UAW collection.

the same union that demanded protections for gay autoworkers in 1996 contract talks with Chrysler. Among the last issues to be resolved, discussions on this demand went all the way to Chrysler's CEO, Bob Eaton. The late Jack Laskowksi, a UAW vice president, described this top-level meeting. There were two unresolved economic issues. Union President Stephen Yokich put them on the table, then turned to Laskowski and asked, "Is there anything else?" Laskowski tacked on the gay rights demand. Eaton wouldn't hear of it. With all other points resolved, gay rights became a potential strike issue. UAW dropped it, believing the union could not mount a national strike over gay rights.[35] I think that is probably true. As an outsider and in hindsight, I am uneasy about questioning the wisdom of UAW leaders at that critical moment. Nevertheless, at the time, I had a lingering doubt. Did the union abandon this demand too readily? Short of a strike, were there other forms of public pressure that could have been applied?

At the point of decision, a rancorous argument took place between union delegate Ron Woods—a lone, gay holdout for the demand—and other UAW members. The question of how much crass homophobia figured in this hostile exchange is wide open. On the surface, however, it played out as a debate between class and identity politics. In the male-intensive auto industry, with its culture of masculinity, a muscular vision of working-class solidarity prevailed. The "weaker" claims of social identity were abandoned. In this connection, the distinction that Laskowski made between economic and noneconomic issues is of interest. For Chrysler (and for straight employees), the gay rights demand was not perceived as an economic issue— not a cost factor, like wage increases or fringe benefits. But for lesbian and gay workers who face discrimination in hiring and promotional opportunities, protections against discrimination have everything to do with economic security.

While no one knows what percentage of auto workers are gay and lesbian, I think it's safe to say only a small minority of them are out at work. Thus the voices of gays and lesbians were muted in this class-identity debate and were generally absent from the culture of organizing in this and other industrial sectors.[36] At the *Voice*, by comparison, the union dropped a number of its demands in the course of bargaining, but it was unthinkable in this workplace of ex-hippies, war refuseniks, feminists, and queers to forsake rightful demands for equality of benefits and representation. This comparison between differing sectors within a single union points to the uneven and fluctuating development of an identity-based class culture. The class compact of an earlier, industrial era is encoded in the bone-crushing handshake between white and black laborer that is still the AFL-CIO's logo. This vision of class solidarity persists in many sectors of the workforce. But even in its strongholds, it has been challenged, and increasingly it is mediated by newer, fuller conceptions of class that acknowledge sexual identity along with gender and race.

An interesting sidelight to the *Village Voice* story is the process of education that went on, on *both* sides of the negotiating table. Zeke Cohen, the union's chief negotiator, was an old-style laborist with deep working-class roots. The son of poor Jewish immigrants, he had risen to union leadership from the ranks of a small quilting shop in Manhattan's garment center. His trade union values were learned from class-conscious radicals in the 1940s. In some ways he was as ill-prepared by his experience to bargain for same-sex domestic-partner benefits as the guys and gals in suits on the other side of the table. Yet, in short order, Zeke was not only held in high esteem by the *Voice* workers, he was loved.

Zeke was not comfortable with the lingo of identity politics. "What's this shit?" he asked, when the *Voice* workers presented him with a "politically correct" preamble they wished to include in their first collective bargaining agreement. Curiously, the *Voice* workers took irascible comments like this in stride. They seemed to trust Zeke's good instincts, and they were right. Zeke had the advantage of an experienced organizer, whose ear is attuned to what is *not* said. If only intuitively, he understood the terms of class solidarity among these workers and modulated his own rhetoric of class to inflect it with the language of identity politics. By the end, he had earned the right to speak in family terms. He could have called a dyke a dyke without being misunderstood.

On reflection, Zeke was not so much intuitive as well trained in daily exchanges with the "broads"—a group of young women organizers, including me, who worked under his supervision. We would rattle on to him about the ugly sexism of his male colleagues. He would listen seriously. "Yeah, that guy's a real putz. Tell him to go and fuck himself," he earnestly advised us on one occasion. Then, with transcendent self-irony, he said, "Now, you broads, go into my office, take off your clothes and lie down. I'll be right in." It was a moment of high parody. Zeke flashed an impudent smile, and we were overcome with laughter. On another occasion, Zeke barged into my office and stopped dead when he saw that a colleague of mine was there, nursing her infant daughter. He blushed to the roots of his slick black pompadour. "Sorry, wrong restaurant," he muttered and turned on his heel.

Like the *Voice* workers, the "broads" took Zeke Cohen for who he was—not a poor benighted fellow of his times, but someone blundering his way into the contemporary moment. Admittedly, my interpretation of "Cohen's rehabilitation" depends on a hunch I have: that radicals-for-life are distinguished by their capacity to change with the times, to stay tuned to "the struggle," even when it appears in unfamiliar forms. All the same, it took a lot more than tolerance and humor to get us through the transition from class to identity politics. It was quite a battle, illustrated in another anecdote from my early union experience.

Among the most forward-looking of union leaders, District 65 President David Livingston was an early champion of white-collar organizing. In the mid-70s, he hired a group of women to lead campaigns in the female-intensive publishing and higher-education industries. With a history of civil rights activism going back to the Scottsboro case, District 65 was always race-conscious and had had a Black Affairs Committee for some time.[37] Following this example, the new women leaders attempted to establish a committee as well. A radical of the old CIO, Livingston clung to his belief in the universality of class. He was irritated. "Why do you need a women's committee?" he asked. "A worker is a worker. We make no distinctions based on sex." "But what about the Black Affairs Committee?" we asked. In characteristic manner, Livingston brushed off the apparent contradiction and continued to resist our demand. He could not—or would not—see the logic in our effort to link gender to race, in the politics of both class and identity.

Increasingly, however, the union was focusing its attention on offices and nonprofit institutions, where women employees were in the majority. As a consequence, male leaders of District 65 were drawn deeply into feminist struggles both inside and outside the workplace. An organization founded on the principles of social unionism, District 65 and its older leaders remained sensitive to rank-and-file aspirations. Though it may have been difficult to abandon old notions of class, it did not take a great leap of imagination to grasp the potential power of union-minded feminists. Eventually, the women got their committee. By 1982, District 65 members at the *Village Voice* had formed one of the first gay union caucuses in New York.[38] Though this story is particular to one union, and a small one at that, I venture to say it suggests larger continuities between CIO social unionism and identity politics of a later time.

Since the 1980s, industrial unions like the UAW have been broadening their base to incorporate white-collar and professional units. In 1992, for example, the National Writers Union affiliated to the UAW. That year, they sent representatives to the union's national convention and lobbied successfully for an amendment to the UAW constitution, adding sexual orientation to the existing articles of nondiscrimination. Later, after the setback at Chrysler, UAW Vice President Jack Laskowski vowed that an antidiscrimination clause covering gay workers would be in the next Chrysler contract.[39] And it was. On September 25, 1999, UAW members at DaimlerChrysler set the pattern for Ford and GM, ratifying a contract that added sexual orientation to the existing "Equal Applications" clause. Then, on June 8, 2000, the agreement was augmented to provide domestic-partner benefits to same-sex couples among the 466,000 employees of DaimlerChrysler, Ford, and GM. Although Chrysler workers in Canada have had these benefits since 1993, this union agreement is the most sweeping of its kind in the North American industrial sector and hopefully will encourage more LGBT industrial workers to come out of the closet and take a forceful stand for workplace rights.[40] And, hopefully, Ron Woods will be recognized for the enormity of his contribution to this victory.

Gay workers (even in heavy industry) are taking their place at the table, and they are changing the language and culture of organizing in the process. It is a small sign, but the morally loaded term "sexual preference" has been replaced in many union contracts by "sexual orientation," the term of choice in gay communities. "We're queer, we're here," is not unheard of on the picket line. Even the concept of queer strategy has entered the mainstream labor movement. Red days at Barneys department store—where the majority of employees are gay—is a good example.

Every Tuesday during contract negotiations in April 1996, employees (members of the apparel workers union, UNITE) defied the all-black dress code. Men in bright lipstick and women in red waited on customers to the chagrin of buyers and managers. The grand finale of this queer contract campaign was an alternative fashion show outside the store, featuring drag queens and dykes. As they strutted their stuff down a makeshift runway, they flashed UNITE picket signs. One of their demands was an end to excessive overtime. "He can't get his beauty sleep," the (straight) emcee said, as one especially flamboyant queen made his entrance. Cutters, sewing-machine operators, pressers, and finishers from UNITE garment factories stood in the street, cheering the queers on.[41]

If these seem like sporadic examples of gay activism, the national growth of gay union caucuses points to a developing, stable base of organization. Though there had been ad hoc alliances of gay union members since the 1970s, not until the 1980s did these take shape as effective coalitions.[42] The Gay Caucus at *Village Voice* was fundamental to an informal New York City coalition that had been meeting since the early 1980s. Similar groups, such as the Gay and Lesbian Labor Action Network (GALLAN) in Boston, developed in other union towns.[43] In October 1987, queers descended on Washington, D.C., for the second national gay pride march in the country's history. Gay union members marched as a bloc, union banners and signs held aloft among the other insignia of gay pride. On the eve of that demonstration, the AFL-CIO had opened its vast marble lobby for a premarch rally and reception. Among the speakers at that rally were the presidents of the country's two largest public sector unions, Gerald McEntee of the American Federation of State, County, and Municipal Employees (AFSCME) and John Sweeney, then head of the Service Employees International Union (SEIU). Not coincidentally, these unions had perhaps the largest and most active gay caucuses.[44] In 1998, three years after Sweeney was elected to head the AFL-CIO, Pride at Work—a national caucus of gay, lesbian, and transgendered trade unionists—was affiliated to the AFL-CIO, joining the Coalition of Labor Union Women, the Coalition of Black Trade Unionists, the Labor Council for Latin American Advancement, and the Asian-Pacific-American Alliance, all of which had affiliated during the Kirkland administration. The historical development of a new class conjuncture was symbolically complete. Will this symbolic gesture be translated into something more tangible? In their essay "Getting Serious about Inclusion," La Luz and Finn say no—not until the constituency groups are "redefined as organizing groups."[45]

In an important respect, John Sweeney is both the product of a new class formation and its representative. He has acknowledged as much himself: "The secret to our success, and the greatest potential for organizing, is among women, people of color, and young workers."[46] This comment, made in his first days as president of the AFL-CIO, has been augmented to include lesbian and gay workers. In "The Growing Alliance between Gay and Union Activists," an essay that appeared first in the winter 1999 edition of *Social Text*, Sweeney says, "We must draw gay and lesbian union members into our programs for leadership development and provide opportunities . . . to become leaders in their workplaces and in their unions."[47]

The emergence of a gay rights movement within the ranks of labor is intimately connected to the growing power of a new, identity-based class coalition. The history of this class formation was present, if unacknowledged, in the leadership transition itself. Some months prior to the 1995 AFL-CIO convention, the heads of several unions mounted an open campaign to oust federation president Lane Kirkland. Leading the insurgents were—again—McEntee and Sweeney. Built in the last thirty years—the "dark ages"—their public sector unions probably represent more women, people of color, and gays than any other. It is no accident that these unions were the advance troops for change in 1995. Nor was Sweeney's opposition slate constructed out of mere political expediency.[48]

Sweeney's running mate was Richard Trumka, President of the United Mineworkers of America (UMWA), a union so small now, it is barely viable. But Trumka was young, and he was an outspoken, even brash, critic of the old guard. His fiery speeches were laced with the rhetoric of class struggle. He had gained a reputation for charismatic leadership during the 1989 UMWA strike against the Pittston coal company and several other coal operators in Appalachia. Won against great odds, the strike represented a triumph of class solidarity over corporate power and government intervention.[49] With Linda Chavez-Thompson of AFSCME, the Sweeney slate demonstrated more than progressive and potentially militant class struggle. It was also recognition of the diversity principle in representation. The AFL-CIO Executive Council had included a few women since the 1980s, but no woman, and no person of color, had been elected by convention delegates to executive office before Chavez-Thompson.[50] No one who knows the labor movement could miss the symbolism, but its basis in historical process may not be taken into full account. Before the AFL-CIO convention in October 1995, black labor leaders had presented both presidential candidates with demands for greater representation by African Americans. A constitutional amendment, passed at the convention, provided for expansion of the Executive Council, with ten seats designated for women and people of color.[51] True, no openly gay woman or man holds office in the federation, but the new emphasis on multiculturalism suggests it is no longer inconceivable.

In his first public statements as president of the AFL-CIO, John Sweeney committed the federation to a vigorous, new, and multicultural organizing effort. He has expanded that vision now to include an organizing agenda specifically directed at lesbian and gay workers.[52] Of the 74,000 home health-care workers who won union representation in 1999, the majority are women, people of color, and immigrants. Gays and lesbians are present among them, as they are in every sector of the workforce. As organized labor struggles to rebound in the new millennium, it must reach out to the many thousands of low-wage, exploited workers who have been left behind in the shuffle of deindustrialization. At the same time, it must continue to target new sectors of the workforce. Together, at least four major unions—the American Federation of Teachers, the Communications Workers of America, the Hotel Employees and Restaurant Employees Union, and the UAW— have already committed millions to organizing university teaching and research assistants, for example. Demands made by university workers characteristically foreground identity-based claims, such as affirmative action and domestic-partner benefits for gay as well as straight couples.

To bring this story full circle, I come back to the Columbia Teach-In and its aftermath. In May 1997, teach-in founders met with John Sweeney to discuss the institutional potential of a labor-intellectual alliance. Sweeney agreed to support the establishment of Scholars, Artists, and Writers for Social Justice (SAWSJ), and an interim steering committee was developed. The question of diversity was first and foremost on the minds of some new participants. After heated discussion, a decision was made to delay formation of the organization until women, people of color, students, and other activists were fully represented in the group.[53] Within a year, the organization had made progress toward this goal. Scholars, Artists, and Writers for Social Justice held its first annual meeting in April 1998. In marked contrast to the teach-in of '96, two rank-and-file leaders shared the speakers' platform with intellectual and labor elites. Of eight keynoters, four were people of color and three were women. Though the question of sexual identity had slipped to the background of internal SAWSJ discussions, it was kept alive by a few members of the steering committee and surfaced at this founding convention with a screening and discussion of *Out at Work*. At the next annual meeting, a workshop was devoted to the subject of gay labor rights. It included Charisse Mitchell, transgendered herself and a public advocate for the rights of transgendered workers.

Living Class

Historian Robin Kelley has said that "class is lived through race and gender."[54] It is the word *lived* that captures my attention. To *live* class implies an engagement. At its most intense, this engagement is described rhetorically as class struggle. I like Kelley's maxim very much, precisely for the degree of agency it implies, but I have wondered why he did not include sexual identity. I tried it out: "Class is lived through race, gender, and sexual identity." Given the extent to which rights, privileges, and social position are determined by sexual identity, my reformulation feels right. More so, when I consider the history of workplace struggle for gay and lesbian rights. Much of that history is necessarily absent from this discussion.

While the account I have offered points to a few victories for those who have been historically underrepresented in the labor movement, it omits years of struggle and defeat. In 1970—even in San Francisco—gay firefighters and teachers were denounced by local union leaders for displaying affection on a picket line and carrying progay signs. The San Francisco Central Labor Council later issued a condescending plea for tolerance, calling the group a "small, unschooled, and new" sector of the movement.[55] This is but one example in a dramatic history of struggle for sexual representation in the workplace and the labor movement. While historians and analysts of contemporary labor have increasingly focused on race and gender, in the main, they have failed to recognize the vital signs of class struggle in contemporary movements for gay and lesbian workplace rights.

At the risk of oversimplification, I would suggest that the mere fact such movements have developed in the workplace—the fact they have been advanced through workplace struggle—demonstrates that sexual identity is intimately connected to class and to the ways class is asserted. This is made more obvious to the extent straight workers and union leaders have incorporated these struggles in the broad pursuit of workers' rights. This is not to say there is a single broad agenda for workers' rights. Class is not monolithic and class struggle is not all-embracing, all the time. Nevertheless, in the crossings and partings that mark the various ways workers identify themselves, points of solidarity emerge. Sexual identity is a lived experience for *all* workers. Of course, workers who identify as straight live it very differently. They live it in the comfort of social approbation and with all the rights and privileges that come from respectability. Never mind that straight workers routinely engage in sexual practices that might be considered deviant— promiscuity, homosexual affairs, sex-work-on-the-side. What straight folks do in bed is mostly nobody's business when it comes to workplace benefits. That is not the case for those who are openly gay, lesbian, bisexual, or transgendered. Straight workers and advocates for workers' rights may not be ready to abandon heteronormative standards of sexual propriety, but they are becoming more conscious of inequities in this double standard. In that sense, the potential for solidarity across lines of difference is nowhere more evident than in the struggle for gay and lesbian workplace rights.

Notes

In studying labor history, I have sought to understand my own experience. If I have understood anything, I owe it to my mentor in the union and my enduring comrade, Milton Reverby. This essay is dedicated to him with thanks and love. I am, of course, indebted to the scholarship of others, principally Stanley Aronowitz, Lizabeth Cohen, Michael Denning, Miriam Frank, Robin D. G. Kelley, Nelson Lichtenstein, and Daniel Walkowitz.

1. Under pressure from the heads of eleven oppositionist unions, Lane Kirkland retired in August 1995. The AFL-CIO Executive Council elected Tom Donohue—Secretary-Treasurer of the federation under Kirkland—to fill out Kirkland's term. Thus, Donohue (not Kirkland) was actually Sweeney's opponent in the October 1995 election.
2. Michael Denning, *The Cultural Front: The Laboring of American Culture in the Twentieth Century* (London: Verso, 1996). For a general description of the period, see

also Lizabeth Cohen, *Making A New Deal: Industrial Workers in Chicago, 1919–1939* (Cambridge: Cambridge University Press, 1990).

3. I attended the Columbia Teach-In and base my comments on recollections of Rorty's speech and the audience reaction.

4. In 1974, District 65 was an independent union, with a jurisdiction covering both blue- and white-collar workers. In 1980, District 65 affiliated to the United Automobile Workers union. By 1990, most locals of the District were assimilated into regions of the UAW. District 65 no longer exists as an entity.

5. Daniel Walkowitz, *Working with Class: Social Workers and the Politics of Middle-Class Identity* (Chapel Hill: University of North Carolina Press, 1999). The "fluidity" of class identity is a central theme throughout this study.

6. A spate of news and journal articles on the future of American labor followed in the wake of John Sweeney's election and has continued. Between its summer and winter is- sues in 1998–99, for example, *Dissent* magazine carried a debate on the subject of union democracy, sparked by Steve Fraser's article in the summer edition, "Is Democracy Good for Unions?" A qualified defense of bureaucratic decision making in labor organi- zations, Fraser's essay was critiqued in separate pieces by Stanley Aronowitz, Herman Benson, and Gordon K. Haskell. The series concluded with a rebuttal by Fraser. This de- bate continued in the "Letters" column of *New Labor Forum* (spring/summer 1999).

7. Jeremy Brecher and Tim Costello, "Labor's Day: The Challenge Ahead," *The Nation*, September 21, 1998, 11.

8. Ibid., 17 and throughout.

9. Gregory Mantsios, ed., *A New Labor Movement for the New Century* (New York: Monthly Review Press, 1998), xv.

10. José La Luz and Paula Finn, "Getting Serious about Inclusion: A Comprehensive Approach," in ibid.

11. Robin Kelley has argued these points with clarity and passion. See *Yo Mama's DisFUNKtional!: Fighting the Culture Wars in Urban America* (Boston: Beacon Press, 1997), chapters 4 and 5. Nelson Lichtenstein's comments on this subject are also in- structive. See his essay, "Falling in Love Again? Intellectuals and the Labor Movement in Post-War America," in *New Labor Forum* (spring/summer 1999): 25–26.

12. *Out at Work: Lesbians and Gay Men on the Job* was released in 1997. A second ver- sion of this documentary, *Out at Work: America Undercover*, was produced for HBO and aired first in January 1999.

13. Perry Anderson, *The Origins of Postmodernity* (London: Verso, 1998), 89.

14. See Lichtenstein, "Falling in Love Again?" 19. In commending progress made by the Sweeney administration, Lichtenstein points not only to gains in the minimum wage, but also to the defeat of fast-track legislation and to the AFL-CIO's Union Summer program, aimed at recruiting young organizers from campuses across the country. The figures on new organization between 1997 and 1999 were supplied by Mark Splain of the AFL-CIO organizing department.

15. In this regard, the International Ladies' Garment Workers Union is an obvious ex- ample. ILGWU was conducting educational and cultural programs within fifteen years of its founding in 1900. *Pins and Needles*—an ILGWU production with music by Harold Rome—is perhaps the best remembered of CIO theatrical productions. It was first performed in the summer of 1936.

16. For an analysis of workforce and union participation by blacks—and black women in particular—during this period, see Jacqueline Jones, *Labor of Love, Labor of Sorrow* (New York: Random House/Vintage Books, 1985), chapters 6 and 7.

17. Michael Denning goes further to argue that CIO labor was "the base" of the Popular Front. See *The Cultural Front*.

18. Nelson Lichtenstein, *Labor's War at Home: The CIO in World War II* (New York: Cambridge University Press, 1982). The number of wildcat strikes between 1942, when the WLB was established, and 1945, when it was dismantled, is a measure of rank-and-file discontent. For a summary of strike activity, see Lichtenstein, 133–35.

19. See Denning, *The Cultural Front*, 24.

20. In *Labor's War at Home*, Nelson Lichtenstein provides a full account of these debilitating effects on postwar unionism. For a summary, see the epilogue.

21. Basic industry refers to the giant smokestack industries, such as steel and auto. Lichtenstein puts union density in these industries at 80 percent by the late 1940s. See Lichtenstein, *Labor's War at Home*, 233. Stanley Aronowitz offers a variation in *From the Ashes of the Old!: American Labor and America's Future* (New York: Houghton Mifflin, 1998). By the late 1940s, he says, over 40 percent of all U.S. factory workers were organized. See *From the Ashes of the Old*.

22. Daniel Cantor and Juliet Schor, *Tunnel Vision: Labor, the World Economy and Central America* (Boston: South End Press, 1987), 41–47. AIFLD was implicated in a series of anticommunist intelligence activities in the Dominican Republic, Guyana, and Brazil. In 1964, AIFLD trained workers who participated in the coup that ousted Brazilian President João Goulart.

23. See Aronowitz, *From the Ashes of the Old*, 11.

24. See Steven Greenhouse, "In Biggest Drive Since 1937, Union Gains a Victory," *The New York Times*, February 26, 1999, sec. A, p. 1.

25. See Aronowitz, "The Rise and Crisis of Public Sector Unions," chap. 2 in *From the Ashes of the Old*.

26. See ibid., 61.

27. In my union, District 65, the bulk of new organizing from 1974 onward took place among professionals and paraprofessionals, including cultural workers in publishing, museums, bookstores, and offices. (Perhaps the largest number of professionals in 65 were university employees, childcare workers, and lawyers.) The National Writers Union, which affiliated to the UAW in 1992, began organizing in the late 1980s. The Graphic Artists Guild, which had begun merger talks in the early 1980s, affiliated to the UAW in 1999.

28. The American Federation of Teachers, the American Federation of State, County, and Municipal Employees, and the Service Employees International Union are obvious examples in the public sector. In the private sector, District 65 is one example. A costly campaign among major publishing companies—including Simon & Schuster, Random House, and Harcourt Brace—failed, despite organizing efforts over a five-year period. Victories at Boston and Columbia universities came only after ten-year campaigns and several lost elections.

29. For a profound analysis of this class transformation, see Walkowitz, *Working with Class*.

30. See John Hoerr, *We Can't Eat Prestige: The Women Who Organized Harvard* (Philadelphia: Temple University Press, 1997), 227.

31. Yvette Herrera, Director of Mobilization and Education for the Communications Workers of America, recounts a telling exchange: At a workshop on sexual diversity, a steward objected to the recognition of gay rights on religious grounds. Discussion later turned to the case of a gay worker, fired because he was HIV-positive. This same steward took an aggressive position in defense of the gay worker. The union would not tolerate discrimination against any member, she said, and proceeded to describe how she had handled a grievance in this case. See "Homophobia, Labor's Last Frontier?" in this volume.

32. References to the *Village Voice* and to District 65, throughout, are based largely on my

own experience as a 65 organizer from 1974–1989. I was the lead organizer of *Voice* employees in 1977 and remained the *Voice* contract administrator for several years.

33. For a history of the *Village Voice*, see Kevin Michael McAuliffe, *The Great American Newspaper: The Rise and Fall of the Village Voice* (New York: Charles Scribner's Sons, 1978.) My account is also based on personal knowledge of *Voice* history, gained in the years I served as staff organizer for the union of *Voice* employees.

34. The *VV* contracts of 1979 and 1982—along with other documents pertaining to health coverage and affirmative action—are preserved in the files of UAW Local 2110.

35. Jack Laskowski described these final negotiations in the HBO film, *Out at Work: America Undercover.* My account of these negotiations and the internal debate that ensued is based on two other sources: a January 3, 1999, interview with UAW *Solidarity* magazine staffer Michael Funke, and "Coming Out at Chrysler," an article by James B. Stewart in the July 1997 issue of *The New Yorker* magazine.

36. See Yvette Herrera's discussion of this phenomenon in "Homophobia, Labor's Last Frontier?" this volume.

37. The Scottsboro case began in 1931, when nine young black men were indicted for the alleged rape of two white women in Scottsboro, Alabama. The case dragged on through a lengthy appeals process, ending with convictions of four defendants in 1937. (A fifth was convicted of lesser assault charges.) The District 65 photo archive contains a picture of union leaders, who had chained themselves to the pillars of a Washington, D.C., courthouse to protest the travesty of justice.

38. Miriam Frank, "Lesbian and Gay Caucuses in the United States Labor Movement," in *Laboring for Rights: A Global Perspective on Union Response to Sexual Diversity*, ed. Gerald Hunt (Philadelphia: Temple University Press, 1999), 21. For the purpose of page references, I use an earlier, unpublished version of the essay.

39. See Laskowski's comments in the HBO version of *Out at Work.*

40. See Keith Bradsher, "Big Carmakers Extend Benefits to Gay Couples," *New York Times*, Friday, June 9, 2000, sec. C, p. 1.

41. The fashion show was videotaped. It was also covered by the *Village Voice* and *Women's Wear Daily*. See Andrew Ross, "Strike a Pose for Justice: The Barneys Union Campaign of 1996," this volume.

42. Teachers in New York and San Francisco were among the first to establish such groups in the 1970s. See Frank, "Lesbian and Gay," 2.

43. See ibid., 21.

44. See ibid., 8–19.

45. La Luz and Finn, "Getting Serious about Inclusion," 180.

46. Kelley, *Yo Mama's DisFUNKtional!* 129, 206 n. 8.

47. John Sweeney, "The Growing Alliance between Gay and Union Activists," in *Social Text* (winter 1999): 31–38. The article is published again in this volume.

48. Robin Kelley's investigation of this very point helps enormously to support my claim. See Kelley, *Yo Mama's DisFUNKtional!*, chap. 5. Citing the importance of what he calls "the changing face of labor," Kelley says, "[T]he victory of John Sweeney (president), Richard Trumka (secretary-treasurer) and Linda Chavez-Thompson (executive vice president) . . . depended to a large extent on their position vis-à-vis the so-called minority workers."

49. The strike lasted nine months and spread to ten states, with wildcat strikes erupting at several mining operations across the country. In the seventh month of the strike, ninety miners occupied a main coal-processing plant in Virginia and remained inside for several days, in defiance of a governor's order. I was among thousands of supporters, including UMWA members from other parts of the country, who converged on the scene, keeping vigil in front of the plant. State police, armed with rifles, stood at

the ready outside the plant gates. Ultimately the governor guaranteed amnesty, and the ninety miners ended their sit-in.

50. Interim officers, elected by the Executive Council after Kirkland's retirement, included Barbara Easterling of the Flight Attendants union.

51. See Louis Uchitelle, "Blacks See Opening in AFL-CIO Leadership Fight," *New York Times*, July 15, 1995, p. 6. See also David Kaneras, "Constitutional Changes Focus on Leadership," *AFL-CIO News*, November 6, 1995, 7.

52. See Sweeney, "The Growing Alliance," 36–37.

53. I base this account on my own experience as a member of the SAWSJ Steering Committee.

54. See Kelley, *Yo Mama's DisFUNKtional!* 109.

55. See Gaile Whittington, "Gay Labor Pain," *Berkeley Tribe*, January 30, 1970.

The Growing Alliance between Gay and Union Activists

John J. Sweeney

I still recall the day in October of 1983 when a resolution condemning discrimination on the basis of sexual orientation came up on the floor of the AFL-CIO's Fifteenth Constitutional Convention. Seventeen years ago, the resolution was something of a landmark, a declaration of the labor movement's support for a group of workers whose identity and particular concerns had never been acknowledged or addressed before. At the time, I was president of the Service Employees International Union (SEIU), which had sponsored the resolution. I rose to speak in favor of it. Since that day, I have spoken out many times for the rights of workers, regardless of sexual orientation. And I am proud to say that the labor movement has since made many advances in the fight for gay and lesbian rights. This document affirms our commitment to that struggle and contains my first published statement of a specific agenda for labor.

Seventeen years ago, six of the most respected union leaders in the country joined me in supporting the AFL-CIO resolution on sexual orientation. As I looked around the room, I could sense the hesitation. Union members, after all, aren't much different than the public at large. Which is to say they've been reluctant to open their hearts and minds to people whose sexual orientation is different than their own. I knew there were unspoken questions—questions I had heard before and have heard many times since: Is it a good idea to put rights for gay and lesbian workers on the labor movement's agenda? Is it possible to organize workers who can't easily be identified, much less mobilized? Is there enough public and membership support to organize around their issues? And yet, not one convention delegate spoke against the resolution. It passed overwhelmingly.

What happened that day is something I've seen happen in the labor movement many times over the years. When faced with a choice, no matter how difficult, more often than not our commitment to equality floats to the top. Equality is a value Americans hold most dear—not only in the labor movement but across the country. We feel strongly that employment discrimination is unacceptable, and that applies whether the bias is based on race, gender, or religion, or whether it's based on the selection of your partner. In fact, according to a 1998 study of public opinion polls by the National Gay and Lesbian Task Force Policy Institute, 84 percent of the public believes that it's unfair to discriminate against or fire someone for being gay. Perhaps more important, we know that the only way to protect and improve everyone's standard of living is to prevent any group from being singled out for discrimination. Basic human and civil rights are meaningless unless they apply equally across the board. Barriers that separate workers along lines of race, gender, religion, or sexual orientation fundamentally weaken the labor movement and our ability to make life better for all working Americans.

The passage of that AFL-CIO resolution in 1983 was a small but significant first step toward formalizing and nurturing a budding alliance between gay activists and union activists. In 1997, we reached another milestone when the AFL-CIO Executive Council voted unanimously to recognize Pride at Work—an organization of lesbian/gay/bisexual/transgender (LGBT) union members—as an official constituency group of the AFL-CIO, thereby guaranteeing gay and lesbian workers a voice in determining the labor movement's agenda. I don't mean to romanticize the American labor movement or overstate the progress we've made in promoting the rights of gay and lesbian workers. No one would deny that it's been a slow and painstaking process getting to where we are. And we still have quite a long way to go. Historically, unions have had to be challenged and prodded before opening the door to people their members view as "different." For gay and lesbian workers, in particular, that remains a hard reality to this day. But time and again, the labor movement has shown itself capable of broadening to include and represent every class of workers. Today, in fact, women and people of color represent the fastest-growing and most dynamic sectors of the labor movement. Their issues—equal rights, equal pay, and equal opportunity— are squarely at the top of labor's agenda. Through their unions, they are narrowing gender- and race-based income disparities. While, on average, union members earn 32 percent more than their unorganized counterparts, unionized women earn 39 percent more than non-unionized women; African Americans who join unions earn 45 percent more; and unionized Latino workers earn 54 percent more.

Now the question is: Can the labor movement embrace a similar agenda for gay and lesbian rights in the workplace? I believe so. For one thing, those of us who work and lead in the labor movement have already come to a much better understanding of how and why gay rights is a union issue. Due largely to the leadership of unions such as the American Federation of State, County and Municipal Employees (AFSCME) and SEIU—and the strong and active LGBT caucuses within those institutions—we're increasingly aware of the fear and discrimination gay men and lesbians experience in the workplace. Slowly, we are rising above reservations and skepticism within

Susan Moir, emcee of an AFL-CIO reception for LGBT workers, pins John Sweeney with a pink triangle the night before the 1993 March on Washington. Sal Roselli, president of SEIU Local 250, San Francisco, addresses the audience. Photograph by Jim Klebaug/Page One Photography; reprinted with permission.

our ranks to include equality and fairness for gay and lesbian workers in our bargaining and legislative priorities. But I hasten to add that ours is not the only cynicism that is being overcome. If we have made progress in forging a gay–labor alliance, it is also because more gay and lesbian workers are casting aside their doubts about unions. Over the years, growing numbers of gay and lesbian workers have come to recognize that the labor movement—for all of its flaws and shortcomings—represents their best hope for achieving equal rights and equal benefits in the workplace.

Congress has yet to pass a federal law guaranteeing rights and protections for gays and lesbians. And only eleven states have such laws. At a time when legislative initiatives have failed to yield the antidiscrimination protections gay and lesbian workers need, trade unionism looms large as a faster and more effective alternative. Collective bargaining, by definition, emphasizes equality. It is inherently designed to ensure that every worker has the same rights, opportunities, and rewards for good work. Moreover, trade unionism is in principle the most democratic of America's institutions. Every member is entitled to a voice. Thus, for many gay and lesbian workers, trade unionism has emerged as the means of coming out—being honest about who they are, without fear of harassment or discrimination in the workplace. Unions are a way for workers to take charge of their own lives, to help themselves make life better by working together. More than just public institutions, unions are vehicles for change, available to any group of workers—provided the group is willing to take necessary risks to win union representation. Because our labor laws are slanted so heavily in favor of employers, workers who publicly support unionization risk being intimidated, harassed, and even fired. For gay and lesbian workers, obviously, the risk more than doubles. In an unorganized workplace, coming out as gay and coming out as a union supporter both require enormous acts of courage. Nevertheless, as more gay men and lesbians go public with their sexual orientation, more are also organizing—in their workplaces, in their unions, in their communities, and in legislative and political arenas.

As far back as the 1970s, gay/lesbian union members were mobilizing inside their unions and standing up for their rights at the bargaining table. In 1974, a group of union bus drivers in Ann Arbor, Michigan, negotiated what is believed to be the first collectively bargained ban on discrimination based on sexual orientation (though at the time it was referred to as sexual "preference"). During the 1980s and 1990s—particularly as the AIDS epidemic heightened both homophobia and fears about the HIV virus—some unions, notably SEIU, AFSCME, and the Communications Workers of America, developed model workplace education programs, which, in part, helped to keep people with AIDS in their jobs. At the same time, gay and lesbian union members all across America were forming caucuses and organizing for the same protections won by the Michigan bus drivers. Today, you can find such antidiscrimination provisions in union contracts covering workers ranging from grocery store clerks in Chicago to janitors at the Seattle Public Library to auto workers in Spring Hill, Tennessee, to nursing home workers in southern California. The grassroots organizing efforts of gay and lesbian union members began producing results in other ways, most notably in the area of equal employment benefits. UAW members at the *Village Voice* and Museum of Modern Art in New York, for example, were among the first to win health insurance and other benefits for domestic partners. Public employees represented by AFSCME throughout the country have since successfully bargained and lobbied to extend to domestic partners the kinds of benefits enjoyed by married couples. Largely in California, but also in other states, private-sector workers represented by SEIU, the Office and Professional Employees International Union, the Teamsters, and many other unions also have negotiated domestic-partner benefits—which are now offered by an estimated four hundred public and private-sector employers nationwide.

While gay and lesbian workers were forming committees and caucuses within their local and national unions, a broader partnership of the gay rights and workers' rights movements was also emerging. Gay and lesbian workers were urging their unions to address their concerns through political and legislative avenues. At the same time, trade unionists were waking up to the fact that to improve living and working standards, through bargaining as well as legislation, they must build broad and diverse coalitions that could unite around a common agenda. That realization was inspired in part by an effective boycott of Coors beer in the mid to late 1970s. In that struggle, gay and labor activists united in opposition to the homophobic and antiworker policies of the giant brewing company. From that, a network—which came to be known as the Lesbian/Gay Labor Alliance—was formed in San Francisco. In 1978, by using their combined political strength, gay and union activists successfully defeated California's Proposition 6, known as the Briggs initiative. Had this ballot measure passed, gay and lesbian teachers would have been barred from California schools. In 1986, this gay–union alliance also defeated the LaRouche ballot initiative (Proposition 64), which could have quarantined people with AIDS.

By the early 1990s, alliances similar to the one in California were up and running in New York, Boston, and several other cities. Gay and union activists were working together to defeat antigay measures that were cropping up on ballots throughout the country. Increasingly recognized as a pivotal political force in a number of cities, gay and lesbian activists became an important part of progressive coalitions that included not only labor but consumers, senior citizens, and other advocacy groups. In 1994, gay–labor alliances joined together to form Pride at Work (PAW), a national organization that held its first convention during the Stonewall 25 anniversary celebration in New York City. For the next several years, Pride at Work organized and lobbied to become an official voice for the concerns of gay and lesbian workers in the labor movement. PAW urged AFL-CIO unions to get behind an affiliation effort that would establish PAW on an equal footing with such AFL-CIO constituency groups as the Coalition of Labor Union Women, the A. Philip Randolph Institute, the Coalition of Black Trade Unionists, the Labor Council for Latin American Advancement, and the Asian Pacific American Labor Alliance. That goal was realized in August 1998, when PAW was officially established as an AFL-CIO constituency group. In the years ahead, the AFL-CIO will look to Pride at Work for leadership in developing an agenda for gay/lesbian rights in the workplace—one that can build a stronger and more united labor movement and raise living standards for all working Americans. We know we have work to do on many fronts:

Raise awareness. We must educate both union members and the general public about gay and lesbian workplace rights. We must build a strong consensus on this issue within the labor movement and work to create an environment in which it will become easier for gay and lesbian workers to come out in their workplaces and in their unions. We must also effectively reach out to these workers and capture their imagination with a vision of how unions can tangibly improve their lives.

Develop leadership. We must draw gay and lesbian union members into our programs for leadership development and provide the opportunities and skills they need to become leaders in their workplaces and in their unions. We must encourage the creation of caucuses and committees at every level of the labor movement to ensure that gay and lesbian workers have a voice in the policies and programs of their unions. And we must support the efforts of Pride at Work to recruit new members, strengthen local chapters, and build a stronger organization that can speak for gay and lesbian workers.

Build broad coalitions. Working with our natural allies is the most effective course for pursuing goals of equality and for bringing all people into the mainstream of American life. Through the AFL-CIO's "Union Cities" initiative, launched in 1997 and designed to rebuild the labor movement at its grass roots, local unions throughout the country are already forging stronger alliances with community groups to advance the cause of workers' rights and civil rights. With Pride at Work as a foundational building block, the AFL-CIO and its affiliated unions must expand efforts to build effective and long-lasting community coalitions and to encourage the participation of gay and lesbian organizations.

Pursue legislative remedies. The vast majority of Americans today live in one of the thirty-nine states that do not prohibit employment discrimination based on sexual orientation. To remedy such discrimination, Congress introduced the federal Employment Non-Discrimination Act (ENDA) in 1994, and the AFL-CIO joined forces with gay/lesbian organizations and other civil rights allies to lobby on behalf of the bill. Though it was narrowly defeated in the Senate in 1996, a similar version has been reintroduced and is currently pending in Congress. Working with Pride at Work, the AFL-CIO and its affiliates will continue to educate union members and mobilize grassroots support for the passage of ENDA as well as to promote state legislation that guarantees the civil rights of all persons without regard to sexual orientation.

Negotiate to protect workers' rights. In the absence of legal and legislative protections, collective bargaining may be the most effective way to guarantee gay and lesbian workers the same job opportunities, protections, and benefits other workers take for granted. We must be certain that union contracts not only protect workers against biases based on race, gender, and religion but also on the basis of sexual orientation. We must make domestic-partner benefits a higher bargaining priority. And we must effectively use our bargaining power to fight for income equality.

Restore the right to organize. Union representation is central to the pursuit of equality in the workplace. By providing an equal voice to all workers, unions can reduce income inequalities caused by discriminatory employment practices and actively promote equal pay and fair treatment on the job. Unfortunately, today's outdated and lopsided labor laws fail to guarantee workers the basic right and freedom to form unions. Workers who try to unionize are likely to be threatened, ostracized, or fired, and the law can do little to protect them. Gay and lesbian workers who are without protections against discrimination on the basis of sexual orientation are particularly vulnerable.

For gay and lesbian workers, as for all workers, restoring the right to organize must be our top priority. And I believe that by standing together—gay and union activists, friends and neighbors, community and political leaders—it can be done. We can challenge employers who use coercion and intimidation to interfere in workers' rights to choose union representation. And we can make such conduct unacceptable in our communities. We can reassure workers that the community stands behind them and helps them exercise their rights, win unions, and a voice on the job. We can educate policy makers and the public about the right to organize and lay the groundwork for legal reforms that will restore the fundamental right to form a union—and bring democracy and equality to the American workplace.

By working together, and by building broad coalitions and partnerships around our common goals, we can and will advance the cause of gay rights in the workplace. I have never felt more confident of that than I did on September 10, 1996, the day the Senate voted on ENDA. True, the legislation was defeated by a harrowing 50-to-49 margin. But as I sat in the Senate reception room watching the votes come in, I was inspired by the gathering of leaders from the human rights, civil rights, and women's movements, who also had come to show their support for the legislation. And I couldn't help feeling hopeful that next time, when ENDA comes to the floor for another vote, the combined power of our progressive movements will help America's commitment to equality float to the top, once again.

Beyond Gay: "Deviant" Sex
and the Politics of the ENDA Workplace

Patrick McCreery

In July 1996, the *Washington Post* reported allegations that Jeffrey Dion Bruton, a physical education teacher at a local middle school, had worked surreptitiously as an actor in gay porn. Titillating to begin with, the *Post*'s exposé of Bruton's "double life" was made more so by the fact that the allegations came from Bruton's wife, who cited her newly discovered knowledge of her husband's sex work as grounds for divorce. Local television pounced on the story, comparing pictures of Bruton to ones of "Ty Fox," the muscular blonde star of such videos as *Fox's Lair*, *Ty Me Up*, and *Hot Day in L.A*. Citing conduct "detrimental" to students, officials at the Loudoun County (Va.) school board said they would fire Bruton if they determined he had indeed moonlighted as a porn actor. As the Loudoun school superintendent told the *Post*, "We believe that teachers, as people who are chosen to be instructors as well

Schoolteacher Jeffrey Dion Bruton—aka Ty Fox, sometime porn star—working at a Washington, D.C., club in 1997. Photograph by Clint Steib/*The Washington Blade*; reprinted with permission.

as leaders of our young people, should be exemplary in their professional as well as personal lives. . . . What we have here is an allegation of a lifestyle that is not in keeping with that. If the allegations are true, that is not conduct befitting a teacher."[1]

Acknowledging that he and Ty Fox were the same person, Bruton soon resigned from his job and surrendered his teaching credentials. But the story does not end there. Two months later, Bruton became a figure in the battle over the proposed federal Employment Non-Discrimination Act (ENDA), which would ban employment discrimination based on a worker's sexual orientation. The *Post*'s outing of Bruton as a worker in the gay sex industry ultimately resulted in right-wing editorials, speeches on the floor of the U.S. Senate and revisions to the proposed bill.

ENDA was intended to establish protections in the thirty-nine states that currently allow employers to fire or refuse to hire workers whom they know or suspect to be gay. First introduced in 1994 by Senator Edward Kennedy, the bill was supported by President Clinton, the Democratic leadership, and a wide range of liberal groups, including the Human Rights Campaign, the American Civil Liberties Union, and the National Council of Churches.[2] Senators narrowly failed to pass ENDA in 1996, and the bill's supporters vow to bring it up for a vote again.

Bruton's inclusion in the ENDA debate raises a number of issues that are the subject of this essay. Foremost is that ENDA—a bill drafted in part by mainstream gay rights organizations and backed by organized labor—does not guarantee workers the right to engage in whatever sexual practices they choose. Even if ENDA were in place, employers could legally continue to discriminate against workers like Bruton who engage in "deviant" sexual practices. Furthermore, the Bruton case also highlights the pragmatism of ENDA's supporters: fearful that conservative legislators would paint Bruton as a typical gay worker, they narrowed the bill's provisions. Finally, Bruton's involuntary role in the battle over ENDA attests to the extraordinary sway that the discourse of child endangerment holds in contemporary cultural politics.

Although ENDA would extend much-needed workplace protection to many lesbian, gay, and bisexual workers, it does so through an unabashed privileging of normative sexuality—meaning nonfetishistic sexual relations between two adults in a monogamous, committed relationship. This is troublesome but hardly surprising. Few unions, legislators, or mainstream gay activists seem willing to seek protections for workers who face discrimination because they engage in so-called "deviant" sexual practices. Bruton is a prime example of this kind of worker. It seems that everyone involved agreed he should be fired even though students and parents praised his coaching and teaching skills. ENDA's limited and flawed "protections" would not have saved Bruton his job.

If we recognize the workplace as a heteronormative environment, we can begin to understand why no one questioned whether Bruton should be allowed to keep his job. *Heteronormative* refers to the way culture privileges heterosexuality as normal and natural, but its meaning extends far beyond the realm of sexual practice. It includes the social structures and cultural institutions that give heterosexuality meaning and make it hegemonic. Heteronormative culture therefore necessarily includes social realities such as marriage, tax laws, zoning ordinances, and job categories. As this list suggests, heteronormativity is inherently averse to "deviance" of any kind—sexual or otherwise. The work of Lauren Berlant, Cathy J. Cohen, Michael Warner, and others indicates that heteronormative culture fantasizes an ideal citizen who—unsurprisingly—is a straight, white, god-loving, flag-waving jock of a man.[3] More broadly, heteronormative institutions are so fundamental to Western culture that "a world in which this hegemonic cluster would not be dominant is, at this point, unimaginable."[4]

Where does ENDA fit into all of this? The bill reinscribes heteronormative culture by relying on the historically contingent orientations "heterosexual," "homosexual," and "bisexual." By not acknowledging the diversity of sexual practices that workers engage in, or the fluidity of identities they may adhere to, the bill tacitly endorses normative sexual mores and institutions. In short, I suggest that ENDA presumes the existence of normative sexual states and that this presumption is a corollary of heteronormative culture. Therein lies the problem. If we concede that any normative state exists, we will always be divided into "us" and "them," "in" and "out," "right" and "wrong."

ENDA is not completely without merit. But the bill's greatest value is the challenge presented by its deficiencies: how can progressives win protection for *all* workers?

Losing Jobs, Saving Children

ENDA and other legislation seeking to protect the rights of gay workers exist because of one simple fact: gay people continue to lose their jobs and face other forms of workplace discrimination because of their sexuality. In the past three decades, various gay and queer campaigns have achieved a degree of public tolerance of homosexuality. But this "tolerance" is unstable, contested, and highly localized. In most parts of the United States, homophobia-based discrimination against gay workers remains both legal and institutionalized. Factors leading to this homophobia range from religious beliefs to sociohistoric tradition, from fears of nonnormative sexual practices to dread of presumed disease.

All of these individual factors come together in the discourse of endangered children. The child holds a privileged status in heteronormative culture, embodying a supposed innocence whose safekeeping is crucial to the health and continuity of the larger culture. The stated need to "protect" children from the alleged moral, social, and physical dangers of homosexuality, as manifested in the Bruton case, permeated debates on ENDA. These supposed dangers are a long-time staple of antigay rhetoric, remaining a favorite of right-wing activists even as "special rights" for gays has emerged as a volatile issue in the past ten years. This rhetoric reduces to a simple dichotomy: the rights of gay people on the one hand, and the moral and physical welfare of children on the other. The two cannot coexist. In this view, homosexuality is emblematic of hedonism, disease, promiscuity, and moral and spiritual decay, with individual homosexuals abusing children literally and defiling their innocence figuratively. Social historian Philip Jenkins has shown that the discourse of child endangerment is deeply ingrained in American culture and historically has had a negative effect on the civil liberties of homosexuals. His comments about gay rights in the United States in the 1950s are applicable to earlier decades as well as to our own: "Tolerance for homosexual lifestyles was inversely proportionate to the degree of popular sex crimes and threats to children. When public fears were at their height, homosexuals were most vulnerable to vice purges and mob vigilantism, to incarceration and medical intervention."[5]

Something like the opposite is also true, however: whenever activists appear to be on the verge of achieving a major gay rights victory, such as the passage of ENDA, the discourse of endangered child welfare becomes shrill. Over the past twenty-five years, homophobic activists have repeatedly argued that legislation protecting the rights of gay people, especially in the workplace, is inherently harmful to children. In several instances, such rhetoric has helped convince voters to repeal nondiscrimination laws.

A brief history of legislation protecting gay people from employment discrimination will help contextualize arguments made over ENDA in the wake of the Bruton "scandal." This history also illustrates the pervasive power of the discourse of child endangerment.

In the 1950s and 1960s, organized groups of gay activists began limited but concerted struggles to secure their civil rights. The right to be free from employment discrimination was one of their demands, and they met with some success—at least in symbolic terms. For example, in 1967, after lobbying from homophile groups such as the Mattachine Society, the American Civil Liberties Union formally opposed the federal government's ban on employing homosexuals in federal jobs. (Arguing that gay people were emotionally unstable and therefore susceptive to blackmail, the feds had instituted the ban in 1953.) According to historian John D'Emilio, "With the expansion of the field of civil liberties to include homosexuality, the union could begin the long, slow process of finding test cases, amassing a corpus of favorable lower court rulings, and chipping away at the system of legal penalties and discriminatory practices."[6]

The Stonewall riots of June 1969 gave the struggle a more public, somewhat more radical, impulse. In 1970, for example, Chicago Gay Liberation members prepared a working paper on gay rights for the Revolutionary People's Constitutional Convention, held that year in Philadelphia. Employment discrimination was the first item under the heading "Grievances Common to All Homosexuals." Discussing hiring, firing, and income, and acknowledging disparities perpetuated against women and people of color, the document's drafters identified ways heteronormative society regulated the employment possibilities of homosexuals:

> There is a tracking system which determines the positions open to homosexuals where we are able to work in the company of other homosexuals. We often take these jobs even though we may not like them and the pay may be low, just so that we won't have to worry about being found out. . . . There is nothing wrong with those jobs, but the choices should be based on interest and ability.[7]

Made in the context of a civil rights–conscious era, such rhetoric appealed to many progressives' notions of equity and nondiscrimination. By the mid-1970s, some thirty municipalities in the United States had passed nondiscrimination laws. However, these local ordinances generally were enacted by elected officials, not voters, and as such were relatively easy for voters to repeal.

The first and most famous repeal battle occurred in Florida in 1977. In January of that year, commissioners in Dade County, which includes Miami, Miami Beach, and surrounding areas, passed an ordinance banning discrimination against gay people in housing, employment, and public accommodation. At the time, it was the gay rights movement's most significant success in terms of number of citizens affected. Immediately after the vote, Anita Bryant, a local resident, pop singer, and spokesperson for the Florida orange juice industry, launched a drive to repeal the law. She argued that "[t]he ordinance condones immorality and discriminates against my children's rights to grow up in a healthy, decent community."[8]

It is significant that Bryant, the mother of four, invoked the discourse of child endangerment even though the ordinance's purview did not extend to public schools. Nonetheless, she repeatedly asserted the need to protect children from the alleged dangers of homosexuality. Save Our Children, Inc., the group she founded to organize the repeal effort, took out full-page newspaper advertisements linking gay men to kiddy porn and child molestation. Ads and leaflets alleged that gay people—gay men, especially—were eager to infiltrate schools and Big Brother/Big Sister programs in order to "recruit" impressionable children. Issues unrelated to children, such as the ordinance's possible economic impact on employers, barely registered in the campaign.[9]

Many gay activists in Dade County responded to Bryant's charges in a way that would become distressingly familiar in similar campaigns over the next two decades: they adopted a strategy that ultimately limited "extreme" displays of gay identity. For example, in order to enforce a conservative depiction of gay life, they discouraged leathermen and drag queens from campaigning for the ordinance in public. Indeed, mainstream gay leaders honed the countersubversive message that the ordinance was more about principle than practice, that gay people actually were not interested in expressing their sexuality publicly. As Jack Campbell, a leader of the pro-ordinance campaign, told Newsweek, "My dentist is gay, my doctor is gay, the people who clean my pool are gay, even my exterminator is gay. . . . Most of them are reserved, conservative people who want to keep their sexuality private."[10]

Despite gay activists' low-key approach, Bryant galvanized broad public support against the ordinance. Save Our Children gathered sixty thousand signatures calling for a repeal referendum—even though only ten thousand were needed to force a public vote. In June 1977, Dade County residents voted two to one for repeal, and Bryant subsequently vowed to expand her group into a national organization.[11]

The campaign received national attention and motivated other conservative activists. Within a year of the Dade County referendum, voters in St. Paul, Minnesota, Wichita, Kansas, and Eugene, Oregon, repealed antidiscrimination ordinances in their cities. In California, state senator John Briggs, who had campaigned with Bryant, authored a proposition that would have forced the firing of gay teachers and banned any discussion of homosexuality in California schools. The proposition failed, but many gay activists suspected the vote reflected a rejection of the measure's vague wording and not an endorsement of gay teachers.[12]

At this time—the mid to late 1970s—organized labor had a mixed record of support for gay rights. Some unions, notably those representing bus drivers in Michigan and *Village Voice* employees in New York City, achieved protections for gay workers. Other unions actively resisted such coverage. In New York City, the police and fire unions bitterly opposed Mayor Ed Koch's 1978 executive order banning discrimination on the basis of sexual orientation in city employment. The president of the firefighters' union argued that homosexuals should be excluded from the department, saying, "If homosexuals were admitted to the Fire Department, we would have to seriously consider providing separate bathrooms, shower and living facilities for gays."[13]

Despite the problems encountered in getting local ordinances passed and keeping them in place, many activists found local governments to be the most receptive to gay-rights legislation. States were moving slowly, and proposed federal legislation was going nowhere. In 1975, Representative Bella Abzug introduced the first federal gay-rights bill. It would have amended the Civil Rights Act of 1964 to prohibit discrimination on the basis of "affectional or sexual preference." But only four representatives agreed to cosponsor the legislation. More bills were introduced in Congress in subsequent years. Some were general gay-rights measures; others dealt solely with employment discrimination. None ever came up for a vote.[14]

In June 1994, when ENDA was first introduced in Congress, eight states, the District of Columbia, and approximately 120 municipalities had enacted some form of nondiscrimination legislation. These laws varied in scope: California prohibited discrimination only in employment and community redevelopment, and it exempted employers with fewer than five employees; Minnesota forbade discrimination almost everywhere—in education, housing, public accommodation, and employment.[15]

In this context, we can view ENDA as a limited, cautious attempt to counter discrimination against gay people. Unlike Abzug's bill or some earlier bills in the Senate, it would apply only to employment because its backers, probably with some justification, argue that a full gay civil rights bill is unpassable in today's political climate. Consequently, ENDA does nothing to address sodomy statutes that are still on the books in at least twenty states; it explicitly affirms that employers are not required to extend benefits to workers' domestic partners; and it exempts the armed forces and most religious institutions from its provisions. (Like the Civil Rights Act of 1964, it also exempts employers with fewer than fifteen employees.)

But ENDA's focus has grown ever narrower over its relatively short life. For example, of the four versions of ENDA introduced into Congress thus far, the 1994 version gave the broadest definition of "sexual orientation," saying that the term "means lesbian, gay, bisexual or heterosexual orientation, real or perceived, as manifested by identity, acts, statements, or associations." In contrast, the 1995, 1997, and 1999 versions defined sexual orientation as "homosexuality, bisexuality, or heterosexuality, whether such orientation is real or perceived."[16] Chai Feldblum, a professor at Georgetown University Law Center and one of ENDA's drafters, said the bill's sponsors removed the "as manifested" phrase in order to deny critics a "hook" to discuss specific sexual acts the bill could be accused of endorsing.[17]

This brings us to the crucial point regarding ENDA (and most of the nondiscrimination laws enacted on the local and state levels to date). ENDA does not seek to ensure the *sexual* rights of workers. Instead, by enacting its protection through the paradigm of sexual orientation, it would mandate only that employers treat gay, bisexual, and straight workers equally. ENDA therefore would prohibit an employer from firing a worker simply because the worker is gay but would allow an employer to fire a worker who had sex in public places, such as parks or alleys. The employer would only have to establish that she would fire *any* worker—straight *or* gay—who engaged in public sex. In doing so, she would not be discriminating on the basis of sexual orientation; she would be discriminating on the basis of deviant sexual practice—discrimination that ENDA would allow to continue.

Actually, that example of a worker being fired for engaging in public sex is only probable because it is unclear exactly which sexual practices ENDA would protect and which it would not. Equally unclear is how courts would determine if a specific practice were even sexual in nature. Cross-dressing, for example, is a practice that is not overtly sexual but that nonetheless is often considered sexually deviant. Cross-dressing and public sex are just two of many issues that ultimately would have to be adjudicated through test cases. According to Professor Feldblum, ENDA protects activity that is "quintessentially related" to one's orientation. As such, the law would be both status-based in that it protects suspected, outed, or self-proclaimed homosexuals, and conduct-based in that it protects people who engage in same-sex relations. However, Feldblum says that courts probably would interpret ENDA as protecting only those "kinds of sexual practices that most straight people engage in and want to keep their jobs," meaning kissing, masturbation, and oral, vaginal, and anal intercourse; perhaps some leather; maybe some light s/m. She doubts it would be interpreted as protecting public sex, hard-core s/m, and many fetishes. "The bill is premised on equality. It is not premised on sexual freedom," Feldblum said. "In reality, it is conservative in terms of sexual freedom."

All of which brings us back to Bruton.

Arguing ENDA

That the Republican-controlled U.S. Senate even voted on ENDA in 1996 was something of a surprise. GOP leaders agreed to the vote only four days before it occurred. They did so to ensure that the Defense of Marriage Act (DOMA), a bill barring federal recognition of same-sex marriages, would be voted on and passed. A bipartisan majority of senators supported DOMA, as did President Bill Clinton, and gay-friendly senators were eager to keep the bill from coming up for a vote. In the end, they attempted to attach the pro-gay ENDA to it as an amendment. Their hope was that the Senate would not vote on the marriage bill at all if passing it guaranteed even a limited degree of gay rights. After much maneuvering, Republican leaders blocked the effort to link the two bills but grudgingly allowed a separate vote on ENDA. In short, in 1996 few senators made the rights of gay workers a priority. Instead, it was the Senate's eagerness to deny gays the right to wed that was the true motivation behind the vote on ENDA.[18]

Given that the Senate's attention was focused on DOMA, it is not surprising that debate on ENDA lacked luster. Anti-ENDA senators predictably invoked the discourse of "special rights" for gays and warned of rafts of lawsuits against employers should the legislation pass. Just as predictably, they warned of children threatened by the putative dangers of homosexuality. Some referred explicitly to Bruton, whose transgressions had come to light in the *Washington Post* only two months earlier. Even before ENDA was scheduled for a vote, right-wing commentators invoked the now-unemployed teacher as a symbol of the homosexual horrors that the bill would inflict on American children. As Robert Knight, director of cultural studies for the Family Research Council, wrote in the *Washington Times*,

> Under ENDA, 'sexual orientation' is defined as 'homosexuality, bisexuality, or heterosexuality, whether such orientation is real or perceived.' This covers everything from foot fetishes to starring in gay porn films. Mr. Bruton could have argued that he was unfairly targeted because most people might reasonably assume that an actor engaged in homosexuality in a film was homosexual. He could then claim school officials were bigoted against his 'orientation' rather than his activities per se.[19]

As if teachers who made porn films were not objectionable enough to *Times* readers, Knight went on to link homosexuals with child molesters. "ENDA could cover pedophilia, because many people believe (with good reason) that pedophilia is disproportionately homosexual. So a pedophile could argue that since people rightly or wrongly perceive him to be homosexual, he is a victim of 'sexual orientation' bias."[20]

ENDA's framers cringed at Knight's implication that all sorts of fetishes and "deviant" sexual practices could somehow fit into the neat troika of sexual orientations on which they had built the bill's protections. In deference to the repressive social climate, they had not intended ENDA to protect most nonnormative sexual practices. Nonetheless, Knight's political scaremongering was so troubling that they included a "construction clause," Section 11, in the version of the bill the Senate voted on. The clause, which Feldblum says was written "to counter the 'Ty Fox' argument," made explicit what the drafters had understood all along:

> Nothing in this Act shall be construed to prohibit a covered entity from enforcing rules regarding nonprivate sexual conduct, if the rules of conduct are designed for, and uniformly applied to, all individuals regardless of sexual orientation.

The inclusion of the clause seems to have impressed nobody. During debate, Senator Orrin Hatch blithely suggested that Bruton's work in gay porn was evidence that Bruton was in fact gay, something Bruton himself had not acknowledged. Hatch further argued that because Bruton was gay, ENDA would certainly have prevented him from being fired. He referred to Section 11, but only to link it to senators' fears of same-sex affection. He argued that if a school allowed a male teacher to kiss his wife goodbye in a school yard (a "good thing for the children to see"), the school would be forced to allow a gay teacher to kiss his male partner goodbye as well. Hatch found such occurrences unacceptable. "This provision [Section 11] provides little help to the people of Loudoun County and across the country who have similar concerns. Its fundamental flaw is that in order to enforce rules under this section, homosexuality and heterosexuality must be treated entirely alike."[21]

ENDA's supporters in the Senate followed the lead set by gay activists in Dade County twenty years earlier. They tried not to discuss sexual activity; when forced to, they quickly condemned "extreme" forms of sexual expression. Perhaps ironically, it was Senator Edward Kennedy, the bill's chief sponsor, who gave one of the more prudish defenses of ENDA:

> Like other civil rights laws, the Employment Non-Discrimination Act does not protect bizarre behavior. . . . This legislation allows employers to discipline homosexuals and heterosexuals whose behavior is illegal or unsafe or

that compromises their ability to perform their job—the examples given earlier . . . would clearly fall under those standards. These policies must simply be applied to all employees—heterosexual and homosexual. . . . School systems can discipline teachers who appear in pornographic movies or other kinds of activities, but they must discipline both homosexuals and heterosexuals similarly.[22]

Senator John Chafee agreed, saying,

An employee whose behavior in the workplace is inappropriate deserves no protection from sanction. A gay employee who makes inappropriate statements or otherwise conducts him or herself in an inappropriate manner should not be countenanced. That is clear. The same would apply to a non-gay individual who conducts him or herself inappropriately. That conduct would not be tolerated.[23]

The Senate voted on ENDA on September 10, 1996. AFL-CIO President John Sweeney and other pro-ENDA labor leaders watched the vote from the Senate's reception room, while gay activists held a silent prayer vigil on the steps of the capitol. The bill failed by a surprisingly close 49-to-50 vote, and commentators later suggested that many senators voted "yea" out of fear of political retribution from gays angry at the passage of DOMA.

Since ENDA's failure, various efforts to secure the rights of gay and lesbian workers have met with mixed results. In 1997, the legislatures of Maine and New Hampshire adopted nondiscrimination laws, bringing to eleven the number of states that protect gay workers. However, right-wing activists in Maine immediately attacked their state's law and ultimately forced a referendum. Once again, conservatives invoked the discourse of child endangerment, with the Christian Coalition distributing tens of thousands of flyers asking: "Do you want to send your children or grandchildren to Day Cares, Pre-schools and Schools that are forced to hire homosexuals?" In February 1998, voters repealed the law by a 52-to-48 percent margin.[24]

On a brighter note, twenty-one years after voters repealed Dade County's original nondiscrimination ordinance, members of the Miami–Dade County Commission again adopted gay-rights legislation. The 1998 law bans discrimination against gay people in housing, employment, credit, finance, and public accommodation. Moreover, the discourse of child endangerment played only a minor role in the campaign. Far more important was the impact of gay tourism on the local economy—in the two decades since Bryant's campaign, gay tourists had begun flocking to the coral sands of Miami Beach, and commissioners did not want to risk losing the newfound tax dollars.

Gay workers in Dade County still are not completely secure in their rights, however. The ordinance's opponents vow to fight the measure—by referendum, if necessary.[25]

Political Expediency, Sexual Intolerance

So where does this leave us? ENDA was reintroduced in both houses of Congress in June 1999. This latest version is even narrower than its predecessors. At the insistence of Representative Barney Frank, ENDA's chief Democratic sponsor in the House, the bill now explicitly forbids affirmative action aimed at gay and lesbian workers. Although ENDA's drafters had never intended the bill to include gay workers in affirmative action programs, conservative legislators were "hitting us over the head" with the issue, Frank told reporters. Frank also refused to rewrite ENDA so that its provisions would cover people who are gender-different, saying that such a move would doom the bill. Despite Frank's pragmatic politicking, many commentators say they doubt the bill will come up for a vote in the Republican-controlled 106th Congress.[26] And, frankly, I'm not sure that ENDA's future is as important as the troubling questions the bill raises for progressive gay and labor activists. I fear that in the interest of getting ENDA passed we are forgoing the possibility of a society in which a diversity of sexual practices is welcomed, not punished.

Both supporters and critics of ENDA have crassly attempted to manipulate discussion of the issue of workplace discrimination against gays. Of course, it almost goes without saying that obfuscation and occasional outright deception permeate the world of politics. Something odd happened in the battle over ENDA, however. Both the mainstream LGBT movement that supported the bill and the conservative legislators who opposed it became invested in denying the diversity of people's sexual practices. This underscores a simple but far-reaching fact: a fear of "deviant" sex permeates ENDA and discussions about it.

The political pragmatism of the mainstream gay activists who wrote ENDA and lobby for it is clear. First, they focused solely on workplace discrimination because they realized that a general gay-rights bill—one that would at least protect gays from discrimination in housing, education, health care, and public accommodation as well as employment—probably would not succeed in today's political culture. They exempted the military and religious groups and excluded issues of transgenderism and gender conformity.

OLD COUNTRY STORE

FOR IMMEDIATE RELEASE:

Cracker Barrel is founded upon a concept of traditional American values,
quality in all we do, and a philosophy of 100% guest satisfaction. It is
consistent with our concept and values, and is perceived to be
inconsistent with those of our customer base, to continue to employ
individuals in our operating units whose sexual preferences fail to
demonstrate normal heterosexual values which have been the foundation of
families in our society. Therefore, it is felt this business decision is
in the best interests of the company.

For any further information, please contact:

>   Mr. William A. Bridges
>   Vice President of Human Resources
>   Cracker Barrel Old Country Store, Inc.
>   P. O. Box 787
>   Lebanon, TN 37088-0787
>   (615) 444-5533

-30-

Legal in thirty-nine states: in February 1991, this policy statement was read aloud to
employees in the Georgia Cracker Barrel restaurant where Cheryl Summerville worked.
Throughout the company, at least eleven workers lost their jobs. This document is
reprinted as it appeared in *Out at Work: America Undercover,* a documentary produced
for HBO TV by ANDERSONGOLD Films. Reprinted with permission from
ANDERSONGOLD Films.

They wrote ENDA as an individual law rather than as an amendment to the
Civil Rights Act of 1964, in effect ranking homophobia as something less
than, and independent of, institutionalized racism and misogyny. Finally, and
most importantly, they provided workplace protection primarily if not exclusively to people who engage in sexual practices that are construed as normative. In short, they chose to seek only what they believed to be obtainable.

Their pragmatism is further evidenced by their characterization of the
workers ENDA would protect. A good example is Cheryl Summerville, who
was featured in the documentary film *Out at Work* and who also testified at
Congressional hearings on ENDA. In 1991, Summerville was fired from her
job as a cook at a Cracker Barrel restaurant in Georgia for violating company
policy that all employees should demonstrate "normal heterosexual values."
The company instituted a blatantly homophobic though perfectly legal employment policy and Summerville, because she proudly insisted on being

43

recognized as a lesbian, lost her job. Interestingly, Summerville said her bosses told her that the policy's intended targets were effeminate male wait- ers whose jobs required them to interact with the public. Had Summerville not confronted her bosses about the homophobic policy, she might still be working in the relative privacy of a Cracker Barrel kitchen today. In any case, Summerville's only clear "transgression" against heteronormative culture was that she was gay: she was in an apparently stable and monogamous relation- ship; at the time she was barely political, much less an agitator at work; and she was not accused of engaging in any "bizarre" sexual practices. Both in fact and as mediated by ENDA's supporters, Summerville's story makes painfully clear the simpleminded bigotry behind so much of the discrimination that gay workers experience. More pertinent, I suggest, is that Summerville is portrayed as typical because she is a *politically acceptable embodiment* of workplace discrimination.[27]

Opponents of ENDA clearly followed their own politics of pragmatism. If Summerville was ENDA supporters' stereotypical worker harmed by workplace discrimination, then Bruton was ENDA critics' poster boy waiting to corrupt American children. Of course, the right's invocation of Bruton in the context of ENDA was misleading given the bill's construction clause, which I discuss above. Almost certainly, any court interpreting the law would have allowed the Loudoun County School Board to fire Bruton. School offi- cials would only have to establish that they were prepared to fire *any* teacher who appeared in pornographic films.

If this is clear from even a layperson's reading of the bill, why did con- servative activists and senators invoke Bruton as an example of ENDA's alleged dangers? I suggest they wanted Bruton to fulfill two roles: he should illustrate the "extreme" ways some people arrange their sexual lives and, si- multaneously, he should induce amnesia regarding the comfortable banality of the more typical gay figure, represented by Summerville. Conservatives opposed ENDA because they construed it as a challenge to heteronormative culture; they then invoked Bruton as a politically potent symbol of all that the nonnormative might encompass. His case, unlike Summerville's, raised issues beyond a gay person's right to be out in the workplace: Bruton was married but most likely an adulterer; he portrayed himself as straight but had sex with men; he violated the idealized intimacy of the sexual act by participating in a very public form of sexual activity; he exchanged sex for money; and, not least, he breached the cultural standards of masculine char- acter and ideals expected from coaches of young boys.

In retrospect, conservative debates over the bill are somewhat ironic. In pragmatic terms of blocking passage of ENDA, conservatives manipulated the Bruton case successfully. However, they falsely interpreted ENDA as a challenge to heteronormative culture. If anything, with its reliance on the paradigm of three separate and presumably inviolable sexual orientations, ENDA clearly seeks not to subvert heteronormative culture but rather to assimilate gay workers into it. As written, ENDA attempts to categorize and organize sexuality, not to acknowledge its fluidity or instability. Once this categorization is accomplished, ENDA then gives employers and judges a distressing capacity to distinguish between what is supposedly normative (and therefore acceptable) and what is not.

This reflexive defense of heteronormativity helps explain why the specter of homosexual interaction with children carries so much social and political power. The fears manifested in the discourse of child endangerment seem to be twofold. First, adults worry that children exposed to any sexual activity, and "deviant" sexual activity in particular, would be either defiled or titillated by the exposure. In either case, the child might then develop into an adult whose experiences lead him or her to transgress the confines of normative sexual practice. Second, the specter of adult-child sex is so repugnant to so many people that it effectively stigmatizes all nonnormative sexual practices. This mode of thinking is a transitive equation: if cross-dressing is deviance and child molestation is deviance, then they must somehow be related. What gets left out of this argument, of course, is an acknowledgment that all cross-dressing and child molestation have in common is their "deviance" *relative to* heteronormative sexual practice.[28]

Conclusion

In closing this essay, I would like to bring together the threads of my discussion—ENDA, Bruton, child endangerment, and heteronormative culture—with a call for greater conversation and cooperation between queer, labor, and intellectual activists. Only a coalition of these forces can begin to challenge the heteronormative culture that constrains and limits us all.

Having said that, I must admit that I am not entirely sure how such a coalition might function or what its specific mode of securing workers' rights might be.[29] Instead, I offer this triad of forces as the logical starting point given the range and scope of the protections that are needed. Workplace protections are necessary for people who identify as gay, lesbian, or bisexual; they are necessary for people who identify as straight; they are necessary for people who claim confusion or who simply refuse to label themselves; and they are necessary for people who are gender different. Workplace protections should not rely on inherently discriminatory hierarchies of sexual identities, orientations, or practices. Finally, and most importantly, the process of establishing workplace protections should entail an open and ongoing acknowledgment of the diversity of sexual practices and institutions within heteronormative culture itself. This process would (and must) unveil the culture's alleged normality and naturalness to be the sham it is.

Some of this work has already begun.

In a campaign to identify that which oppresses, some intellectuals have turned their focus to the concept of heteronormativity. I have already mentioned the recent work of Lauren Berlant, Cathy J. Cohen, and Michael Warner. Intellectual inquiry into heteronormativity began some years earlier, however, and its genesis seems to lie primarily in the work of Michel Foucault and Gayle Rubin. In her canonical essay, "Thinking Sex," Rubin explains how mainstream society has established a gradation of sexual practices it labels deviant. She terms this gradation the "sex hierarchy." The "good sex" in her hierarchy is reproductive monogamy in the confines of a committed heterosexual relationship. The "bad sex" is any that involves transvestitism, transgenderism, fetishes, sadomasochism, prostitution, or pedophilia. The contested area between these poles includes sex involving, in descending order of acceptance, unmarried straight couples, promiscuous straights, masturbation, long-term gay couples, and promiscuous gays.[30]

This hierarchy helps explain why gay people are likely to be harassed or arrested for engaging in "deviant" sexual practices, such as consuming pornography or having sex in public places, that straight people often engage in with impunity. Although Rubin did not factor race into her hierarchy, many other cultural analysts have described Western culture's historical construction of whiteness as sexually pure and blackness as irretrievably libidinous. Consequently, people of color, like homosexuals, are often if not typically viewed as inherently sexually suspect. In short, society grants varying amounts of privilege to actors in the sexual realm depending on their race, gender, class, and sexual practices. This raises questions of what is truly transgressive, of whether some "deviant" sexual acts performed by straight people are a subversion of heteronormativity or, instead, a privilege of it. I suggest that the answer depends on the social status of the actor(s) performing the act in question.

Moreover, Rubin's hierarchy should resonate with labor activists, for certainly it is the monogamous straight (white) folks at the top who experience the least amount of workplace discrimination because of their sexuality. The farther down the hierarchy one goes, the more discrimination one finds and the more overt and obnoxious it becomes, so that the known transsexuals and prostitutes at the bottom can rarely find "legitimate" work anywhere.

Perhaps most importantly, Warner and other intellectuals have introduced many of us to queer theory, which rejects putatively natural categories of sexuality such as the trio of orientations ENDA embraces. Almost by definition, queer theory opposes heteronormativity, which relies on these same categories for coherence. In rejecting the naturalness of sexual categories, queer theory encourages a form of sexual liberation based on feelings of pleasure and desire that may change over time or by situation. Finally, its rejection of sexual categories has encouraged activists to resist those aspects of the dominant culture that seek alternately to identify, define, regulate, and police sexual "difference."

I dwell on queer theory because I want to distinguish between "queer" and "gay" and, in doing so, suggest that the former offers a more liberating view of sexuality. Perhaps following Rubin, who as early as 1984 encouraged us "to think about sex," queers place sexual desire and activity at the forefront of identity and activism.[31] Sexual desire and activity are ambiguous subjects for many gay activists, however. Increasingly, mainstream gay organizations like the Human Rights Campaign seem to want to maintain the paradigm of sexual orientation while disconnecting it from the reality of sexual practice. But in reality many gays—just like many straights—cross-dress, pick up strangers, have multiple partners, masturbate to porn videos, screw in parks, play with sex toys, dominate and submit. And sometimes we lose our jobs for doing so. By supporting ENDA without question, mainstream groups compromise the rights of people who engage in "deviant" sex. Given that, how effective can they be in producing a society that acknowledges and welcomes sexual diversity?

For their part, queer activists in recent years have targeted laws and institutions seeking to regulate or deny people's sexual freedoms. In New York City, the group Sex Panic formed in response to Mayor Rudolph Giuliani's systematic crackdown on "queer zones" throughout the city, some of which encompassed commercial areas that contained bars, dance clubs, and porno shops, others that consisted of public spaces such as parks, streets, and piers. This crackdown climaxed in October 1995 when, at Giuliani's instigation, the city council passed a zoning ordinance that relegated most sex shops and strip joints to the fringes of the city. Sex Panic not only publicized the homophobia inherent in Giuliani's "quality of life" campaign, but also singled out gay neoconservatives such as Andrew Sullivan and Gabriel Rotello, whose attacks on sexual liberation were seen as complicit in the crackdown. According to Douglas Crimp,

Their program calls for us to conform to a narrow standard of sexual expression, essentially limited to monogamous relationships or marriage. They believe that the distinctive sexual culture we created should be abandoned in favor of imitating the most constricted, institutionalized forms of heterosexual conformism. . . . The primary right we've had to fight for—and still have to fight for—is the right to be sexual.[32]

This is far from the rhetoric that emanates from mainstream LGBT rights groups. Much in the same way Queer Nation and ACT-UP infused gay activism with a queer, justifiably angry sensibility, groups like Sex Panic remind us that sexuality is an integral aspect of identity, and therefore always under threat.

Finally, in recent years progressive elements within organized labor have initiated a public embrace of gay rights that could greatly improve the lives of lesbian and gay workers. In 1983, the AFL-CIO passed a resolution condemning discrimination against gay workers, and in 1998 it established Pride at Work, an organization of LGBT union members, as an official constituency group. Perhaps even more important than these largely symbolic moves have been union-led efforts to secure the economic rights of gay workers. Many unions, especially those representing large numbers of women and people of color, now regularly negotiate contracts that prohibit employers from discriminating on the basis of sexual orientation and that extend health care and benefits plans to the partners of gay workers. In one or two instances, unions have even agreed to organize workers in the sex industry. In April 1997, for example, the Service Employees International Union (SEIU) negotiated a contract for the seventy strippers at the Lusty Lady Theater in San Francisco. Although the Lusty Lady campaign came about only after a great deal of discussion between dancers and SEIU organizers, not to mention within the union itself, it demonstrates that progressive elements within organized labor recognize that workers in the sex industry are just that—workers.[33]

It is this kind of recognition that engages heteronormativity, but it is also, in many ways, the antithesis of the political and intellectual arguments put forth in ENDA. Many intellectuals, queer activists, and union officials recognize the diversity of sexual practices in which people engage, and some even celebrate that diversity. It remains to be seen, however, whether we find commonality in that recognition, whether we form activist coalitions that seek to end discrimination against people who engage in "deviant" sex, and whether our collaborative activism occurs not only in the workplace but in other contested spaces such as the home, the school, the bar, and the street. In short, it remains to be seen whether any coalitional efforts would truly seek to transform heteronormative culture or, like ENDA, would only assimilate more people into it.

Notes

1. Victoria Benning, "Loudoun Coach Allegedly Starred in Sex Videos," *Washington Post*, July 19, 1996, sec. D, p. 1.
2. Kennedy's bill was S.R. 2238. Its counterpart in the House, H.R. 4643, was sponsored by Representative Gerry Studds, D-Mass.
3. See Lauren Berlant and Michael Warner, "Sex in Public," *Critical Inquiry* 24 (winter 1998): 547–66; and Cathy J. Cohen, "Punks, Bulldaggers, and Welfare Queens: The Radical Potential of Queer Politics?" *GLQ* 3, 437–65.
4. Berlant and Warner, "Sex in Public," 557.
5. Philip Jenkins, *Moral Panic: Changing Concepts of the Child Molester in Modern America* (New Haven: Yale University Press, 1998), 62.
6. John D'Emilio, *Sexual Politics, Sexual Communities: The Making of a Homosexual Minority in the United States, 1940–1970* (Chicago: University of Chicago Press, 1983), 213.
7. Chicago Gay Liberation, "Working Paper for the Revolutionary People's Constitutional Convention," in *Out of the Closets: Voices of Gay Liberation*, ed. Karla Jay and Allen Young (New York: New York University Press, 1992), 347. I invoke the term "heteronormative" here advisedly because Chicago Gay Liberation members did not use it themselves. Nonetheless, I believe they were referring to a cultural, systemic privileging of heterosexuality that seems remarkably similar to what I understand as heteronormativity.
8. "Bias against Homosexuals Is Outlawed in Miami," *New York Times*, January 19, 1977, sec. A, p. 14.
9. For more on the Dade County campaign, see John Loughery, *The Other Side of Silence: Men's Lives and Gay Identities: A Twentieth-Century History* (New York: Henry Holt and Co., 1998), 371–88. For a contemporary account of the referendum, see *Newsweek*, June 6, 1977, in which the collection of cover stories is titled "Anita Bryant vs. The Homosexuals."
10. Richard Steele, "Battle over Gay Rights," *Newsweek*, June 6, 1977, 16.
11. B. Drummond Ayres, "Miami Votes 2 to 1 to Repeal Law Barring Bias against Homosexuals," *New York Times*, June 8, 1977, sec. A, p. 1. Soon after the Dade County vote, the charity group Save the Children objected in court to Bryant's choice of name for her organization. A judge ruled that the names were confusingly similar, and Bryant renamed her organization Protect America's Children.
12. For more on the Briggs' Proposition, see Randy Shilts, *The Mayor of Castro Street: The Life and Times of Harvey Milk* (New York: St. Martin's Press, 1982).
13. Edward Ranzal, "Bill on Homosexuals Is Planned in Council," *New York Times*, January 4, 1978, sec. A, p. 16.
14. Abzug's bill, introduced during the 94th Congress, was H.R. 166. To my knowledge, no one has published a systematic analysis of the many gay-rights bills introduced into Congress since 1975. For the text of this and other federal bills, I refer readers to the Library of Congress's wonderfully detailed website: http//thomas.loc.gov.

15. The states that had nondiscrimination statutes on the books in 1994, when Kennedy introduced the first version of ENDA, were California, Connecticut, Hawaii, Massachusetts, Minnesota, New Jersey, Vermont, and Wisconsin. Rhode Island passed a nondiscrimination law in 1995. Maine and New Hampshire enacted protective statutes in 1997, though Maine voters repealed their state's law in 1998. Nevada provided protections in 1999.

16. For simplicity, I refer to the different versions of ENDA by the year they were introduced. The "1995 version" refers to H.R. 1863 and S.R. 2056. This is the version—with one change that is noted later in this article—that the Senate voted on. The "1997 version" refers to H.R. 1858 and S.R. 869; the "1999 version" refers to H.R. 2355 and S.R. 1276.

17. Professor Feldblum and I spoke via telephone on November 18, 1998, and her quotes in this essay are from my notes of that conversation. I thank her for her candor, time, and good-natured guidance.

18. For more on the Senate's votes on DOMA and ENDA, and the events leading up to the votes, see Eric Schmitt, "Senate Weighs Bill on Gay Rights on the Job," *New York Times*, September 7, 1996, sec. A, p. 12; Eric Schmitt, "Senators Reject Both Job-Bias Ban and Gay Marriage," *New York Times*, September 11, 1996, sec. A, p. 1; and J. Jennings Moss, "Jilted," *The Advocate*, October 15, 1996, 23–27.

19. Robert Knight, "Prelude to Sexual Legal Anarchy?" *Washington Times*, August 22, 1996, sec. A, p. 15.

20. Ibid.

21. *Congressional Record*, 104th Cong., 2d. sess., 1996, 142, pt. 121.

22. *Congressional Record*, 104th Cong., 2d. sess., 1996, 142, pt. 122.

23. *Congressional Record*, 104th Cong., 2d. sess., 1996, 142, pt. 123.

24. Goldberg, Carey, "Maine Voters Repeal a Law on Gay Rights," *New York Times*, February 12, 1998, sec. A, p. 1.

25. Mireya Navarro, "Two Decades on, Miami Endorses Gay Rights," *New York Times*, December 2, 1998, sec. A, p. 1.

26. With these changes, ENDA became so diluted that even some mainstream organizations began to reassess their support for it. On June 16, 1999, Kerry Lobel, director of the National Gay and Lesbian Task Force, released a statement saying, "Without the inclusion of transgendered people, NGLTF cannot endorse ENDA. We do not oppose ENDA, but advocate adding language that is more inclusive." For the full text of the statement, titled "NGLTF Supports Transgender Inclusion in Employment Non-Discrimination Act," see www.ngltf.org/news/index.cfm. For news reports on the latest version of ENDA and the controversies surrounding it, see Lou Chibbaro Jr., "New ENDA Bill 'Bans' Affirmative Action for Gays," *Washington Blade*, June 25, 1999, p. 17; and Tracey Eckels, "Frank Angers Transgendered Community," *New York Blade*, July 2, 1999, p. 10. See also Riki Anne Wilchins's remarks regarding ENDA in this volume.

27. Summerville is featured in the documentaries *Out at Work: Lesbians and Gay Men on the Job* (ANDERSONGOLD Films, 1997) and *Out at Work: America Undercover* (HBO, 1999). These are two separate films, both made by Tami Gold and Kelly Anderson. I do not differentiate between the two films in this context because both give basically identical accounts of Summerville's story, using the same footage.

28. I do not mean to diminish or dispute the fact that some adults do sexually abuse or otherwise brutalize children, though I certainly would argue with assertions that gays are any more likely than straights to molest children.

29. I suggested in an earlier version of this paper that ENDA's limitations and lack of engagement with heteronormative culture challenge progressives to work for a law that

would protect all workers regardless of sexual *practice*. Currently, ENDA's protections are based on the paradigm of sexual orientation. I understand now that a law forbidding discrimination on the basis of sexual practice might jeopardize other laws that ban sexual harassment in the workplace, and so I withdraw my first suggestion. The earlier version appeared in *Social Text* 61 (winter 1999): 39–58. I thank Lisa Duggan for sharing her concerns with me.

30. Gayle Rubin, "Thinking Sex: Notes for a Radical Theory of the Politics of Sexuality," in *Pleasure and Danger: Exploring Female Sexuality*, ed. Carole S. Vance (Boston: Routledge, 1984), 267–319.

31. Ibid., 267.

32. Douglas Crimp, "Liberation Backlash," in "Sex Panic!" (pamphlet), 11–12, n.p., n.d. E-mail: sexpanicnyc@geocities.com. My understanding is that Sex Panic has focused on resisting attacks against sexual diversity and freedom in general and has not been active in issues of workplace discrimination. Although I would like to see Sex Panic get involved in workplace issues, I invoke the group here as an example of a progressive collective of queer activists and intellectuals who are challenging the heteronormative standards that are the basis of workplace discrimination.

33. I thank Heidi Kooy for drawing my attention to this campaign, which she writes about in "Trollops and Tribades: Queers Organizing in the Sex Business," in this volume. Kooy acknowledges that Lusty Lady dancers had no actual *physical* contact with their clients. It would be interesting to know if this fact made their organizing efforts more palatable to some members of the labor movement. To my knowledge, organized labor has made no overtures to two of the most exploited groups of workers in the United States—prostitutes and people, such as Bruton, who appear in pornography.

What Is This Movement Doing to My Politics?

Cathy J. Cohen

HELP!
BOYCOTT
COORS
BEER

It seems to me that we have reached a critical moment in the politics of Lesbian, Gay, Bisexual, Transgender, Two-Spirit, Queer (LGBTTSQ) communities. Specifically, we seem to be fractured as never before. While there have always been tensions and divisions among LGBTTSQ people, at this moment in time the differentiated organized interests that exist among our national organizations are especially visible and appear to have a vicious edge. In part, this tension is the result of the proliferation of groups representing the varied interests and politics of queers. Technological advances also allow us to monitor the actions of "our" elites in ways not previously possible. However, for many of us, it has been the transformation in our status from unredeemable deviants to a possibly legitimate minority group that has heightened the stakes in "our" movement. Having received the gestures toward recognition from dominant institutions, we are now facing the possibility of actually being heard. Ironically but probably appropriately, in response to such advances we are witnessing heated and important battles over whose vision and politics will guide this "movement" through its next phase.

Probably in no other year (1998) have the limits of identity politics, at least in LGBTTSQ communities, been so apparent. These are just a few examples: the narrow self-interest evident in the Human Rights Campaign's endorsement of conservative former senator Alfonse D'Amato in the New York senate race; the Log Cabin Republicans' honoring of Ward Connerly, the black frontman for California's antiaffirmative action Proposition 209; the increasing corporatization of our national organizations, with the National Gay and Lesbian Task Force receiving and eventually returning a "gift" from Nike, which sells apparel produced in sweatshops, and the Gay and Lesbian Alliance Against Defamation accepting a "gift" from Coors, whose corporate, union-busting parents have long supported right-wing causes; the move to sanitize, whitenize, and normalize the public and visible representations of the LGBTTSQ community, as was evident in the response from national gay organizations to a right-wing ad campaign featuring "ex-gays." Examples like these indicate the need to reconsider a basic question: not, "What is the movement doing to my politics?" but "Can I have my politics and be a part of this movement?" Increasingly, I am sorry to say, I'm not sure.

Howard Wallace, leader of the 1973 Coors boycott, protests Coors sponsorship of a gay film festival in 1997. Photograph by Kaucylia Brooke; reprinted with permission.

As someone committed to progressive, radical politics that are anti-capitalist yet democratic; antisexist and feminist; antiracist and queer; international and global in focus, I am beginning to question whether those politics can coexist with a movement that has seemingly decided that the way to gain power is through assimilation. This form of assimilation is different from the assimilationist strategies of many early gay organizations, which fought for acceptance, but under the rubric of being a distinct and legitimate minority group. Instead, too many of our leaders today would have us conform and blend in, negating any claims we might have to a distinctive culture, distinctive understanding of family, and distinctive relationship to sexuality and sex that could revolutionize this country. Our new rediscovered goal—let us not forget we experienced a similar move to the normative right among our organizations during the McCarthy era—is to work the system for its currently structured benefits as opposed to challenging a system for the benefit of those more marginal and excluded. Don't believe their lie; our inclusion in and of itself will not make things different.

I want to be clear: I never understood the organizations in question or our movement as a whole to be committed to a truly progressive agenda—one that at the very least is willing and ready to look critically at the distribution of power in society, generating a response that advances the interests of those most marginal. I did, however, expect this movement to engage in some form of liberal transformative politics of inclusion, where our participation in the larger society would signal the reconsideration and reconstitution of basic categories like "citizen" and "family." The key here, of course, is the idea that as a movement we would actively participate, challenging and confronting the values, norms, and politics that previously denied our presence. Unfortunately, however, too many of our organizations seem to be buying inclusion at any cost. These community leaders would have us adopt the oppressive rhetoric and ideals of the right not only for a seat at the table, as is commonly articulated, but also because some believe in the society as it is presently constituted—except for that minor problem of their own personal experiences with exclusion. As a community, we are confronted with multiple identities, differentiated locations within oppressive systems, and the reality that we queers don't all suffer equally the process of marginalization. It is in this context that we each confront the question of whether inclusion is in fact enough for each of us individually and for others we consider a part of our community.

Again, let me be clear. I do not mean to denigrate the idea of inclusion, because the process of receiving formal recognition and rights has been, and continues to be, a very important achievement. Historically, across marginal communities, formal inclusion has been an important marker of economic, political, and social advancement. Ranging from the Thirteenth, Fourteenth, and Fifteenth Amendments during Reconstruction to the enactment of civil rights legislation during the 1960s to the legislative battles seeking basic civil rights for gays and lesbians in the 1990s, recognition of previously excluded groups has necessitated at the very least some minor redistribution of resources toward those most privileged in the newly incorporated group. Thus, through formal inclusion, some of us get benefits, some of us are recognized, and hopefully more of us get rights. However, despite such advances, we still confront the question of whether inclusion can be the only or the most important goal of our work. This is a dilemma that is especially pertinent to those who stand on the margins—those who through some combination of race, class, gender, sexuality, and/or national background find themselves excluded from the benefits of our supposedly democratic society. Those on the margins experience firsthand the race, class, gender, national, and sexual warfare being waged against the most vulnerable in our communities, not only by the right wing, but also by those who claim to be our liberal supporters. Thus, a liberal process of inclusion into this country as it is currently constituted is rarely sufficient, for inclusion is most often extended only to those who demonstrate the possibility of assimilation and conformity. Left perpetually on the outside are those marginal groups that members deem most deviant and aberrant. These group members, instead, suffer the consequences of our liberal politics of inclusion and face yet another system of exclusion.

For example, through a liberal politics of inclusion, we have experienced the destruction of welfare and witnessed the implementation of the 1996 Personal Responsibility and Work Opportunity Reconciliation Act, national legislation that rejects the state's long-term responsibility to aid those most defenseless. This policy instead forces on a population composed mostly of women, and disproportionately women of color, yet another works program that is often insufficient in the financial compensation it guarantees, as well as the work conditions it provides. In numerous cities across the country, reports are being made public of poor women forced into the workplace through our new "welfare policies" at hourly rates that will not raise them out of poverty and under work conditions that jeopardize their health and safety. Additionally, through the current politics of liberal inclusion, we have seen program-by-program and state-by-state attacks on affirmative action, immigration, and bilingual education, denying marginalized racial, ethnic, and immigrant populations equal opportunities for advancement and, indeed, basic rights. Harsh new immigration laws treat many immigrants—a great number of them people of color—as unwanted aliens, stripping them of fundamental rights accorded so-called "legal" residents, including access to health care and education. Moreover, under a politics of liberal inclusion, we have seen our liberal "allies" impose the silencing policy of "Don't ask, Don't tell," while our own national organizations tried to organize—largely through a closed process—a Millennium March that would bring together gay, lesbian, bisexual, transgender, two-spirit, queer, and supportive allies under the proposed conservative theme of "families and faith." In this case liberal inclusion is predicated on adherence to, or at least the appropriation of, traditional images and ideals like those of family and Christianity.

Of course this list of liberal acts of "inclusion" could go on. The point, however, is not to enumerate a list of political atrocities originating from the hands of liberal allies and colleagues, but instead to illustrate how a politics of mere inclusion or liberal accommodation will not serve the needs of most gay and lesbian people. As noted above, this process of inclusion is based on group members meeting the normative standards of a dominant white, heterosexual, capitalist class. The consequences of accepting this social contract is to exclude large segments of LGBTTSQ communities. Furthermore, such a list also underscores the fact that the society we live in, and are trying to move into, is not static but constantly in flux, spurred by the constant engagement of mobilized groups and individuals in the politics of the state. Some of the battles sparked by these engagements are instigated and waged by individuals and groups ideologically located on the right. These struggles may be assessed as reactionary efforts to keep the status quo in place or, better yet, to return the country—politically, economically, and most importantly socially—to years gone past. Other battles—unfortunately far too few—are fought by those we might place ideologically on the left, who hopefully are busy promoting what we would expect to be an agenda for progressive social change. Finally, other conflicts are waged by pockets of resisters situated somewhere between these two convenient and imagined ends of the left/right continuum. Thus, as a movement (if that is what we are) we have to ask: What shape will our intervention take, and in what direction will it go? If society is constantly being recreated in response to struggles over social change, what fight will we wage?

The direction our politics will take, while undoubtedly informed by our identity, must extend beyond our particular circumstances and take root in a larger vision of how we actualize, at the very least, a just and equal society. Such a dictate necessitates that we not only be consumed with raising money, mobilizing bodies, and passing legislation, but also with articulating visions of the society we seek to produce. Without dialogue and debate about what greater good we are working for, we may in fact achieve inclusion, but inclusion in an oppressive society. Therefore, we must be prepared to struggle with one another about what politics, ethics, values (yes, values), and visions are shaping LGBTTSQ organizations and more generally "our" movement. Struggle of this kind will be easier in some cases than in others. For example, most of us can agree that we stand against racism and those who espouse such beliefs. But what about those who claim to stand against racism while embracing conservative positions on issues dealing with gender or sexuality or class? I am clear that I am unwilling to associate myself in any long-term formation with conservative forces, whether those entities be black conservatives such as the Nation of Islam, which has continually engaged in rhetoric and behaviors meant to replicate heteronormative capitalist structures in black communities, or queer conservatives such as the Human Rights Campaign, the Washington-based gay-rights lobbying group whose endorsement of Alfonse D'Amato was tacit approval of his race-baiting, antipoor politics. Shared identity just does not go that far for me. However, such a broad declaration may not be as forthcoming from others. Thus, standing against racism may be the "easy" part. Constructing an analysis of racism that recognizes the multiple contours and intersections of racist oppression may be the more difficult task in front of us.

Class and class exploitation are still other issues we have to analyze in terms of the multiple forms they can take, especially as they are relevant to our movement. Organizations and groupings within LGBTTSQ communities have to figure out a praxis concerning issues of economic exploitation. Fundamentally, we have to reach beyond those class or worker issues that are clearly bound to gay and lesbian identities, such as domestic partnership, to other class issues that structure the daily lived condition of "queer" people more generally. So, for example, when national gay and lesbian organizations meet with corporations and companies to encourage the provision of domestic-partner benefits—an incredibly worthy effort—we must demand that they also include on their agenda questions concerning the workplace environment of gay, lesbian, and other workers. As we fight for domestic partnership we must also fight for a living wage for all workers, independent of sexual orientation, because it is part of our progressive vision of a just society. And as we struggle for transformative inclusion, we must struggle to transform the workplace, guaranteeing at a minimum that everyone has the right to organize.

However, beyond workers' rights, there are other class issues that have been represented as tangential to gay and lesbian identities but demand the attention of any progressive movement. As a movement, how have we and

will we respond to such issues? Were we prepared to talk about and participate in efforts to defeat the 1996 Work and Responsibility Act, which promoted workfare in many states? From my political vantage point, I think we
should have been on the battle lines of this fight—not just because we are
everywhere; not only because there are queer women who are exploited by
this legislation; not simply because the ideological roots of this legislation
promote as normal nuclear, working, heterosexual families, while demoniz-
ing every other family structure, but also, and just as importantly, because it
was the progressive battle to wage. In our local communities, are we prepared to find out about the working conditions of employees in gay bars, gay
cafes, and gay bookstores? Are we prepared to boycott those establishments
we call our own if they don't pay their workers a living wage? And are we
prepared to suffer the consequences, in terms of lost benefits, in order to
challenge the continued corporatization of our movement itself?

I understand that these are difficult and possibly controversial positions;
that some will argue these issues go beyond our collective identity as "gay"
people. But that is exactly the point. I think we have reached the moment
where the politics of recognition demand that we articulate a political vision,
transforming the basis of our unity from identity to identity politics. Such an
endeavor will mean that some who share our identity will not share our politics and will choose to disassociate from certain political formations, developing new political groupings that speak to their vision of society. That is a
natural, healthy, and inevitable consequence of what we might call the "second wave" of identity politics. Refining our political analysis forces us to reexamine the basis of our unity and explore just how far we can proceed with
our current political configurations. It would be a mistake, however, to suggest that individuals, activists, and organizations are not already engaged in
these discussions. In our neighborhoods, on the Internet, even in our newspapers, talk of differences, divisions, and confrontations abound. Discussions
of this kind will continue and as a result of our reevaluations, the LGBTTSQ
movement may not look like the movement or groupings we have right now.
My guess is there will be a call from those excluded and alienated from the
current structure of LGBTTSQ politics for new organizations, both nationally and locally, and new strategies—not necessarily abandoning identity politics, but building on or working through identity politics. Organizations like
the Audre Lorde Project in New York, a LGBTTSQ people of color organization committed to progressive organizing around queer issues across communities of color; Esperanza, the San Antonio Peace and Justice center committed to pursing social justice while serving communities of color; and the
Black Radical Congress, a national organization of black leftists committed

to radical liberatory politics, show us that we can have progressive politics, based on—and using—identity. We can come together around a shared identity and a shared political vision. Moreover, we can divide across political lines without completely negating the collective history of oppression and struggle we share. We're confronted with difficult choices but also wonderful opportunities to rebuild our organizations, reevaluate our politics and, most importantly, recommit ourselves to the communities that help to define who we are and where we struggle.

Note

This essay is based on remarks I made to the National Gay and Lesbian Task Force (NGLTF) Creating Change Conference, held in Pittsburgh, Pennsylvania, November 12–15, 1998. I want to thank NGLTF for inviting me to speak on the panel titled, "What Is This Movement Doing to My Politics?"

Sexuality, Labor, and the New Trade Unionism:

A Conversation

Amber Hollibaugh and Nikhil Pal Singh

Until there's a cure, there's ACT UP

Amber Hollibaugh is an organizer, writer, and filmmaker whose work centers on HIV-AIDS and sexuality. Nikhil Pal Singh is assistant professor of history at the University of Washington in Seattle.

NIKHIL PAL SINGH: We want to discuss the relationship between sexual politics and the labor movement, a subject that you have given a great deal of thought and active effort to. Perhaps you could begin by telling us about some of the organizing work that you have been doing around issues of sexuality in the workplace.

AMBER HOLLIBAUGH: About ten years ago, I was at the AIDS Discrimination Unit of the New York City Human Rights Commission. At that time, we were already looking at discrimination issues and the union movement. The hospital workers union, 1199, was concerned about HIV, but the only way they knew how to deal with it or think proactively about it was in terms of safety or barrier methods for health-care workers. They talked about needle sticks and those kinds of issues. They thought their members should be trained about safety measures, but—as in most unions at the time—there was a deafening silence about the fact that union members were dealing with HIV in their own personal lives. HIV only made it more obvious that people had to choose between their private lives and the way they saw themselves as workers. It was profoundly isolating. Everything that put them at risk was considered a part of their private life, and the only thing that could be dealt with in the public sphere was a risk in that workplace setting. Union officials always thought the conversation was about homosexuality—that we were trying to tell them there were closet cases in the union movement. Well, yeah, that was true. But what we were really trying to talk to them about was class, sexuality, and what had been considered privacy. It was an almost impossible conversation.

I remember meeting a business agent who had worked for years in one of the municipal unions. He was terrified because he wasn't out about his sexuality. He didn't actually identify as a gay person, but he had sex with men. He was HIV-positive at a time when one's health was vulnerable very quickly, and he didn't know what to do. He had to have health care, but he was terrified to have his HIV status known. When he came forward to talk to other union officials about it, they laid him off but agreed to continue paying his health care. He was isolated and so didn't feel he could challenge it. And I thought, oh, this is really horrifying. This can't be allowed to stand.

I asked myself, how could we begin to have a different conversation about drug use and sexuality inside the union movement? How could we challenge the union movement? I think that challenge needs to start by saying that our understanding of human experience is fundamentally different than it was twenty years ago. Then private life was not really seen as a component of organizing work, whether it was organizing from the left, from progressive movements, from the antiwar movement, or from the civil rights movement. Since then, we have learned that if you can't talk to people about the literal lives they lead, you can't convince them to see the union movement— or any other movement—as a community. If people are terrified of speaking out, of ever articulating the particularities of their own lives, they won't sign a union card. They won't speak up when there's a grievance. They won't shut a line down. Their spirit is broken precisely in the place where they need to have a voice.

The newest and most interesting organizing strategies of the AFL-CIO are not just economically based. They are very specific, long-term, community-building strategies. They're based on a very different understanding about immigration, gender, and race—and race not just as black or Latino, but also as South Asian and African. Given who labor has now identified as the people it wants to organize, issues of sexuality and HIV status become fundamentally important as clues to what a new and revitalized union movement needs to take on proactively and progressively. Sexuality and HIV are the life issues that those people are dealing with. Good organizing needs to speak to the complexity of private life as well as public life. If you can't speak to that, you can't create a space where people can acknowledge what things they struggle with, and ultimately you haven't created a space that makes it possible for people to talk about what affects them as they try to survive economically. That to me is a bottom-line consideration for the new union movement: Will it build a different sensibility and a union culture that's deeper and richer?

NS: We're talking about a fundamental distinction that organizes modern capitalism: the split between private and public and the ability to cordon off "the private" as a preserve of sanctified property and self-possession, justified and buttressed by forms of ascription that aren't named or identified, but rather naturalized. The most historically notable forms of ascription (male-ness, whiteness, straightness) have thus been located (along with the prop-erty relations they uphold) "outside" of power, or any kind of public ac-countability or political contest.

The greatest achievement of social movements in the 1960s, it seems to me, was that they offered unprecedented challenges to the public/private distinction, in the recognition that "everything is political." They did this not only by rejecting the stifling economism of the existing trade union move-ment. In fact, in some ways they challenged the public/private distinction in terms that may have been closer to the old communist and radical left than we now realize. The latter, after all, attacked the validity of private property, but without fully recognizing the forms of proprietary individualism and as-criptive logic that underpinned the property system. In some ways, what we are talking about today is bringing together forms of radical theory and prac-tice that have remained separate for far too long, in effect bridging the old and new left divide.

AH: Yes. To look at it from the other side, some of us have been trying to challenge social identity-based movements to take on class. As much as the union movement is conflicted about taking on "identity politics," identity-based movements have been terrified to take on class. There's a reason that lesbian AIDS is invisible in the self-identified "lesbian community." Why? Because those working-class dykes with AIDS were never the dykes that the white, middle-class, identity-oriented lesbians wanted at the table. They never wanted butch/femme dykes with two years of high school to be the people who articulated the political agenda of that social movement.

NS: When social identity movements do not interrogate class, their goal in some ways becomes being able to enjoy the same privileges of privacy, to have a kind of sanctified, legitimated identity that is ultimately no different from any other, to basically enjoy the same kind of proprietary privileges, protected and insulated by property and well-being that so-called straight people, or other people who are similarly placed, enjoy. So ironically, social identity movements come to be about class aspiration. In certain ways, what we're doing in this conversation is showing what it would mean in a practical sense to deconstruct what we mean by class and thus to begin to really rec-ognize the universality of class struggle—with all its deviance, and with all its material messiness.

AH: Yes, the real point is that deviance isn't something that's homosexual. Deviance or difference isn't something that can ever be bracketed or privatized. Difference, including differences that are problematic and that people don't know how to talk about, are embedded in the way that individually we come to understand ourselves. It may be a fantasy in our mind; a way we dress; a place we go to; a set of people we love. These are the kinds of things that actually are the most unique qualifiers about how we live as working-class people.

To take another example, the Black Radical Congress was extraordinarily influenced and fundamentally affected by the fact that a lot of the organizers were in the union movement. They were union organizers who didn't say that somehow their union work was outside their black community work or their radical politics. They brought unionists into dialogue about the need to create a progressive black voice that could speak to the issues and the class base of that black community. The reason I feel strongly about the union movement—despite my criticisms—is precisely because I know how necessary it is. And it cannot be bypassed. You cannot take class out of sexuality. You cannot take class out of race. You've got to insist on the right to the real differences that someone understands within their lived experience as a working-class person.

NS: One question that immediately comes to mind, though, is the specificity of sexuality—and of gender I suppose as well. It does seem that the new union movement, which is rooted in social movements, is taking off in all kinds of ways. There are many examples of how union organizing has been very effective in incorporating questions of race and ethnicity and even the private and the domestic—the various aspects of people's "identity" or embodied subjectivity. At the same time, it seems to me that there's still often a normalizing impulse at work. For example, there's a willingness to talk about "women's issues" so long as they're cordoned off from anything that might be outside prescribed ideas of gender. Or there's a willingness to talk about issues of concern to a particular racial or ethnic community, but within terms that are already defined by that community. In this way, oppressions that may already exist within communities are in certain odd ways reproduced.

One of the striking difficulties of the sexual liberation movement—which in certain ways took the personal as political to the farthest degree it could be taken—is the extent to which that movement is not really identifiable with community as such. The movement cuts across self-identified communities and communities of interest, sometimes presenting itself as universal, as something like the economic. So, I agree that issues of HIV status and sexual practice pervade people's everyday life. But what happens when you're organizing in a community that also wants to repress these questions? Isn't it still necessary to organize around the specificity of HIV-positive people and gays and lesbians in the workplace?

AH: It's going to be interesting to see how the new union movement takes that on. Twenty years ago hardly anyone was out in the workplace. Now people are out. To my thinking, labor needs to be provocative and brilliant about taking the reality of lived experience as the basis for doing its organizing work. If you take that on, you take on a combination of issues, seeing them as different but profoundly important and influential in the way the workplace is organized and the way people understand themselves in the workplace.

If I'm a single mother and raising kids, everybody gets it that I'm going to have a very different kind of life than if I have a permanent partner who's employed. Organizers probably would be willing to bring that situation up. But people seem to think HIV status should be kept outside of organizing work. Maybe some unions will take a liberal "Don't ask, don't tell" attitude: they might say to organizers, "You can be queer, but you don't have to talk about it when you're out there doing your work. You don't have to bring it up unless somebody asks."

But why do you have to leave it at the door—your health status, your sexuality, the way you parent, the way you partner, whether you're monogamous or not? If these are things you never bring up at a union meeting, then to me you're not building a different kind of union movement. I think the only reason people believe in the union, rather than just need it, is if it literally empowers them to understand and take charge of their own lives. I don't think any union movement can survive if people don't see it as a part of their culture. By that I mean a class culture with very different dynamics for the various people in it. They don't have to be identical to each other, but the issues that are specific to their individual social experience have to emerge. The class reality of the workplace is a commonality. If that's the principle that generates organizing, then unions don't have to tell their organizers to leave a part of themselves at home.

NS: I was reading about a Service Employees International Union (SEIU) policy directive in the aftermath of the fantastic victory in Los Angeles County in the organization of home health-care workers.[1] The directive said something to the effect that male organizers couldn't have visible piercings—pierced ears, pierced tongues, or pierced eyebrows—and that women organizers couldn't have any multiple ear piercings. It also specified a dress code: male organizers had to wear jackets and ties and so forth. All of this was based on the idea that, well, the workers they are organizing are mainly Latinos, they are Catholic, socially conservative, churchgoing people, and so on, so the organizers need to present themselves in a quiet, nonprovocative, well-dressed manner.

Although it may seem trivial, to me it is an interesting example of both the potential cultural radicalism of the new labor movement (who are all these pierced organizers, after all?), and the way that radicalism gets normalized or new barriers get put up, in part because strategic calculations are made. I think these calculations are often made by union leaders on the pragmatic if not cynical basis that winning the loyalty of workers is in part a negative process of not giving offense, of meeting workers where they already are, of not issuing any challenge beyond the wage demand, rather than a more radical project of activating people to ever wider imaginations of their circles of affiliation. Organizing should not be based on reductive notions of sameness but on a sense that we live our experiences differently through different modes of representation and desire, but that fundamentally we're engaged in a common struggle. We should not, in order to be sympathetic and understand each other, have to imagine ourselves as the same.

AH: Having done AIDS work for over fifteen years, this is what I heard about AIDS work, too. You had to be really cautious; you couldn't be too explicit, the only way to be respectful was to leave out anything that could be considered provocative or challenging—anything about yourself that might upset the people you were speaking to. I have to say, that is the most useless kind of strategy. To think that HIV somehow isn't there, that piercing isn't there, that homosexuality isn't there—that it's somehow in somebody else's community, somebody else's neighborhood, somebody else's issue, is not to get what's really going on. All the things that put people at risk or that make people exciting and interesting and sometimes vulnerable are present in every community.

NS: The lie of normalcy.

AH: Right, the lie that it only happens to certain people or under certain circumstances. Sometimes organizers don't want to deal with AIDS—not because it's not going on in the communities, but because they don't feel capable of talking about the fact that a woman they're trying to convince to join the union is fucking three guys and doesn't have a clue about how to insist that a man use a condom. That organizer doesn't bring it up and never talks about the kind of issues that put that woman at risk. In the meantime, the workplace may be the one institution she pays attention to—the only place she gets information. If that place isn't giving her information about her private life, she has no access to it.

NS: I would like to throw out a parallel example, which comes from Yale, where I organized as a graduate student. We couldn't talk about abortion there. "It's going to divide the union down the middle if we take any 'official' stand on this." That kind of sentiment is about effectively curtailing the union as a political entity in the public domain. According to this rhetoric, a union can't act politically because—for its members—the union isn't political, it's economic. But, at the same time, by staking a claim for yourself in a radical democratic culture and in doing this kind of organizing that you're talking about, you're taking the path of most resistance in certain ways because what you're suggesting is that the union should take on every issue that affects the quality of the lived, embodied experience of people who are working.

AH: One thing that blows me away about the left—not just the union movement—is its inability to understand how desire affects the workplace. So someone will say to you, "Sexuality doesn't have anything to do with the way you organize a workplace." And then you think about all the eruptions that happen in the workplace because somebody gets pregnant, somebody has an affair, somebody finds out they're HIV-positive, somebody is having sex with somebody else behind the factory building. These are the kinds of explosive issues that actually animate most people's human experience. The one place where they experience the most hope and the most despair is at the level of their personal lives—it's about the quality of their relationships with their children, with their partners, it's through their sexuality—because personal life is one of the few things that isn't entirely negotiated through economics.

NS: The perhaps more vexing question about what it means to practice an antiracist, antisexist, antihomophobic political agenda is trickier in the context of organizing if only because your proposal of bringing desire into the workplace and being sensitive and attuned to difference is a nonlegislative model, whereas we have generally tended to understand these questions in terms of legislation, prohibition, and censorship. Thus, to be antiracist means saying that racial jokes, stereotypes, and caricatures are not acceptable in our workplace. Now, obviously, gross racial caricaturing still goes on. If anything, it's on the rise in a lot of workplaces. Sexism clearly doesn't disappear with sexual harassment legislation. Homophobia, if anything, remains the absolute norm. So how, as an organizer, do you root those things out? How do you foster a different culture within the union, while continuing to insist that, "This is not acceptable. We cannot have this as part of our movement"?

AH: I don't think these are easy questions. The union movement reflects the contradictions and complications that everyone in our society is trying to deal with. The union movement is neither responsible for, nor the exception to, any of these rules. It has always been confronted with where it draws the line. Does it take on race and racism? Does it take on gender and sexism? Does it take on sexuality? Does it take on provocative issues that are considered political? When it has failed to do those things, it's paid a terrible price.

NS: It's still paying a terrible price.

AH: Nonetheless, very few institutions operate the way the union movement does, representing diverse constituencies and organized around class. For that reason, I think unions need to grapple with the question of sexuality and sexual behavior. That makes me ask of any organizing drive whether it will be prosex, whether it will understand that human desire is fundamentally organized around the hope of how your partner or how you feel about your body. That includes abortion, pregnancy, reproductive health, and all kinds of homosexuality, not just the kind that looks like heterosexuality except that it's between two girls or two guys. I'm talking about the things real people do. Those things are not marginal. If labor can speak to them, then it's a movement that also can understand how deeply rooted those issues are in people's lives and how people are vulnerable in the workplace because of them.

A lot of people think of these issues as social, but to me a revitalized union movement has got to be a social world.

NS: Right. It's about constituting a genuine alternative, one that really does, as you say, construct an "alternative social world." Given the impoverishment of the discourse of class in this country, there's a way in which the images we have of class are hangovers from antecedent times. You're talking about reimagining solidarity, outside reductive ideas of class that have been inherited from older models where the typical worker is a male industrial worker and the head of a family. When we're talking about organizing around class as the site of materiality, we're required to talk about all of the things you have mentioned. It's not about a bunch of different issues that add up, it's about the fact that material, embodied reality is lived through all of the things that we're talking about. In a sense, it's about what class is.

There's a lot of talk about union democracy right now. The fact of the matter is that the ossification of the trade union movement in this country during the Cold War, the growing impoverishment of internal democracy in the governance of many unions, the acceptance of an economistic compact with government and corporations, was integrally connected to the failure of the AFL-CIO to fully confront the contradiction of race in the 1950s and 1960s, and beyond this the failure to take on the range of issues that have stemmed from the contradictions to democracy in American life. So what we're talking about is the failure of the American labor movement to develop as a significant counterculture, a "parallel civil society," as Mike Davis suggests. It has not developed as an alternative space for governance of the pressing social questions and needs that are not dealt with by corporate culture, that are not dealt with in the Beltway, that are not dealt with by local government.[2]

There has to be a way of thinking and talking about these questions within the union movement. There are real signs of that, but still tentative ones. As soon as those signs appear, there also seems to be an impulse to retreat. I guess what bothers me is that there is still some way that the discussion of the "new union movement" betrays a failure of imagination. It's as if the revitalization of American labor is something that comes from on high—from John Sweeney's election, and so forth. This ignores all the energy that's been infused by rank-and-file organizers—many of whom were active in other arenas. You see this activist energy on every college campus today—around labor and employment issues, the no-sweat movement, student radicalism around education and access, the new abolitionists working on race and incarceration issues, the anti–police brutality protests . . .

AH: And that's also been generated by the activation of new immigrant populations, like New York City taxi drivers.

NS: Yes, and generated by organizing around race and ethnicity, sexuality and gender. I think it's a fascinating question, because it turns the "identity politics versus class politics" debate that we've heard ad nauseam from the old New Left—mostly white men—on its head. It says that the reinvigoration of class politics has derived from all those places where innovative, interesting organizing has been going on.

AH: The question is not whether a flat, unimaginative definition of class will engender organizing, because it won't. It may succeed in a particular drive because there's a particularly good organizer or because there are extreme needs at that moment, but over time it will fail. The ability to create new conceptions of organizing and union building will depend on a much more dynamic understanding of who is in the class.

The union movement needs to acknowledge the complexity of the material lives people lead. It needs to recognize that identities are not rigid or always obviously defined to have a complex understanding of diversity. If you want to bring all the players to the table, then you have to understand who the players are, what their issues are, and how their own issues color the way they see issues of commonality. When the union movement fails to recognize that, it is, in effect, containing the workplace. Frankly, it's operating like the employer, who does not want difference and only uses difference to divide people. They want the generic worker they can control and manipulate.

If you think about who should be targeted in new organizing drives, the demographics are almost identical to who the Center for Disease Control (CDC) has identified as being most at risk for contracting HIV. It's the working poor. That's where HIV is, where parenting without marriage is, where having kids or trying to get abortions is, where racism and illegal immigration is.

NS: That's where issues of criminality come up as well. Here, again, we have come up against a very sharp boundary and test for the new union movement. Today, illegality and incarceration are principal sites for perpetuating both racialization and forms of civil death that have primarily affected African American people in this country. As attacks on the working and workless poor, these kinds of things are clearly an immediate threat to any viable working-class movement, especially insofar as quasi-forced prison labor is on the rise. And yet it seems that these are the things that most unions don't want to touch with a ten-foot pole. Criminals are really beyond the pale.

AH: I've done prison work for more than thirty years now. Working with women in prison, you see the hopeless lives that people lead when they have no choices. "Let's see, what shall I do? I will let my kid starve, but I won't try to get $250 off a blow job that gets me busted." That's what you see. When people are poor, they're one step away from incarceration. That's what they know. If we're going to build a new understanding of race and gender, then we have to come to terms with that.

Again the questions are: Will the union movement be an institution that understands the nature of economic justice and economic injustice in all its nuances? Or will it have a more limited understanding? Will labor shy away from the issue of prisons and say, "That's not about us. We don't have anything to say about it, nor do we want to intervene in it"?

NS: When you put this together with what you said earlier about CDC statistics, it's a remarkable convergence. Sex work and street-level drug dealing and drug use are the places that produce the most risk around HIV, and they are also the places that have been targeted for the heaviest forms of policing over the last two decades. It's the place where we have concentrations of women and people of color in the greatest numbers. Actually, it's not a remarkable convergence. It's terrifying.

AH: The women's side of Rikers Island has five hundred inmates, and 60 to 70 percent of those women are HIV-positive. They're all going back into the community, and they're all going to be looking for work. They are who the union movement will be organizing. What will unions do about these women's HIV status? What will they do about foster-care programs that have custody of these women's kids?

It's interesting to me that in Mexico, in the border towns where U.S. industry has gone, so many of the women who work in *maquiladoras* do sex work to supplement impossibly low wages. Frankly, that doesn't happen only on the U.S.-Mexico border. It happens in Albany and in the South Bronx. You do what you need to do in order to put a roof over your head or buy your kid some shoes. Unions have no choice, it seems to me. If they want to organize people in industries that suffer the most from not being organized, they've got to deal with race, immigration, HIV status, and sexuality.

Most recently, I did HIV prevention work with women as National Field Director for Women's HIV Prevention Services at the Gay Men's Health Crisis (GMHC). But prevention work, when it is embedded in an AIDS organization, is already too late. By the time a women gets to an AIDS organization, she's already positive. In order to do prevention work, you've got to partner with the primary institutions in a women's life that are not connected to HIV—the church, the union movement, the hair salon, the neighborhood park, the dry cleaners. You've got to go to the places where people live their lives. If union training programs included issues around health care and positive preventive health maintenance—and if that training included discussions of sexual partnering, of sexually transmitted diseases, HIV, pregnancy and options to pregnancy—then HIV would be a discussable topic in the workplace.

NS: Health care is a frontline issue in employer/employee battles right now. A radical health agenda for unions is crucial, not only in securing benefits that are being eroded, but in safeguarding the health of workers. If it were possible to wage a deeper battle against the corporate culture that we all live in, it would save a lot of people a lot of money in wasteful, unnecessary medical expenditures.

AH: It would save a huge amount of money and it would save a lot of lives. We need to take on mental health, for example. It's one of the things that people don't want to talk about. Admitting that you have an alcohol problem or are depressed is difficult and also provocative in terms of taking these issues on in the workplace. But alcoholism has always been acknowledged as a problem in white working-class communities. So in the last twenty years, alcohol rehab programs have become fairly common in unions. When it comes to the more socially controversial issues of substance abuse, HIV, or domestic violence—issues that are deeply connected to race, gender, and sexuality— unions have been reluctant to give those problems a high priority. Domestic violence, for one thing, has to be part of the union agenda in the same way that racism has to be—because it divides a workplace. If a guy treats his wife like shit, trust me, he's not a nice guy to the woman who works for him. These are not separable issues. Social attitudes are reflected in human relationships. If I'm a racist at home or in my neighborhood, then I probably am at work, too. If no one calls me on it and if the union lets me get away with it, then the union movement has lost an opportunity.

When you speak up, people may not agree with you. But if you've built real relationships so that people respect who you are, then they will engage in discussion with you about issues where you may disagree. That's the kind of engagement that needs to happen. It won't be simple or easy.

NS: Again, we're talking about creating a transformative political culture in the union movement. It's like radical teaching—you provide a kind of "exit" for people from various kinds of behaviors, attitudes, and identities that are crippling or damaging to themselves and to other people. An exit is the representation of some credible alternative, the sense of a different, more enabling way of being. That exit is something that you have to be able to show, represent, and constantly rearticulate. But you have to have real credibility yourself to be able to do that. It isn't legislation. It's persuasion.

AH: It's persuasion and also engagement. People don't have to agree with me, but they do have to engage with me. That's why I'm a good organizer and can do what I do. It's not because I have all the answers. It's because I'm willing to bring up the things that are difficult and make it possible for people to talk about why those issues are both so profound and so troubling at the same time.

NS: It's a missed opportunity when unions don't engage people. When you're organizing people, and when people are challenging power around economics, it's the scariest thing anyone can do. And there's an assumption that, when you're doing it, you have to keep everything else constant, otherwise you won't be able to fight the battle. But in fact the opposite is true. It's amazing how our personalities can be reshuffled in an instant. People can be completely transformed when they're fighting. They see other people on the picket line, for example, and suddenly the whole world is reorganized. Then you do have an "alternative social world"—assuming you've managed to articulate things like race, gender, and sexuality and show that they're central, as opposed to trying to re-privatize them and push it all away. If you just say, "We're all here because we're fighting the same thing, and we all want the same thing," that's an immensely squandered opportunity.

AH: It is. The union movement saw what trade unionism at its most literal and pragmatic led to. It led to racism and sexism—where a certain sector of white men were seen as the only credible and important speakers for union politics. What I always found interesting was that the union movement wanted to reflect its radical past without having any of its radical politics. For example, people would talk about the Flint, Michigan, sit-down strikes. But if you ever suggested sitting down at your own plant, your union would tell you all the reasons you couldn't do that, that you had to be in conversation with management. But, you know, if you want to be a voice for economic justice, then you have to take on the forces that create injustice. That means you have to be willing to speak to those injustices as they are lived by the people in the workplace. A union movement that doesn't have a vision may still be able to obtain something for workers who have no economic power. But the only way that movement can last and grow is if it gives people genuine hope for improving their lives.

Most of us will never be creative workers who can find satisfaction in isolation: we can't all make a movie or write a book. Most of us live engaged lives where we work, and the quality of our job has a lot to do with the quality of our life. When our labor is something that gives us honor, we are really proud to be workers in the places where we do our jobs. We don't have to go somewhere else to feel decent about what we do. To those of us who come from backgrounds where we were poor and scared, the union movement represented a way we could begin to speak for ourselves—in a place where we thought we had no power. Why would we want to ignore all the other places that represent us but where we have been silenced against our will? If the labor movement can encompass all those sites of personal identity, people will stay when things get hard. They will help to build belief in a union movement that can organize a workplace—organize not around the bitterest antagonisms but around the most generous of our common experiences. In that kind of movement, no worker has to be humiliated when they're forced to take a job because they have to pay the rent.

The union movement has to be brave enough to have a vision that individual people often are afraid to hold out for. The politics of such a vision are not just little variations on a theme. They are not about whether I get to hold hands with my girlfriend at work, not that that's small. But it's not the symbolic acts, it's about being a movement that reflects the best about human life and human possibility. And you have to ask yourself: where else but the union can that happen?

NS: I think we have been rightly focusing on the state of the current trade union movement and all of these issues on the assumption that this is an extraordinary and incredibly exciting moment. It has emerged out of new thinking in the labor movement and new behaviors and new identities, which in turn are being encouraged by the labor movement. At the same time, we still have advocacy politics, with different agendas, that are outside the scope of trade unionism. Given the work you've done around AIDS and sexuality, how do you see these other sites operating in connection to these issues and to the union movement? To what extent does the current incarnation of the gay rights movement take on issues of class politics and employment and see them as central? Do they need to?

AH: The reason that you and I are having this conversation is both because the union movement has created a new dialogue about hope and organizing and because the limits of the class, race, and gender politics that drive social identity movements have become more and more obvious. These things have become especially obvious to those of us who were in those social identity movements because we didn't know how to be in the union movement and be out sexually. But while unions have begun to do a huge amount of organizing around sexual identity and many other issues, social movements that are advocacy movements—the queer movements, the sexuality movements, the HIV movements—have come to reflect more and more fundamentally the class of the people who dominate them. So those movements advocate for specific class agendas in an endlessly infuriating way. Take the way the military issue was dealt with: The queer organizations in conflict with Clinton's "Don't ask, don't tell" policy said the policy discriminated against guys at West Point. They didn't ask, "Who are the majority of gay people in the military?" The majority are poor women and men of color who joined the army or navy or air force because they had no job options where they were. Policy on gays in the military is most felt by the foot soldier, by the guy who is a faggot who flies a helicopter or a dyke who drives an army supply truck. Not having those people represented as the driving force behind an agenda for gay rights in the military reflected the class politics of those movements and the economics that fueled those campaigns.

Many of us did AIDS work in reaction to the class politics of social movements, because in AIDS work you have to be able to deal with the complexity of race and class as well as sexuality. Much of the gay movement, in my experience, has been willing to forgo substantive discussion about anything of concern to anyone but a privileged and small part of homosexual society in this culture. The politics of these gay movements are determined by the economic position of those who own the movement. You see contradictions over and over again in what they think a gay issue is. Is immigration a gay issue? Oh no! Is workplace organizing a gay issue? Oh no! Are prisons a gay issue? Absolutely not!

For a lot of us, the reason we are so fierce in our hope for this new union movement is because we need to come home. We need to bring the skills and gifts we possess into the bigger organizing drive that has to embrace working-class communities, because we are part of those communities. At least in my life, if you were a lesbian, the only choice was to be quiet or to leave. In the trailer parks I came out of, man, those were the options. You could be a homosexual and get the shit kicked out of you at work all the time, or you could leave and try to have a life with other gay people. That no longer is true. It's not the same dynamic anymore, precisely because we have done so much to change the dialogue about lesbian and gay life. Now it's really embedded in a much bigger world. Most gay people are working-class people. All the issues they have in their lives are working-class issues. They need to be able to bring their queer, working-class selves out to the unions, out to the workplace, out to HIV, out to sexuality. We are not outside agitators. We're absolutely the backbone of those movements, in terms of our gender, our color, and our sexual orientation. Does the union movement want its children or not? That's the real question. If the union movement wants us at home and out, it's got to see that our identities reflect the ways in which we are also working class.

Organizing sex workers—that's got to have a home in the labor movement. Issues like that are not irrelevant issues that concern only a small number of people. They are broad social issues that engage many working-class and poor people. We need to be able to represent ourselves as we are and as we live. Most of the women with whom I do HIV organizing are precisely the women who are organized in the home health-care movement, who are doing the poorest paid jobs in hospitals, who are trying to figure out how to get a GED because they spent six months in jail instead of in high school. That's who they are. They are also dykes. It's not either/or: they need decent-paying jobs; they're lucky if they have a high school diploma; they have two kids they had before they were eighteen; they're trying to figure out how to survive in families that are conflicted because they are lesbians. The union movement's got to help them in all that. These are people who have no idea about the Human Rights Campaign or the National Gay and Lesbian Task Force. Maybe they come to Gay Pride once a year because, well, it's not in the Bronx so, fuck it, they can go to a march. They're lucky if they even know there's a Gay and Lesbian Community Center.

NS: It seems very important to recognize the fact that the forms of cultural innovation and identity performance that the gay and lesbian movement and the black movement pioneered as a part of the dynamic of protest have transformed the public sphere by creating much of the emotional and dispositional space for "difference" to appear in public. That's a huge, undeniable achievement. At the same time, it is amazing how the political movements have narrowed and narrowed to things like defense of marriage, affirmative action, and the most watered down kinds of nondiscrimination politics.

AH: If we're going to have progressive politics, the union movement has to be a part of the dialogue about what progressive politics means in this current historical moment. Part of what progressive politics now means is engagement around things like affirmative action and nondiscrimination, to be sure, but also an engagement around the ways this culture more and more rigidifies, reduces, and alienates the possibilities of human expression and experience. I think there is going to be an explosion in this culture over exactly these kinds of issues. The question is whether the union movement will capture the power of that explosion and give it voice.

NS: Underneath the veil of normalcy is the culture of racial hatred and violence, self-hatred and despair, the inability to deal with difference or fathom difference, an absolute obsession with militarism . . .

AH: And it's all killing the cultures and communities that the union movement knows it has to organize. For that reason, unions have got to take on HIV—and prisons, because prisons reflect the racism of the culture. It's how racism is practiced daily.

NS: And that's why we are talking about things that of necessity must go beyond affirmative action. It's not just about developing a response that's adequate to the reactionary constraints of the late twentieth century. It's about identifying the modalities of racism and sexism in the current moment, because they have also shifted and changed.

AH: They have shifted and changed globally. There are very few institutions in this country that can speak from a global perspective and represent class. The union movement can, because it knows that it's got to deal with the impact of the global market. Organizing in the United States is fundamentally affected by what's going on globally and so labor has to speak to class in global terms. Everywhere, our world is radically altering around issues of race and sexual orientation and gender. It's not happening only in the United States and not in India. The developing world is being devastated by HIV. The workforce is being wiped out in Southern Africa, because it's working-class people who are dying of AIDS. The trucking industry across the Middle East is dying from HIV. The wives of HIV-infected workers are giving birth to kids who are HIV-positive. All of this is reflected here in the United States, and it's reflected elsewhere. There's a way in which these complex issues can be made to appear as if they are outside the limits of general discussion. In that context, AIDS isn't anything except a set of secrets and taboos. That's all it's about—powerlessness engaged in desire. Why do we think it's so different—what you do in your workplace and what you do in your bedroom?

It's always amazing to me. People tell me things because I'm gay and because of what they feel about homosexuality. They feel homosexuality is forbidden. So that allows them to tell me what they feel is forbidden for themselves. What you learn from that dialogue is that everybody has something forbidden. That's what you learn—not about your own homosexuality but about how much people live inside a forbidden subjectivity. That's what they carry, whether it's a fantasy or a secret. I want to create a political movement where that kind of understood, lived experience can have value or not, depending on whether it's relevant to what's going on, but a priori won't be decided that it's not a part of the dialogue about the workplace. If this experience could be engaged in the workplace, then deviance wouldn't be about homosexuality, it would be about desire. What you have to understand about desire is that this culture has given people no rights around desire, although it's given some men power. But it's given nobody any intelligence or training or education about their bodies, the way they live in their bodies or how they feel desire through their bodies. That has meant that women have always paid, poor people have always paid, and queers have always paid. If that's who the union movement wants to organize, then it has to speak to the bodies that it's organizing, the ways that these bodies are acted on by the culture and the expectations that people live through their bodies. It can't be separate from that. It can't be.

NS: That's wonderful. Let's stop there.

Notes

This discussion took place on April 30, 1999, in Nikhil Pal Singh's office at New York University.

1. A struggle for unionization that began in 1987 came to victory in February 1999, when 74,000 home health-care workers in Los Angeles won representation through the Service Employees International Union.
2. Mike Davis, "Why the U.S. Working Class Is Different," in *Prisoners of the American Dream: Politics and Economy in the History of the U.S. Working Class* (New York and London: Verso, 1986).

Strike a Pose for Justice:
The Barneys Union Campaign of 1996

Andrew Ross

The days are over when union pride alone could sustain an audience for commercial entertainment. The high watermark remains *Pins and Needles* (1937–41), the famous musical revue sponsored by the ILGWU and performed by garment workers, which turned into one of the longest running musicals in Broadway history. This immensely successful production, which irradiated the popular show tune with overtly political lyrics ("I'm on a campaign to make you mine / I'll picket you until you sign / In one big union for two," and "Sing me of wars and sing me of breadlines / Sing me of strikes and last minute headlines"), was a full-blown extension of the vibrant culture of union organizing and working-class solidarity that had flourished in the course of the 1930s. While nothing since has matched this feat—Hollywood's one-off feel-good *(Norma Rae)* or feel-bad *(Matewan)* features don't rate—the tradition of drawing on entertainment and showbiz to lend some spice and dash to labor campaigns has far from died off. Sometimes, when it's done right, it can make all the difference.

Under the Stars in Chelsea

If you were standing on a certain street corner in Manhattan's gentrifying Chelsea neighborhood on an unseasonably chilly April evening in 1996, you would have witnessed one of the most striking uses of that tradition. The New York fashion world's fall shows ("Seventh on Sixth") had just wound down. But there is one more runway show in town, "Seventh on Seventeenth," on the street corner synonymous, since 1923, with Barneys—a New York institution in retail that had grown, mercurially, from its rag trade beginnings into the largest men's clothing store in the world, and then shot off, at a tangent, into the air-kissed stratosphere of chic taste in the course of the 1980s decade of greed.

By 7:15 P.M. on this Saturday evening, there is quite a scene to behold. From a brightly lit catwalk mounted on a flatbed truck, speakers are pumping out house music anthems as the models begin to strut, sashay, and swirl on stage. The crowd, numbering in the hundreds and hemmed in by police

Photograph by Teru Kuwayama; reprinted with permission.

street barricades, cheers wildly and strikes up chants more appropriate to a football game than a fashion show. One by one, the models either don or expose clothing and caps bearing the insignia of UNITE, the garment workers union. Emcees reveal each model in turn to be a Barneys worker, with their very own workplace concerns to parade in public:

> Here comes Michael. This fierce, fun-loving contract negotiator [in a long blond wig, with tight gabardine pants and a UNITE T-shirt tied up around his midriff] is fighting for all our concerns to be heard. Work it, Michael!

> Next up is Kelley [in a little white dress with high black boots], our blonde bombshell, who is worried about job security because her job might be cut in half. Was her dress cut in half?

> A big hand for Timothy from the cosmetics department, Queen Bitch for Glamour. Here to show unity—it's a family affair—is his sister Sharon (with silver coat, boa, and white go-go boots) and Chanel poster puppy Bon-Bon, his puppy. He [in a full-length sharkskin overcoat, the pooch painted green] is a firm believer in an ironclad contract as long as management can no longer be trusted.

> Come on up, Efron, a seasoned union veteran (all black from head to toe) who wants to be assured our health and pension plans remain secure in our union contract. Work it, homie!

Please welcome Philippe, a popular Parisian from couture [in bhanji-style street wear] who is against mandatory overtime because he needs to get his beauty sleep. He looks like he's been sleeping for quite a while!

Here comes Brenda (in leather jacket and miniskirt). This Puerto Rican party girl has one problem—productivity! Well, she sure looks productive tonite!

Step up, Matthew [in classic unstructured Armani]. He is one of the top producers in his department. He fears merit-based increases because he knows he won't get one!

Loretta, our babe from Brooklyn, is in the house (hair slicked back, in a double-breasted pimp suit). She says she's never seen such unity at Barneys. We are stronger than ever and will not be ignored.

Next up is Erving, an up-and-coming designer [in a sparkly vest and pin-stripe pants] who wants to make sure that nonselling employees get a fair in-crease. Work, girl, work!

Sure to bring the house down is absolutely fabulously fierce David [voguing to the max in a see-through organza dress, festooned with UNITE buttons, and with full flamenco plumage on top]. With more hair colors than Linda Evangelista, David worries about stock levels and how they affect compensation, not to mention keeping his manager happy. He certainly looks happy, doesn't he?

Photograph by Teru Kuwayama; reprinted with permission.

Lastly, we have Gaston [in full Naomi Campbell drag, with a silver body sheath], who makes Ru Paul look soft. Gaston is concerned about fair pay increases and transfer procedures, and he knows that, yes, we are Barneys, but we are also UNITE.

Across the street, more soberly garbed employees from Barneys legal and management ranks look on, amused and astonished as the "fragrant MCs from cosmetics," whip the crowd into shrill appreciation of the vamping models-for-a-day and the union name. Even louder is the announcement that it is the workers who represent the company: "We are Barneys! We are Barneys!" These managers and lawyers are weary from weeks spent in the fractious negotiations following the company's filing for Chapter 11 bankruptcy protection, and some of them pause to wonder if they themselves represent Barneys any longer. Far from providing comic relief, albeit at the expense of the svelte fashionistas to whom the company now caters, the runway show is a stark reminder of union strength and the role that these workers have insisted on playing in the bankruptcy proceedings that will decide the future of their jobs. For the last seven days, union employees at Barneys' three Manhattan stores have been working without a contract, and this show is the culmination of a public campaign, aimed directly at store customers and neighborhood residents, to win job security, fair compensation, and sound agreements on health and pension benefits, overtime rates, and productivity standards. The campaign has included ads in trade organs like *Women's Wear Daily* and the *Daily News Record*, lunchtime rallies and leafletting outside Barneys' lush Madison Avenue uptown store, and posters all around town heralding tonight's event:

> What's in Fashion This Year? A Fair Union Contract!
> See Real Cool People in Real Hot Fashions!
> Get the Inside Scoop on Life at Barneys!
> Strike a Pose for Dignity!
> April 6th
> Don't Miss "7th on 17th"
> Under the Stars in Chelsea!

Everyone agrees—this is a unique way to put contract demands in the public eye. But there's more to this event than a routine round of contract negotiations. Just before the models strike a pose, Fred Kaplan, manager of UNITE Local 340, addresses the crowd: "We will not take a backseat to the insurance companies and the banks!" The workers certainly know what he is talking

Photograph by Teru Kuwayama; reprinted with permission.

about, but so do many New Yorkers, who have been voyeurs of the messy legal spectacle of a famous business partnership gone sour.

The bankruptcy petition centers on a nasty dispute with partner Isetan, the Japanese department store giant, landlord of Barneys' three flagship stores in New York, Chicago, and Beverly Hills, and financier of its expanding empire of provincial outposts of taste in Seattle, Dallas, and Troy. Keeping company with Isetan are a host of creditors, from construction subcontractors to big shot designers like Hugo Boss and Donna Karan, left holding millions of dollars worth of unsecured invoices. A bankruptcy court judge has recently barred the company's attempt to evict the union's Amalgamated Insurance Fund from the creditors' committee. Barneys workers, through the union, have a high stake in the outcome of the bankruptcy filing and are not about to be ignored. It's not just the fate of the Pressmans, New York's most famous retail family, that hangs in the balance. Six hundred workers, in jobs that have been union for over forty years, stand to fall along with the storied owners of the clothing empire.

But before I explain how this came to pass, let me clarify a thing or two about the scene that evening. Among the crowd was a host of residents from Chelsea itself, lately established as New York's youngish and upwardly mobile gay male neighborhood of choice. Many were from Splash, the club opposite. In fact, the runway show, minus the UNITE schmattes and labor voice-over, pretty much resembled amateur drag night at any one of a legion

Photograph by Teru Kuwayama; reprinted with permission.

of gay clubs in the city. It was a simple extension of baseline gay culture. In addition, the show was an extension of workplace culture. Every holiday season, management organized a runway event—called "Christmas Kick–Off "—solely for employees, and primarily to build unity and loyalty among them. The purpose of the event was to model a new line, but it mostly involved drag roles in skits and spoofs of the usual high-fashion rituals. Management took part, playing roles like Patsy and Edie from *Absolutely Fabulous*, while employees did drag impersonations of over-the-top Barneys customers. The high jinks of these affairs were combined with a lavish breakfast for the entire workforce. So, too, the extravagant holiday parties the Pressman brothers threw for workers had their performative elements. In other words, some of the models on the runway that night were doing repeat performances of roles they had pioneered in a much safer, nonpolitical environment, where workers mingled with management in a festive and almost saturnalian setting.

There was an easy continuity, then, between "Seventh on Seventeenth" and queer-inflected practices within the workplace and within the neighborhood itself. Of course, the overlay of union pride and partisan commentary gave them quite a different meaning and design, and a shiny element of political genius lay in this transformation of purpose. It took real courage to move the runway from the protected sanctuary of the store into the public hubbub of the street. Yet these worker-models were taking it all in their high-heeled stride.

Could the same be said from the perspective of the union? This was exotic territory for an industrial union with its roots in the loft-and-tenement sewing and cutting shops. UNITE, sensing that the Barneys campaign was going to be pivotal, not only within the retail business but also from a public relations angle, had lavishly backed Local 340's efforts, providing three full-time organizers and extensive media support for public outreach. While the idea for the runway event and for other internal tactics had come directly from workers themselves, UNITE, the result of a recent merger of the International Ladies' Garment Workers' Union (ILGWU) and the Amalgamated Clothing and Textile Workers Union (ACTWU), lent its newly strengthened resources. There was a palpable buzz at the union's Seventh Avenue office that this campaign was breaking new ground in some way that wasn't fully understood at the time. In fact, there was no indication, in reports published in the UNITE newspaper, that "gay" strategies had proven effective in the campaign.

Was there was any recognition, on any side, of the pioneering use of gay culture in the campaign? If so, it did not translate directly into contract demands that benefited specifically queer employees (very much in the majority in the Barneys workforce) in the form of same-sex domestic-partner bene-

Photograph by Teru Kuwayama; reprinted with permission.

fits. For a while these benefits were on the table, but Barneys and the union decided to establish a new health fund, and, according to the local manager Fred Kaplan, "We didn't want to start a new fund with levels of benefits that had no history." In addition, the company, while receptive to the idea, was reserving the right to review all benefits that could be challenged in a discrimination suit, as sometimes happens with domestic-partner benefits that exclude straight couples (who can legally marry). "Since we didn't want to divide the workforce," Kaplan and the committee aimed, ultimately, "at the greatest good for the greatest number." Katherine Kirsch, a UNITE organizer who worked on the campaign, recalled that the workers themselves did not assign a high priority to these benefits at the time. They were more ready to push in 1999, when the contract was up for renewal, and when the benefits were finally secured. (When this piece was written, UNITE staffers did not yet enjoy these benefits themselves. In 1999 contract negotiations between their staff association, the Federation of Union Representatives, and officers of UNITE, they did finally win same-sex domestic-partner benefits.)

The Barneys workers, it appeared, were ahead of the bargaining curve in putting a queer foot forward with their campaign tactics. The runway on the street may have been a simple expansion of their daily, often theatrical, labor in selling style, but the queer tactics it embodied brought results for the whole workforce, gay and straight. Why did they prove so successful? The answer lies in the story of what Barneys had come to be.

Rise and Fall

"No Bunk, No Junk, No Imitations." This was the sales motto that Barney Pressman adopted when he set up shop as a discount, used-clothing store in 1923, using the five hundred dollars he redeemed from pawning his wife's engagement ring. At that time, the neighborhood was solidly working class, and tied to the thriving Hudson waterfront, a world away from the genteel setting of the uptown emporia of taste like Saks, Bergdorf Goodman, and Bloomingdales. In the classic mold of the first-generation Jewish garment entrepreneur, Barney peddled and wheeled his way to success by selling meat-and-potato men's clothing in all sizes to all comers at bargain prices. By the time his son Fred took control in the early 1960s, Barneys was selling more men's suits than any other retail store in the world.

A color-blind tastemaker who turned his back on the cut-price religion of his father, Fred steered the store onto the path of upward mobility by preaching his own theology of style. Classier merchandise, much of it bought from exacting Italian tailors still working in a preindustrial environment, began to set the profile for a more discerning customer. Ironically, the neighborhood itself was now in the throes of deindustrialization, with its deserted lofts and warehouses abutting an abandoned waterfront. Customers, now more Waspy, or Euro-friendly, and not at all from neighborhoods like Chelsea, were drawn to the store by the new ethos of the designer. While well established in ladies' fashion, designer wear represented a new mode of consumerism in men's clothing that would come to supplant the manufacturer and transform the entire industry. Fred introduced the names of Brioni, Cardin, Givenchy, and, most infamously, Armani. Expanding the retail space by leaps and bounds, he also added departments like the Underground—dedicated to rococo hipster gear, gussied up from the rock 'n' roll counterculture—and, in 1970, the International House, which exclusively featured handmade European and Japanese designer wear set off in individual boutiques. Nothing like this had been seen in American men's stores, and Barneys' name quickly became synonymous with a new masculine self-consciousness that prized individualist flourishes over the mass cult of suit-tie-and-hat conformity. As the 1970s wore on, Fred's store also acquired a reputation for serving the prosperous.

The third-generation sons, flashy Gene and bottom-liner Bob, took this ranking into the realm of the opulent. The steep rise in Barneys' status began with Gene's introduction of pricey women's couture and ended with the mother-of-pearl shelves, silk dressing-room curtains, goat-skinned and platinum-leafed walls, and Carrara-marbled floors that graced the flush uptown palace of Barneys' Madison Avenue store, decorated for a king's ransom, and built by a pharaonic army of laborers, working around the clock. Gene and Bob's reign began with Azzedine Alaia's dresses, for those who "could never be too rich or too thin," and ended in a blizzard of Prada bags, Blahnik heels, Valentino coats, Comme des Garçons shirts, Dolce and Gabbana underwear, Lang pants, and Gucci shades for those who could not afford to be seen without the right items and accessories. Under the sway of the Studio 54 aesthetic, disco prince Gene's departments became a mecca for the mix of Eurotrash, gay underground, and self-glamorizing yuppie hipsters that came to rule Manhattan's high life in the 1980s and early 1990s. Not the uptown bourgeoisie, but the cultural elites that bubbled up from the rapidly gentrifying downtown arts, media, and lifestyle scenes. In no time, the styles and attitudes concocted for these beneficiaries of this cultural capital were hungrily emulated by the city's young finance capital entrepreneurs.

This, at least, was the Pressman family story about Barneys, imaginatively recounted in Joshua Levine's book, *The Rise and Fall of the House of Barneys*.[1]

But what did these sea changes mean if you were an employee? Arguably the most famous, and most highly paid, is Simon Doonan, the acerbic satirist and protégé of Diana Vreeland, awarded directorial control over the design of the store's famous windows from 1984 onward. Doonan's biting, and often bitchy, tableaux vivantes served to broadcast the new shockist attitude associated with the store. The usual camp celebrities made de rigueur appearances: Bette Midler, Cher, Jackie Onassis, Nancy Reagan, Liberace, Louis XIV, Queen Elizabeth II, Barbara Cartland, Martha Stewart. But pride of place, as figures to be ridiculed with punk bravado, was reserved for the patron saints of cultural conservatism, like Margaret Thatcher, Dan Quayle, Jesse Helms, Tammy Faye Bakker.[2] Of all the sins of taste to be pilloried in Doonan's hierarchy, homophobia ranked among the highest. To be hip to this aesthetic you had to aspire to be fabulous, which meant being gay or gay-friendly. Doonan brought a decisively queer, though somewhat unforgiving, sensibility to the public image of Barneys. Increasingly, this sensibility reflected the world outside. Chelsea had become the latest desirable gay male haven, with rents and prices to match, and an insider culture with a distinctive look and esprit de corps quickly branded as "Chelsea Clone."

Inside the store, the new buyers and tastemakers established the color black as the universal rule of thumb in every wardrobe item—put together in austere, minimalist ensembles. The cult of black quickly extended its sway, almost like the Holy Roman Empire, all over the global fashion map. The nature of the labor expected of the selling employees had also changed. Retail clothing, no less than couture designing, has always been heavily staffed by gays and lesbians. While the ability to do the "emotional labor" required in fitting and selling clothes has traditionally been seen as a queer talent, these personal skills had been exercised discreetly, and were indistinguishable from the service ethos of gentility. As Barneys made its way up in the world, it drew more and more openly gay employees into the selling ranks, and with the opening of the Underground and the International House, discretion was no longer a virtue on the sales floor. As in the chic restaurants that studded the gentrifying belts of the city in the 1980s, service employees who were identifiably gay were not just a business asset, they had become an economic necessity. What sold clothes to the hipoisie in this new environment was a frankly camp, though still restrained, behavior, combined with a posture of *folie de grandeur* that verged on parody. At Barneys that blend was perfected for the benefit of customers who needed to be persuaded that their high-end purchases could be worn as a charm to ward off the demons of bourgeois respectability. The attitude that Barneys sold was woven from the cloth of queer labor in more ways than one.

By the mid-1990s, the temple of taste was in serious financial trouble. The women's department had bled money from the outset, the provincial stores had flopped, and the sumptuous Madison Avenue store was sucking Seventeenth Street dry. When the Pressmans sought bankruptcy in January 1996, the writing was on the wall, and workers were galvanized in their campaign to renew and strengthen their contract. There was talk of layoffs and reorganization and much uncertainty about the future. The union needed a highly visible strategy to unite the entire bargaining unit. A membership meeting was called, and workers came up with a bold new tactic, designed to win over customers and clients in a way that simply picketing outside the stores would not.

Soon, customers who visited the stores on Tuesdays began to notice employees wearing swatches of red against the severe backdrop of basic black— a tie, a handkerchief, a scarf, a T-shirt, socks. Some actually wore red from head to toe. It could have been a new trend, so customers took notice. But the red, it was explained, signified unity with the union campaign, and it was the workers' way—through a stylistic flourish—of communicating their contract concerns to customers and management. Why red? To represent the union's colors, and also to contrast with black, though the precedent of AIDS ribbons gave the color some additional resonance.[3] Some of the men in cosmetics went a little wild with their nails, lips, and cheekbones. While this sort of thing could pass, on an individual basis, without too much comment at Barneys, the spectacle of an entire workforce united by the color of union loyalty sent a powerful message to management. "The unity was very visible," recalled Elba Liz, a rank-and-file member at the time. "It showed we were out on a mission to bring the contract home. Coming into the store and seeing our brothers and sisters wearing red gave us an energy and sense of pride. And it made the workers want to be more active. . . . A lot of the workers knew they had a union but they didn't know what it was to be organized, if you will. Getting involved in the process like this made all the difference."

Katherine Kirsch, the main UNITE organizer, agreed. "Rather than having a small minority being active, the overall sense of ownership helped to build the union from the bottom up." In addition, "outrageous was part of our goal. It sent a message to management that we were willing to go wacky on them." Kirsch confesses that she had wondered if some of the top-selling employees would identify, finally, as workers: "They have their own client books and have some bargaining agency as individuals. I was amazed to see workers, earning as much as $95k, who sell two-thousand-dollar Armani suits, and who wear these suits, chanting 'UNION! UNION!' out there on the street." It helped that the tactics didn't associate the union solely with

Photograph courtesy of Elba Liz; reprinted with permission.

"drudgery and militancy," and the employees, who established authorship of the campaign, "felt free to be who they were (or weren't) on the picket lines." Tyler Mayo, a rep from the cosmetics and fragrances floor recalled: "We were friendly and direct, not militant, not mean, and our issues were made very understandable to the public."

Contract negotiations began to get sticky, and it looked as though an impasse might be declared, at which point management would be permitted to implement the last offer. One of the workers in cosmetics suggested the runway show as a public event that might break the impasse. The models, it was agreed, would be able to address the concerns that were still on the negotiating table. Not only was the show scripted by the workers, the fact that it expressed their own identity served to increase their militancy. For many of the employees, the pride in their public flamboyance was part and parcel of their pride in the union, both during the runway show and in the immediate impact it had on management when negotiations resumed three days later. Liz explained: "They really were working the runway, and didn't mind at all that people recognized them as homosexuals, because they were open about it, and felt good about themselves. And every time we went to the table and came back with something we had gained just because of that, it gave them even more ownership and pride. They were happy because 'We got this' *and* 'I was all that.' 'We got to be out there,' and so 'we got it because of my flamboyance.' It was a very proud moment for them."

According to Liz, who served on the negotiation committee and went on to take a staff position with the local, "Management was shocked. They said, 'How did you do all of this?' A few days later, we got job security, and productivity was up for discussion, and the compensation system was negotiated on our terms. We brought the contract home." In fact, the compensation system proved so lucrative that the increase in commissions outpaced the increase in sales, and had to be renegotiated three years later. Especially satisfying were the solid increases that were won for nonselling employees. Straight workers were more likely to be employed in the nonselling ranks, and so here was an example of how overtly queer campaigning was directly benefiting straight workers.

Staving off the threat of a strike was a relief to management, but nothing could stem the heavy losses. After showing a deficit of $97 million for the fiscal year ending in August 1997, the company closed and auctioned off the Seventeenth Street store, along with many of its national outposts. Ownership quickly passed from the Pressmans to its unsecured creditors and two so-called "vulture funds" that specialize in investing in distressed companies' debt. When a reorganized Barneys finally emerged from bankruptcy protection after three years, it was a different creature. With the imposition of the new corporate environment uptown, and much more conventional management, workers quickly realized that the camp ways were no longer encouraged. But the legacy of the 1996 campaign did not die. When contract renewal negotiations started up in 1999, workers revived Red Days, this time on Saturdays. Management tried to exploit the tactic by placing an easel at the front of the store, advising customers to open a Barneys credit card if they "saw red." Peeved that management had tried to coopt their actions, the employees quickly switched to yellow. The most fashion-conscious among the rank-and-file had to swallow some pride to wear this color, and at least one had to fit in two appointments in a tanning booth before his pale, white skin could carry the yellow. Leafletters outside the store handed ingoing customers yellow balloons with smiley faces. Carried inside, much to the chagrin of management, the balloons revealed, on their flip side, "No More Pay Cuts."

Barneys is no longer quite what it was, for its workers, owners, and customers, but the lessons of 1996 and 1999 are worth lingering over. These campaigns were as creative as anything dreamed up in the course of the company's colorful history. The tactics deployed grew directly out of the culture of the workplace and drew upon specific features of queer labor that the company had employed for its own benefit during the glory years of Barneys. So, too, the public and the press responded in kind, rising to the support of this artful expression of workers' concerns. Management was impressed by the ingenuity of the tactics, and the kindred enthusiasm of straight workers, in less spectacular jobs, demonstrated how queer tactics can bring justice for everybody. All in all, there had been little to distinguish gay pride from union pride. Tyler Mayo, the cosmetics rep who worked his way from floor rep in 1996 onto the negotiating committee in 1999, puts it this way: "We are gay and part of the union at the same time. We don't work at Barneys because we are gay, and we're not gay because we work at Barneys, but these all happened to be simpatico at one and the same time, and they are part of the whole picture here."

Notes

1. Joshua Levine, *The Rise and Fall of the House of Barneys: A Family Tale of Chutzpah, Glory, and Greed* (New York: William Morrow, 1999).
2. Simon Doonan, *Confessions of a Window Dresser: Tales from a Life in Fashion* (New York: Viking, 1998).
3. In addition, Doonan had done a series of Red Windows, enlisting designers and artists like Jasper Johns, Robert Rauschenberg, and Ross Bleckner to create works of art using red. Proceeds from the auction of the artwork went to the Little Red Schoolhouse in Greenwich Village and the Storefront School in Harlem. A "bad taste" Nativity scene, which featured Madonna and Bart Simpson, among others, ignited the tabloid and religious press, all of which helped to brand the company, and the color, as notorious in the public eye. See Levine, *The Rise and Fall*, 135.

Conversations with a GenderQueer:

Talking with Riki Anne Wilchins

Patrick McCreery and Kitty Krupat

PATRICK MCCREERY: Before we get to the larger question of the potential for a radical collaboration between LGBT movements, organized labor, and intellectuals, I would like to ask you about gender, which often seems to get left out of this discussion. Why is it that so few activists talk about or work toward transgender rights?

RIKI ANNE WILCHINS: Well, I see we're just going to dive in there. (Laughter.) Of all the things that we convey to each other as human beings, perhaps the first and most fundamental is our gender. It's the reason we put on certain clothes in the morning. It's the reason we style our hair a particular way. It's the way we walk and talk the way we do. Throughout our lives, we carry on a continuous nonverbal dialogue with the rest of the world, saying, "This is who I am. This is how I see my body. This is how I want you to take me." Because of that, the right to one's gender must be protected.

You used the phrase "transgender rights." But that's not how I think of it. In fact, I say "gender" specifically, because the right to one's gender is not a "trans thing." It's also a gay, lesbian, and bisexual issue. And it's also a straight issue. GenderPAC formed in 1994 to work for recognition of gender as a fundamental human and civil right. We look forward to the day when it is universally regarded as such.

GenderPAC also recognizes that neither gender nor the gendered lives we lead are simple, though the identities and movements we build to represent us often are. Our mission statement reflects this idea. We say that we pursue "gender, affectional and racial equality." This means that, while we focus on gender, we continue to link with the other "isms"—with things like affectional preference, race, and class, with the ways different kinds of oppression meet and intersect in our lives. This is because most of us do not lead simple, uncomplicated lives. We don't build our homes on the straightaways of identity but at the intersections where many different kinds of oppression meet and interact. We live complex, messy lives and we need to start building movements that reflect the daily reality of our lived experience.

PM: That sounds like organizing without identities.

RAW: Right. Most of the major rights movements of this century have been identity-based: black civil rights, women's rights, gay rights. But there are a couple of problems with using gender as an identity. The first is that it doesn't really belong to any one group. Everyone is doing a gender; you only become "transgender" when people become aware of it, when you're caught in the act. The second is that gender is so very fundamental that we don't have language for it. It's hard for me to get serious about "transgender" as a real identity when the word didn't exist until about five years ago. And, finally, since gender is not just something I feel but also something I do, people are reluctant to make it essential the way they have race or sex.

KITTY KRUPAT: Can you elaborate on the distinction you make between "feeling" and "doing" gender? How is it felt? By contrast, how is it done?

RAW: When gender-difference was attached to a medico-psychiatric discourse of health versus illness, we learned to speak of "gender identity," some fixed internal *being* which prompted subjective states and feelings which, if they didn't "match" our crotch, was in need of treatment. Of course much the same happened with sexual orientation.

With the recent rise of postmodern discourses from people like Judith Butler, there has been a countervailing emphasis on gender as—not a *being*—but a *doing*. Gender is understood to be a set of social acts—clothing, posture, gesture, inflection, and stance—which, through rigid regulation, solidify over time into the illusion of coherent, natural gendered identities, i.e., the "natural" femininity of women versus the "natural" masculinity of men. As a butch lesbian once told me, "Yes I like wearing high heels sometimes because, damn it, it makes me feel like a woman."

So, gender can be conceived of as both a set of subjective feelings as well as a specific set of social acts. Obviously one question is, why do we regulate both so ferociously? But for me there is a larger, more pressing issue. I am always appalled by the fact that we have centuries of progressive political theory with which to think of oppression against our physical person and our rights. We have political theory to deal with the violence of economic discrimination. We even have some theoretical tools to deal with the political oppression of regulating or punishing how bodies can look and what they can do—for instance, women wearing slacks or men sleeping with men.

But we still have no theoretical tools whatever with which to think about the politics of subjectivity itself. How did we get people who sleep with the same sex to experience themselves as this thing called "homosexual"? How did we get men to fear feeling feminine? How did we make it nearly impossible for a woman to look at her naked body and experience it and herself as masculine? These kinds of subjectivity are not natural at all—they are political accomplishments. To mangle a familiar aphorism, I would say that subjectivity is war pursued by other means.

All of these things are converging and I think you're seeing something very exciting: out of this completely marginalized, stigmatized group is emerging the country's first postmodern, postidentity approach to politics.

PM: Meaning?

RAW: Meaning we are trying to organize based on goals rather than identities. Anyone who is interested in fighting gender-based oppression, anyone who is interested in pursuing gender civil rights, is welcome.

I think it's part of the postmodern moment, in which we are preoccupied with questions of identity construction. People realize that we are constructing the identities we then inhabit, and from which we then launch our struggles. I don't want to fight for the right to be a free transgender person. I want to fight for the right *not* to be transgendered. I want the right to define my primary social identity in ways that are much more meaningful to me. And, believe me, what clothes I put on in the morning or what's between my legs is not the most meaningful thing about me.

PM: So, what does a "postidentity politics" look like?

RAW: Well, this is all very Judith Butler and Michel Foucault. The idea is that institutional power has two sides: negative and positive, or the productive. We're all familiar with the negative—the nightstick, the jailer. The positive is more subtle. It includes the power to create people and their beliefs, to create people as "homosexuals," for example, and get them to believe in, to live within, the reality of that identity. If you can capture belief, if you can make someone believe in something, then you control them in positive ways, ways that negative force could never, ever achieve.

KK: You give, as examples of positive control, the power "to create" people and to "capture belief." That suggests our identities are constructed by outside forces and our beliefs are manipulated in the process. Doesn't that rob us of agency and power? In what sense is that positive rather than negative?

RAW: Well, this is a famous problem with postmodernism. First, if culture is so powerful, what about agency? And second, how did the speaker, with all "hir" insight, successfully escape its clutches?

Personally, I don't mind at all the notion that my identity is a product of culture. That this robs me of a certain kind of agency bothers me no more than the fact that I answer to my name, something else in which I played little part. For me the larger question is: What will I do with the cultural positions I am called to occupy? How will I use the various identities with which this body is clothed by culture?

I think one possible answer is always to look for the margins and always to identify with whatever is despised in the room. So if I'm in a room where transgender is marginalized, I will use my identity as a transsexual woman. If I'm in a homophobic environment, I will own that I am a lesbian and date women. If I'm with a group of radical feminists who despise men with vaginas, then that's what I am for them.

One of the advantages of occupying this body at this time is that it is so radically unstable, that it wears so many identities. You can see that as a loss of agency. But I choose to utilize that very loss as a source of agency itself—to use my body's instability to attack the same oppression that causes it, that names me and hems me into these different boxes.

PM: Doesn't this make identity nothing more than a set of positions?

RAW: Yes, it does. And I believe that cultural identities are not much more than that: a set of positions we occupy. From this viewpoint, the only reason we have a homosexual identity is that culture heavily stigmatizes who we fuck. The only reason we have gendered identities is that culture politicizes gender.

You may recall that handedness used to be heavily politicized: people who were left-handed were presumed to have a particular kind of makeup, to be predisposed to certain acts and feelings, and so on. Handedness itself became a social identity, and parents did anything to prevent their children from growing up left-handed.

We now think, "How quaint, how very primitive." But from where I sit, it's a very, very primitive culture indeed which calls its citizens to have a primary social identity based on where their genitals are parked at night and what kind of clothes they put over them in the morning.

So any political movement must be concerned with both these kinds of power: that which restrains and negates, but also that which produces people, concepts, identities. And, according to Butler, in a postidentity politics, what you are, who you are, is not the foundation for action, but what issues from political action. Identity proceeds from what you do, and it is shifting, mobile.

KK: I don't want to divert our discussion into an analysis of Judith Butler, but for our purposes here, can you elaborate a little—perhaps give an example—to show how political action leads to identity formation?

RAW: People who are working on gender rights are gender activists. This means that, in GenderPAC, we don't have to ask each member, "Are you trans-gendered?" or "Do you belong here?" We don't have to police the boundaries of identity as other movements have done.

PM: And how has this gone over?

RAW: It's difficult. People want identities. And many transgender-identified people want a boundary, a movement of their own. But a funny thing: We're also beginning to draw feminists, young dykes, and college students—people who may not identify as transgendered but definitely understand gender rights.

In a sense, we're still addressing a constituency that does not yet recognize itself as such: the straight man who takes ballet and who is gender-bashed on the street does not recognize himself in a drag queen, who does not see her problems reflected by the butch dyke, who doesn't see her problems reflected in the postoperative transsexual who is fired from her job, who doesn't see her problems reflected by that sixteen-year-old Midwestern cheerleader who becomes anorexic to look "thin enough," who doesn't think about the straight feminist who's oppressed for being "too butchy," who doesn't see her problems in the woman who's harassed walking past the construction site for dressing "too sexy," who doesn't recognize her problems in the FTM who loses the right to see his own children because the courts consider gender queerness to mean he's a threat to his own kids.

Part of our job is to build those connections so people see each other. So they realize they have common cause. At the moment, it's still an uphill struggle.

KK: GenderPAC is a lobbying organization. How do these connections play out in actual practice when you're meeting with public officials?

RAW: Some occasions are better than others. We've had a series of meetings with the Justice Department on hate crimes. They tried to be politically correct and sensitive and kept saying "transsexual" and "transgender." Dana Priesing, our senior Washington advocate, and I simply refused to use either term. We answered every question back in terms of people who were "gender-different," "gender-nonconforming," or "gender-variant." And we talked only about gender-based hate crimes. In effect, we refused to answer them back in terms of identities.

You could slowly see them get it, that we weren't going to use those terms. About twenty minutes into the meeting they starting talking our language back to us. You could almost see these lawyers tasting the phrases. And finally one young man spoke up and said, "If you're going to talk about gender-based hate crimes, well, you're going to have to include rape." And our response was like, "And your point would be . . . ?" They got it that we were concerned with the function of gender-based violence. We weren't concerned with the body on which it happened.

PM: Was there a particular moment when you or others said, "We really need to form GenderPAC," or, "We really need to form an organization to do this kind of work"?

RAW: The Transsexual Menace, which I helped found with Denise Norris and Jessica Xavier in 1993, started out as a street-action group, like Queer Nation or ACT-UP. It had no officers, no offices, no dues, fees, or policies. It was more of a disorganization than an organization. Over time, and after many protests and murder vigils, it became apparent that a sustained movement for social change would require structure, staff, a formal organization, and a long-term approach. That was the founding of GenderPAC, to pursue a national civil rights movement for gender freedom.

KK: What kinds of street action was Transsexual Menace doing?

RAW: We were protesting the American Psychiatric Association, which was pathologizing gender through what it calls GID, or gender identity disorder. We picketed the American Association of Pediatricians with the group "Hermaphrodites with Attitude" on intersex genital mutilation (IGM), the cutting of intersexed infants' genitals so they resemble "normal" male or female genitals. We held Camp Trans outside the Michigan Womyn's Music Festival to protest their policy of evicting transgendered women from the grounds. In fact, some of us are going back there this year, in two weeks.

PM: As GenderPAC or as Transsexual Menace?

RAW: There's no connection, aside from some overlap of people.

Street actions are effective within certain parameters, but we realized that kind of action was not a foundation from which to launch and sustain a national movement for gender rights, certainly not to lobby Congress, or meet with the Department of Justice. That's when we began thinking about a formal organization like GenderPAC to do things like congressional advocacy, grassroots mobilization, media relations, and so on, and to work on long-term issues like gender-based hate crimes and gender-based employment discrimination.

As a group, GenderPAC is far more structured than Transsexual Menace. We have about two hundred members at present and eight staff people, six of whom are volunteers and two of whom are paid for at least some of their time.

PM: Let's move on to the Employment Non-Discrimination Act (ENDA). On your website you make a number of points about ENDA that coincide with points I make in my own essay for this book.[1] Specifically, I criticize ENDA because it doesn't offer protections on the basis of sexual practice. ENDA offers its protections through the paradigm of sexual orientation . . .

RAW: " . . . real or perceived homosexuality . . . "

PM: Right. Of course, the earliest version of ENDA included the phrase "as manifested through acts and identity" and so forth. But the later versions took out that phrasing. The point I make in my essay is that under the current version of ENDA a person could still be fired for making a porn movie, for example, because it's not specifically related to sexual orientation.

RAW: Or fired for even wearing leather.

PM: Or even wearing leather. There seems to be quite a bit of overlap there with issues of gender conformity. How the boss interprets gender and sexuality is all very subjective. A boss can say, "I'm not at all objecting to your sexual orientation; it's about what you do or how you look."

RAW: There's a very fine-line distinction here between dress and behavior. It is clear that ENDA might stretch to cover gender-based behavior in the workplace. For example, a guy discriminated against for being too "nelly" or a woman for being too butch might be covered under the law. This coverage would have to issue clearly from the perception that the workers were homosexual, so it's not a slam dunk by any means. But the potential for protecting at least some instances of workplace discrimination based on "gender" behavior is there, at least on a case-by-case basis.

Gender-based dress is another issue entirely. There is a serious exposure there. Not just the cross-dresser, but also the millions of lesbians who don't want to wear a dress and high heels to work—who want to wear slacks, flats, and a man's-style sport coat. Employers have a long-recognized right to set and enforce reasonable dress codes in the workplace, and ENDA is going to leave these people almost totally unprotected.

PM: You've said that you are not interested in discussing only transgender people. Nevertheless—with regard to ENDA and workplace discrimination—I'm tempted to ask if you think there are any issues specific to transgender people. Any actual, everyday issues?

RAW: Again, I am not interested in specifically discussing only transgender-identified people. I'm interested in discussing gender rights and people who are gender-different. This is why: In my experience, the term "transgender" tends to refer to cross-dressers and transsexuals. One of the problems—one of the challenges—we face, is that when we mention "gender," it is immediately written down and thereby written off as "transgender," as if only trans people were concerned with issues of gender difference.

In my experience, gay, lesbian, and bisexual people in substantial numbers are in some way visibly queer. That is, they are the ones you can spot on the street; they are the ones your mother warned you about; they are the ones who get beaten up in the locker room or on the sidewalk. I think there's a very dangerous type of identity-based discourse going on within the queer movement where whenever one says "gender" one means "transgender." We end up eliminating the more inclusive facets of "gender" from our discussion.

For instance, I would say that the Matthew Shepard murder was also about gender. He was small, slight, gentle, blonde, and young. Gay men who are most often picked out are not people who look like they work out in the gym. In the same way, I would look at the Oncale Supreme Court decision, which was about same-sex harassment, and see gender.[2] Again, you've got a man who was slender and blonde with long hair, and wears an earring. He was repeatedly sexually harassed and verbally assaulted by men he worked with on an oil rig at sea. So, among these hairy-chested drilling-rig types, he was seen as being gender-queer.

When the Other Side bar in Atlanta was bombed, the Human Rights Campaign (HRC) was on television immediately talking about a "gay and lesbian hate crime."[3] But the Other Side, as people in Atlanta knew, was frequented by large numbers of trans and drag people. There was just another case that happened down in Kentucky, which involves the murder of an Army serviceman because he was a man dating another man. But the out "gay man" he was dating was a transgender woman who had been living full-time as a woman.[4]

So whenever something about gender happens, it gets erased. Either it's ignored, or else it's rewritten as something else. You never see it. It's like intersexed people. There aren't any, because as soon as they are identified as infants, they're immediately genitally cut to be "male" or "female." One of the things I do when I speak is to talk about issues of gender and not just the narrower focus of transgender. Gender is a human right and it engages all of us. It's just that trans people, because they are such egregious examples, tend most often to be the ones getting hammered on the anvil of oppression.

KK: Although certainly they do have legitimate concerns in the workplace, just as anybody who is gender-different has, as you are saying.

RAW: Yes, but it's not clear to me, when people talk about transgender in the workplace, where the dividing line is between a stone butch lesbian who wears men's coats, ties, and shoes, and a transsexual man who could answer to that same description but who starts taking hormones and now identifies as an FTM. Once you allow one sort of person to dress in men's clothes, it seems to me that you also have to allow another to do the same. The issues become, if not identical, very, very similar. When we put on our glasses to look at gender in the workplace, we need to have a much wider focus than just looking at trans people. Everyone is doing gender, only trans people get tagged with it. Your gender only becomes transgender when people becoming aware that you're doing it.

PM: Going back to the bar bombing in Atlanta and the "mainstream lesbian and gay movement," I would think that groups like HRC and the National Gay and Lesbian Task Force (NGLTF) would have a vested interest, not necessarily in playing down the gender aspects of that event, but in playing up the bombing of a quote-unquote gay and lesbian bar. Does playing one group against another go on a lot?

RAW: All the time. Even groups that are trying to be supportive tend to erase gender unless something happens to a person they can identify as transgender. When a butch lesbian is targeted on the street and beaten, groups talk about a "gay hate crime." They do not mention that as a "gender hate crime."

PM: Why do you think they do that?

RAW: Gender is something we just don't "see" yet. We don't look for it, and consequently we just don't see it. We've learned to see just gay and lesbian. We don't think in terms of gender. Gender is not something that people recognize as an issue, much less a civil rights issue.

KK: You say we don't see gender as a civil right. Wow! My gut reaction to this comment is that it wipes out historical feminist movements with a single stroke.

RAW: Alas, when American feminists say "gender," what they really mean is "sex." So when feminists talk about gender equality, what they mean is not the right to one's gender, and more specifically the basic right to gender-difference, but the pursuit of a more equal division of the available power between the "two" opposite sexes. I won't argue that that is not a useful goal—

it is. But it falls far short of embracing the right to one's gender as a funda-mental civil right. Indeed, I would argue that by mounting an identity-based movement for and about women, American feminism has actually solidified binary sex rather than breaking it down. For instance, the sixteen-year-old cheerleader who starves herself because real women are supposed to be preternaturally thin or a young man who is humiliated by his coach in front of the whole team because he cries after losing a football game—this is all about gender and about what limits society places on our rights to express gender.

We don't see with that lens yet, and so these things get written off under other categories.

KK: Reams of popular literature have been written about why girls are vul-nerable to eating disorders or why real men don't cry. So, in a sense, these are things we *do* see with great regularity. We've even established a set of verities about them, which are virtually household vernacular. The point you're making, however, is an important one. We may be seeing these things *wrong*. It's *how*—through what lens—we see gender in relationship to things of this sort. Can you say more about that?

RAW: All of us operate more or less unconsciously within a continuous and coercive system of gender regulation. We're simply so used to it, we don't see it. For instance, if you're a man, try any of the following: shop in the women's clothing section of a store, cry openly after a movie, let your wrist bend when you drink a Coke with your boss, pat your hair into place, stand with your feet together and your hands folded in front of your chest while you wait for an elevator.

You will notice that all of this is registered by others around you, and they will find countless little ways to both let you know you have crossed gender lines and to force you *back into your place*. And if you go a little far-ther, say, wear a dress out the front door, well, then chances are you will be beaten to a pulp before you get to the subway.

Gender is regulated everywhere, and at all times. There is no cultural space where we have a right to our gender. The verities that we are so used to, the "naturalness" of gender is not natural at all. Indeed, it is a thoroughly political effect, one achieved only through the most stringent and constant social regula-tion. As a culture, we work long and hard, we expend a tremendous amount of social energy making sure people don't deviate from their "natural" genders.

PM: ENDA doesn't begin to address any issues related to gender. I know that GenderPAC has taken what I think is a terrific stance on the bill—that it must include protections for people who do not conform to typical, meaning traditional and narrow, notions of gender. How do you see this debate regarding ENDA and the question of gender rights playing out within the queer community? How will the debate affect the bill's chances of passing?

RAW: NGLTF withdrew its endorsement of ENDA in 1999, over just this issue.[5] When that happened, I think you saw the opening move in a long slow slide that will leave just one or two groups stranded on the beach saying, "No, no, ENDA's fine protection for just sexual orientation." The movement as a whole has embraced unity, inclusion, and diversity and the question now is when the remaining groups are going to embrace it also.

These are not simple issues, because queer people don't live simple lives. For instance, a transgender woman named Tyra Hunter was involved in an auto accident in Washington, D.C., and the EMS technician providing emergency care at the scene actually backed away from her body after cutting open her pants and finding that she had a penis.[6] (She died later at the hospital.) That was a hate crime, but which one? Was it a transgender hate crime? GenderPAC treated it as such. But Hunter was also a black woman, and it took EMS technicians twenty minutes to get to her in the inner city. Was this a crime of race or class? But then, nobody's really sure how she identified. Maybe she identified as gay or drag. Maybe she'd never even heard the word "transgender." Or maybe that EMS technician saw her as just another fag. So maybe this was a gay hate crime, and we're the ones who were erasing part of her identity.

It's not really clear, when you get to those of us who live complex and messy lives, exactly what kind of oppression it is that results in any one incident. And that's why I think it's important to look at the kinds of things that actually impact people's lives. These simplistic, one-note, identity-based movements are more simplistic than the lives we lead.

PM: But can you protect all kinds of gendered people through legislation like ENDA? Or is the point as Barney Frank might put it: "Some protections are better than no protections. This is a starting point, not an ending point."

RAW: Some protections are better than no protections. But with all due respect, the problem is that neither Barney Frank nor HRC nor anyone else has earned the right to make that argument. Because, to date, no one has actually tried to write an inclusive version of ENDA. Look, if they bust a gut trying to get the sponsors and other supporting groups to back a gender-inclusive version, and it just won't fly, then the handwriting is on the wall. And maybe that's the time to accept that this is the best bill we can get. But we haven't reached that point yet. In fact, the dialogue has not even begun.

As for whether ENDA is a starting point and not an ending point, the problem is that most of us suspect it's both. If gay activists and legislators were to say, "Listen, we accept that gender is a gay issue. We're going to pass ENDA now, but the moment it's passed, we're coming back for you," then I suspect there wouldn't be this sense of do or die among gender activists. But the fact is, none of the players here have accepted that gender is a gay issue. And so the suspicion is that once this ship sails, they're not coming back for us. They'll just move on to another issue. And we'll be left stranded here on the beach, alone, unaided, and still losing our jobs and our livelihoods on every front.

KK: How open are feminist organizations to these questions?

RAW: Every organization is open to these questions. No one is doing anything about them. We held a "National Roundtable on Gender and the Law" conference in Washington, D.C., in 1998. It was cosponsored by HRC and the National Center for Lesbian Rights (NCLR). We got everybody to attend— NOW Legal Defense Fund, Lambda Legal Defense Fund, National Partnership for Women and Families, National Women's Law Center, the American Civil Liberties Union. These are wonderful groups doing incredible work. Moreover, unlike GenderPAC, they've been around; they have real budgets and real organizations behind them. I remember walking into that group that morning and thinking to myself, "We don't need GenderPAC anymore. All these groups are here because they understand gender as their issue."

I thought I would be out of a job, which was not an altogether unpleasant prospect for me. I held that perception for about two hours. And then it became apparent that after you got past the Oncale decision and the Price Waterhouse case, in which a female employee was terminated from a partnership track for being "too masculine," and a few Supreme Court decisions, almost no one in that room had any grasp of state-level case law.[7] And that was because, except for Gay and Lesbian Advocates, Defenders (GLAD), and NCLR, no one was actually litigating gender-based cases, doing impact litigation or filing amicus briefs in gender-related cases. And suddenly GenderPAC was back in business. Because, small and underfunded as we are, we're still the only national group putting horsepower into gender, the only national group working on gender as a primary issue.

PM: Why aren't these national groups more involved in this? Is it because it's a touchy issue and they're scared to handle it? Is it because they see the problem as one that involves only transgender people and there are only a small number of those?

RAW: It's a mystery to me. A lot of nights I go to bed and I wonder, "Why am I doing this? Why is this necessary?" Thirty years into American feminism, wouldn't you have thought gender difference was settled as a feminist issue? But feminism was immediately gay-baited and gender-baited. "Either you're all just lesbians who want to be men, or you're women who are men." And so feminists immediately backed away from issues of gender diversity and instead concentrated on more equally dividing the available power between the two genders.

And then there's gay rights. This is a movement that was started at the Stonewall Inn, by Third World trans people and drag queens of color. They didn't riot against the police that night because they were too lazy to walk to the next gay bar down the street or because the jitney for Fire Island wasn't leaving till the next morning. They fought back because the "better" gay bars didn't want them. They fought because there was simply no place else to go.

And then so many gays, lesbians, and bisexuals are themselves visibly gender-queer and gender-different. These are the ones we all "just knew" were queer, the ones our mothers warned us about, the ones who got beaten up after school or abused on the street.

So you would have thought that it was morally incumbent on the gay movement to take on gender difference as a key issue. But the gay movement was itself gender-baited immediately, accused of being all just dykes and fags trying to masquerade as normal. So here we are, thirty years into a gay rights movement, and the assimilationist rallying cry has become "We're just like straight people. We just sleep with the same sex."

Two of the three great civil rights movements of this century have bypassed gender rights, and it's been left to us to wage this struggle.

KK: Have they done nothing at all?

RAW: No, they have not. Their main thrust has been the amelioration of inequalities between the sexes. Note that it was not until three years ago that NOW finally endorsed a resolution (after much debate) on transgender and transsexual women. And HRC still does not include gender as part of homosexuality, nor do they include transgender as part of their mission. At the national roundtable on gender and the law we held, every single gay and feminist group in the room acknowledged that gender law was an important issue to them, and every single gay and feminist group in the room acknowledged that they were not putting any budget, staff, or resources into gender law. (The National Center for Lesbian Rights remains an outstanding exception here.) Which is to say, we're *still* not on their political map in any significant and fundamental way.

I suspect this is because, unlike gayness and feminism, gender is visible. You can see we're visibly gender-queer because we look and act different. And that means people have a visceral reaction to us. That makes this struggle doubly hard. Because, with very few exceptions, there is no community, no religion, no society, and no country on this earth that wants its gender-queers.

Gender is the last frontier. It is so fundamental we didn't even see it. Feminism was like that. Like trying to see yourself blink, women's rights were so right in front of us that we couldn't see them.

We were just so used to seeing women in the home, on *Leave it to Beaver*, raising kids. What else was there? It's a little bit like what Kate Millett said in *Sexual Politics*: it's hard to critique patriarchy because it's so universal and omnipresent it's hard to conceive of an alternative.[8]

I think it's that way about gender rights. Gender is so heavily regulated that we all fall into the patterns, and it's almost impossible to conceive of what we might be like without regulation, or what a society might be like where we would all be free to make choices about gender.

KK: So why a gender rights movement now?

RAW: There's this very small core of people who simply don't, won't, play by the rules, and who are willing to pay the price for being profoundly gender-different. That's why a gender rights movement has ignited out of the drag and transgender and transsexual communities. These are people who by definition were willing to pay the price.

Now, everyone is starting to look and go, "Oh my goodness, these kinds of harassment, hate, discrimination, and violence are about gender." It's always been there, but until you learn to see it, it's invisible. There was always gay-bashing, but until we named it no one saw it, tracked it, or wrote editorials or legislation about it. But as I said, gender rights is still a lens through which we haven't learned to see clearly, and it's going to take some time for people to begin to make those connections. And gender is going to be, as feminists and gay activists have found, a very tough sell.

PM: Of the eleven states that now offer workplace protections for gays and lesbians, do any of those laws protect against gender nonconformity?

RAW: Minnesota is the only one at present. There are also a dozen or so cities that do now, including Iowa City; Cambridge, Massachusetts; Evanston, Illinois; San Francisco; and New York City. These laws, drawing on Minnesota's language, tend to use existing sexual orientation provisions, and define sexual orientation to include nonstandard expressions of gender not usually associated with one's biological sex.

PM: Do you know of any labor contracts that do?

RAW: Not offhand.

PM: Organized labor is central to this anthology. John Sweeney, president of the AFL-CIO, has written a piece for the book, in which—for the first time— he lays out a course for the union movement to ensure the rights of lesbian and gay workers. He does not speak to the issue of gender conformity.

RAW: What ends up happening, I think, is that gay and lesbian workers who are protected through union contracts, are—implicitly or explicitly—the ones who are gender normative. The quote-unquote faggy gay man or butchy gay women are still at risk of workplace hostility and/or discrimination. Again, that's the problem of what happens when we take queer lives and try to boil them down to just being about sexual orientation. It simply does not reflect reality. Many gay people—perhaps as many as a third—are in some way visibly gender-queer. And they will continue to be targets until people start thinking in those terms and speaking out explicitly.

KK: Is GenderPAC talking to organized labor about this?

RAW: We started discussions with the AFL-CIO and some of their organizers about four years ago, around the issue of managed health care. These discussions quickly petered out. It's like dealing with insurance companies—these are such huge and diffuse institutions that we simply didn't have the resources to pursue a sustained dialogue with more than a few unions. Yet this remains an important goal, we're still trying to fund it. Interestingly enough, when we announced a Fortune 500 Project to change the EEO policies of major corporations, we had little trouble raising money for it. Which I guess means that Nike has cachet to funders, but the United Metalworkers doesn't.

There are so many layers and so many places to go and so many meetings. We just don't have the staff or budget for that, I'm afraid. But it is obviously something we need very much to be doing. In fact, we're planning to contact groups like Pride at Work, an official AFL-CIO LGBT constituency group, about the question of getting protection for gender expression into contracts and policy statements.

And through the Fortune 500 Project, we'll work with the twenty or so major corporations that already cover sexual orientation. We want to get them to add gender protections to their EEO statements.

KK: You said that it's been easier to get funding for corporate outreach than for labor outreach. Elsewhere in this anthology, Cathy Cohen makes a similar point, but as a criticism of LGBT movements. The majority of LGBT people are working class, she says. So, when LGBT groups forge relationships with gay-friendly corporations or political groups, they need to consider where these groups stand on workers' rights, immigration, welfare rights, and so on. Cohen believes LGBT groups often make "unholy alliances" with folks who work against the interests of working-class queers. Has GenderPAC thought along these lines?

RAW: Unfortunately, revolutions are always started by the underclass, paid for by the upper class, and staffed by the middle class. Which means that, yes, national progressive groups often develop an unconscious bias towards money, power, privilege, and established interests. It is an occupational hazard, and I can think only of NGLTF and a few other national gay groups that have successfully avoided it.

PM: Taking all of this together, what then in your opinion is the potential for a collaboration between labor, queer movements, and mainstream gay and lesbian movements?

RAW: As a national and congressional advocacy group, our experiences tend to be more in the political arena than in organized labor. We do the bulk of our work with Congress and queer groups.

PM: How about then modifying my question a bit: Organized labor aside, what are the chances of really bringing the issue of gender to the fore in the workplace in general?

RAW: Well, there's definitely a movement toward talking about gender, or "transgender," as many groups prefer to call it. I think that's an encouraging development, and I hope to see it continue. Exactly where we'll end up, I don't know. I am very encouraged by NGLTF's position on ENDA, which I thought went well beyond what they needed to say. They could have just stopped with a simple statement. Instead, they said, "Listen, we are not going to endorse ENDA until it encompasses the entire movement. End of story." I suspect that in the coming months you are going to see most of the national gay organizations coming out with similar, if not identical, positions. BiNet just sent out a press release that rescinded its endorsement of ENDA, in large part because of NGLTF's stance.[9]

PM: What do you think the future of ENDA is?

RAW: I think eventually it will pass, but not until we have a Democratic House, a Democratic Senate, and a Democrat in the White House. As for gender inclusion, I don't know if we'll get that, but I do know that we'll continue fighting for it every single day. We need an inclusive version of the bill which protects all gender identities, not just the people who are gender normative.

The problem is that there are three main places where society can apply pressure. First, your front door, the right to walk outside on the street; the second is family matters, the right to get married, to raise kids, and have custody; and the third is the workplace.

We already get it in the neck in the first two. It's hard even for me to walk out the door some days just because of what I have to bear. If it's not stares, it's taunts. It depends on where you're going, what you're wearing, and what you're doing. It's like a tax that you pay every place you go. We also get it in marriage. We don't have the right to marry if we're gay. We have to fight for custody rights, and trans people routinely have their kids taken away from them and are denied visiting privileges.

But of all these things, probably the worst is employment discrimination because it's the most fundamental and leaves you the most vulnerable. If you can't get a job, you don't even have a house to walk out of. You don't have the money to get married and have kids. You don't have anything.

You don't even have to lose your job. It's very difficult to survive in a hostile work environment. For instance, when I was teaching remedial English at a college in Cleveland, I had to take Valium every day, just to go into work. From the time I stepped on the grounds until I left at night—walking into elevators, trying to get service when I went to the cafeteria, trying to work with the students I was supposed to work with—it became impossible in that environment to survive. You have to have a certain amount of social privilege, a certain amount of respect in order to function. Without it you can't survive. I would fall asleep every day in my cubicle. My boss would let me doze off, because the Valium was taking hold. It was the only way I could get through.

Even today, as a computer consultant on Wall Street, there are places where I know I don't get the assignment because of who and what I am, and places where I do get the work but get frozen out on the floor. Some places it's almost impossible to work. People stare at me, glare as they walk by, refuse to meet my eyes or answer back. I get the hostility every other time I have to use the women's room. And I have the advantage of being white, well-trained, and living in a liberal, cosmopolitan city.

I have two young women who are supposed to be working part time for me. Both of them have had to leave and are turning tricks. Why? Because they want to? Because they like it? Because they're stupid or ill-intentioned? No, because the day their bosses learned they were transsexual both were fired on the spot. They can't get any other work, they don't have advanced skills, and sex work is the only thing left that puts food in their mouths. People ask why there are so many trannie hookers. Well, in a society that denies us work but both rejects and sexualizes our bodies, it's the one occupation left open to us.

We get calls every month from people who get fired for being gender-different. We can't do anything for them because they don't have a leg to stand on. It is still perfectly legal to fire someone because they are gender-different. And as I said at the outset, this is not just a "trans" thing. You can tell a lesbian, "You keep wearing a men's sports coat and shoes into work, the other women are not comfortable with you, some of your clients don't like it, and we're going to have to let you go." You can tell a gay man, "You just won't tone it down. I'm sorry, you'll have to clean out your desk." All this is perfectly legal, because it's about gender. And if you can't earn a living, you can't put a roof over your head or food on the table. The right to express one's gender is a basic civil right, and GenderPAC looks forward to the day when it is universally recognized as such.

KK: I am very moved by your passionate comments about the workplace—what it means for our sense of identity and self-esteem. What you've said confirms a basic assumption of this anthology: that the workplace is central to our lives in every public and private sense.

RAW: The workplace is also central to our sense of identity and agency. It remains the primary public space wherein we become social beings and actors.

KK: Right, which leads us back to the specific subject of a gay–labor alliance, which is a fundamental theme of this book. Earlier, you said that GenderPAC is interested in grassroots organizing. It seems like the labor movement, with its thousands of queer members, would be a logical place to start a grassroots campaign. Why didn't GenderPAC turn to labor earlier—or at the same time—it looked to corporations and LGBT groups for support?

RAW: Well, GenderPAC is coming late to everything. Remember, we just started five years ago. And it remains unclear that this country is ready even still for a national debate on gender civil rights. It is not just that we are late, but the discourse itself is late. Meaning—no one who came before us wanted to touch it.

Naturally, we're going to work with NGLTF before the ACLU, the AFL-CIO, or IBM. To say otherwise would be disingenuous. That said, we are just starting to look at both corporations and labor. Our work with major corporations has just started getting its initial funding. The check literally arrived last month, and we'll need more grant money before we can make a serious run at it. I don't believe our work with unions is far behind. But in both cases, we will be promoting the rights and interests of people on the job.

PM: Do you think working people and unions are ready to talk about gender on your terms? How do you foresee overcoming obstacles to such a discussion?

RAW: It's interesting. Unions, in my experience, tend to be both amazingly progressive and amazingly reactionary on issues like women workers or homosexual workers. It will be very interesting to see how they handle gender difference on the job. I don't believe anyone knows how that dialogue will shake out yet.

KK: And finally, what does the labor movement have to gain from an alliance with GenderPAC?

RAW: Any organization which is for human rights must see that the right to work means little if holding a job means accepting an oppression of the most fundamental parts of one's experience and character. I would hope that is what unions and labor activists would have to gain from a dialogue with GenderPAC.

Notes

This transcript is based on several in-person and E-mail conversations that took place between August and October 1999.

1. GenderPAC's website is located at www.gpac.org.
2. The court ruled in *Oncale v. Sundowner Offshore Services, Inc.*, 523 U.S. 75 (1998), that same-sex harassment is banned under Title VII of the Civil Rights Act of 1964. To read the unanimous decision, see Cornell University's wonderfully detailed website of important Supreme Court rulings: http://supct.law.cornell.edu/supct/.
3. A pipe bomb exploded at the Otherside Lounge on February 21, 1997. Several people were injured by flying nails.
4. Pfc. Barry Winchell was beaten to death in July 1999. His girlfriend, Calpernia Sarah Addams, was a transgender cabaret performer. News reports generally characterized the murder as a gay hate crime, largely avoiding any mention of Addams's gender non-conformity. For a discussion of the crime and how the media and many mainstream LGBT groups avoided mentioning Addams, see David France, "An Inconvenient Woman," *New York Times Magazine*, May 28, 2000, p. 24–29.
5. On June 16, 1999, Kerry Lobel, director of the National Gay and Lesbian Task Force, released a statement titled, "NGLTF Supports Transgender Inclusion in Employment

Non-Discrimination Act." In part, the statement said, "Without the inclusion of trans-gendered people, NGLTF cannot endorse ENDA. We do not oppose ENDA, but advo-cate adding language that is more inclusive." For the full text of the statement, see: www.ngltf.org/news/index.cfm.

6. Hunter was struck in a hit-and-run auto accident on August 7, 1995. Prostrate and bleeding, she was left unattended for three to five minutes after the EMS techni-cian who was treating her discovered she had a penis. She died later that day in a Washington, D.C., hospital. Hunter's mother subsequently won a $2.8 million verdict against the city and the attending doctor.

7. In 1989, the U.S. Supreme Court ruled against a Price Waterhouse manager who sued the firm under Title VII of the Civil Rights Act of 1964 after she failed to make part-ner. The woman had argued that colleagues discriminated against her because they be-lieved her appearance and demeanor were not adequately feminine. Significantly, al-though the court ruled against the woman, a majority of justices agreed that this form of "sex stereotyping" violated Title VII. However, the high court held that employers need only present a "preponderance" of evidence to prove that their employment de-cisions were based not on gender but on other factors. Lower courts had ruled that employers must show "clear and convincing" evidence, a higher legal standard, when making such claims. See 490 U.S. 228 (1989).

8. Kate Millett, *Sexual Politics* (New York: Doubleday, 1970).

9. BiNet U.S.A. is a bisexual rights group. For more information about the organization, see: www.binet.org.

Trollops and Tribades:
Queers Organizing in the Sex Business

Heidi M. Kooy

Chants like "Bad girls like good contracts!" "Two, four, six, eight, don't come here to masturbate!" and "No justice, no *piece*!" are not run-of-the-mill slogans shouted by workers protesting unfair pay and working conditions. But then, the employees at San Francisco's Lusty Lady Theater were not running the average labor organizing campaign. In the summer of 1996, the dancers, janitors, and cashiers of this San Francisco peepshow decided they were fed up with unfair treatment on the job and sought union representation. Although they were not the first strip club to attempt to unionize, they are the only organized club in existence today.

Photograph by Darcy Padilla/*New York Times* Pictures; reprinted with permission.

Interestingly—but not surprisingly—the majority of the organizing drive's key activists were lesbians, bisexuals, or people who at least slept with the same gender on occasion. There may be many reasons for this phenomenon, but a primary one is that gays and lesbians are no strangers to fighting for fair and equal treatment, especially around sexual issues. Similar to the way the queer community has rallied against heterosexual hegemony, sex workers have organized to convince the general public that erotic labor is a legitimate occupation.

Equally important to explaining the large number of queer activists at the Lusty Lady is the myth that a disproportionate number of lesbian and bisexual women work in the sex industry. The stereotype of the sexually deviant sex worker can be traced back to late nineteenth and early twentieth century medical and psychological discourses that asserted a strong correlation between lesbianism and prostitution.[1] To this day, the convergence of female homosexuality with erotic labor continues to be perpetuated in the porn industry. The sex entertainment business commodifies behaviors that mainstream culture may consider kinky, perverse, or sick. "Girl on girl" sex enacted in porn videos and splattered across the pages of *Penthouse* and other magazines is marketed for the titillation of the heterosexual male. Thus, lesbian behavior is an integral part of sex industry work. Of course, this does not mean that all sex workers are lesbians or that all women in the business engage in, or are comfortable with, homosexual acts. However, since girl on girl sexual acts are a "part of the job," the majority of sex workers seem to have a greater level of comfort with homosexuality than the general public.

In this article, I illustrate the sociopolitical history and context that motivated queers in particular to organize the Lusty Lady Theater. I present the personal and political stories of three lesbian/bisexual activists who were prominent in the organizing campaign. Their narratives focus primarily on why they decided to organize, the difficulties they faced in organizing a strip club, and how being gay influenced their labor activism.

Peepshow Organizing

The Lusty Lady, located in San Francisco's North Beach district, is not a typical strip club where women writhe around on a stage, slowly disrobing for a crowd of cheering men. It is a peepshow that operates like a video arcade. In the privacy of a tiny room the size of a small closet, the customer deposits quarters or bills into a slot. A window rolls up, revealing a waist-level view of four to five nude women sensuously undulating their pelvises in a room mirrored from floor to ceiling. There are thirteen windows in all, as well as fifteen video booths and a Private Pleasures booth, where customer and dancer meet one on one. In all cases, customers are separated by glass from performers, and no physical contact occurs. But whereas dancers performing on the main stage are paid an hourly wage, dancers in the Private Pleasures booth work on commission, negotiating fees for a variety of shows, which can include verbal domination or submission, dildo shows, masturbation shows, or erotic talking. The main stage and the Private Pleasures booth operate from 9 A.M. to 3 or 4 A.M., while the video booths run twenty-four hours. The number of employees at the Lusty Lady fluctuates, but usually there are about sixty to sixty-five dancers and ten to fourteen support staff (janitors, cashiers, and bouncers).

The issue that instigated unionization was one-way windows. At one time, three of the thirteen windows on the main stage were made of one-way glass, allowing customers to see dancers but not the other way around. Dancers often were clandestinely videotaped or photographed. Fearing their images would pop up on the Internet or in low-budget porn videos, the dancers asked management to remove the one-ways. Managers refused, saying the possibility of being videotaped was simply another occupational hazard. Frustrated by management's response, the workers sought help from the Exotic Dancers Alliance (EDA), a group that was working with Service Employees International Union (SEIU) Local 790 to combat oppressive labor conditions in other San Francisco strip clubs. Members of EDA suggested the Lusty Lady employees unionize. They argued that even if the club's management removed the windows as a result of petitions and employee pressures, only a union contract could guarantee that the one-ways wouldn't return.

When the dancers first met to discuss the one-way issue, they realized that there were many other serious problems in the workplace: racial discrimination, favoritism, at-will employee status, pay cuts as a form of discipline, inconsistently applied disciplinary procedures, and lack of a sick policy (dancers were forced to work when ill or suffer a pay cut for a missed shift). Unionizing appeared to be the only way to make the company accountable for all of its unfair labor practices. In May of 1996, about 80 percent of the dancers signed union cards, causing the management to dispose of the one-way windows and plead with the employees to "give the company another chance." Since both the San Francisco and Seattle Lusty Lady theaters had the reputation of being "the best club in town" because they were "woman-run," "woman-friendly," "sex-positive" establishments, the management at the San Francisco theater could not comprehend why the rank and file was now threatening the "Lusty Lady family."[2] The women were not dissuaded from continuing with their union plans, even though the management retaliated by refusing to recognize the union, hiring the Bay Area's most renowned union-busting law firm, Littler Mendelson, and demanding an election for union representation, supervised by the National Labor Relations Board (NLRB).

For the next several months, the Lusty Lady's management team ran a "vote no" campaign, distributing flyers claiming that the union would make false promises, impose outrageous dues, and diminish the rights already given to the employees by the company. The employees, however, remained unified. On August 30, 1996, they voted fifty-seven to fifteen to unionize.

The company then was legally required to negotiate a union contract "in good faith." This was no easy task, as Jane, one of the dancer-organizers, wrote in *No Justice, No Piece*, a guide to labor organizing in the sex trade:

> We spent the months following the election attempting to negotiate a contract with the company. But instead of working out an agreement with us, company lawyers spent most of the bargaining sessions engaged in performance art that easily rivaled our own in caliber and affectation. Like a stripper who waits until the end of the song to wiggle out of her panties, the lawyers kept their client paying by teasing us with lengthy diatribes, each bargaining session's invective more scathing than the last, the union's planned demise just around the corner. They were paid by the hour, and their time-wasting strategies were impressive. For example, they spent days insisting that dancers were "sexually harassing" each other by using the "scurrilous, offensive and derogatory term *pussy*" in the workplace. (Despite the word's "scurrilous" qualities, one lawyer in particular delighted in repeating this term as often as possible.) . . . The lawyers repeatedly ignored our efforts to discuss things like sick pay and grievance rights, and flooded us with their own contract proposals outlawing foul-mouthed hussies instead.[3]

To protest management's stalling tactics, the dancers staged a "No Pink" day, where they continued to perform nude but refused to open their legs for customers and flash the up-close "beaver shots" that the Lusty Lady is infamous for. Management responded by firing one of the dancers. Immediately, the employees set up a picket line outside the theater, and management fired back with a lockout. Since the theater was technically still in operation (video booths featuring a variety of porn flicks but no live nude show), the employees continued to picket, heckling customers who tried to enter the building. Only a handful of men pushed past the picket line, braving the verbal assaults of the angry workers marching outside the establishment. Within two days, managers agreed to rehire the dancer, and they also started cooperating at the bargaining table. In April 1997, the Lusty Lady employees ratified their first union contract.

Decadence, twenty-eight, a bisexual white woman, has been working in the sex industry since 1994. She is a performance artist and editor of the magazine *Fnord*. She describes the union drive at the Lusty Lady and the events that prompted it.[4]

I was working there at the time we started to organize. When we first met, we didn't meet specifically to unionize. We met over some incidents that were happening at work. Some people were videotaping us without our knowledge or consent and definitely without paying us compensation. Sometimes we would see a little red camera light through the glass. We complained to management for years about this, and their response was basically, "Well if you don't like it, go work somewhere else." So finally a few dancers called a meeting.

What happened then and in subsequent meetings was that we started to discuss other problems at work, like being forced to come in when you were sick. One girl had to come in the day she had a miscarriage; another girl had to come in the day she had surgery. The managers were like, "If you don't show up to your shift, you're fired." Or, if you're a minute late for the stage they dock you from twenty-four dollars an hour back to eleven dollars an hour. All these problems started coming out. We started researching what we were going to do about the one-way windows. Our first thought was to organize a petition. But we were really concerned about individual dancers being scapegoated and fired, because that happened on a regular basis. People were treated unfairly. A dancer could get away with coming in late if she was blond and had big tits or if management just happened to like her; whereas other dancers they didn't like would be fired for the most minuscule offenses.

During the time we were doing research on our different options, we got in touch with the Exotic Dancers' Alliance. They told us that the only way that we would have any sort of protection would be if we unionized. We didn't originally meet to unionize; but it became the only way we could have any sort of legal protection, any way to force managers to make the changes we wanted them to make.

We realized that not only could we force them to take out the one-way windows, but we could also address some of the other problems. We had a stack of union cards signed by most of the dancers. We approached management at one of our staff meetings and said that we are a union and you can either recognize us now or call for an election.[5] That day they took out the one-way windows and they haven't been back since. I think they thought that if they gave us that we wouldn't go through with unionization. But the thing was that they could put the one-ways back at any time. Unless we had a contract, there would be nothing to stop them from doing that. Plus they wouldn't have to negotiate a contract with us, unless we unionized.

June, who was the manager at the time, said she felt betrayed: "We don't need a union here, we're already the best company in the city." Well, that may be true but we still had problems. That summer was so tense. We had this three-month election campaign. Every time I went in there I had knots in my stomach. I was like, "Oh God, all this shit being thrown back and forth." Like letters from management and then our response and their response. It was all this paper plastering the walls. It was crazy. But we employees were incredibly unified. There wasn't this huge contingent of people who would vote no. Management would give us all this information but we saw through their lies. When we had the election at the end of August, we won.

According to our union [SEIU Local 790], we had one of the best-run campaigns of the union. Our local was incredibly supportive, but there was definitely some tension from the International not taking us seriously. We're sex workers and our union was mostly health-care workers and service employees. But, whatever, we were a group that wanted to organize. We had a rad campaign and won.

Julia is a thirty-year-old Jewish lesbian who has been working as a stripper since 1995. Currently, she is pursuing her master's degree in social work and finishing a documentary about the unionization of the Lusty Lady. She got involved in the union drive partly to combat what she believed were the management's racist employment policies.[6]

I had never been involved as a worker in a labor organizing effort before working at the Lusty Lady. I had been raised to support union efforts and the workers' cause, but I hadn't ever worked at any place where there was any sort of struggle to be a part of. Before I started working at the Lusty Lady, I said to a friend, "They should unionize there," and I'm sure a lot of people said that. My friend replied, "Oh, it'll never happen." I started to believe that. When I was working at the Lusty Lady only a few months, a new girl arrived and said, "We should unionize here." And I said, "It will never happen."

Then when the one-ways became an issue, it wasn't something I cared about. I didn't really care about being videotaped because I didn't think that any video would make it into distribution. I felt the stage at the Lusty Lady was a limited scene and you couldn't do a whole lot with it. I was kind of naïve. Then I realized that guys don't need scene changes; it's not like you need a movie with a plot. It's just not about that. In that way I was wrong, too.

I wanted to unionize because I was pro-union. For me the biggest issues were the [potential] to be fired for no reason at all, not having any safety in your job environment, and the racism. All of this produced a general level of anxiety that was really oppressive and tortuous. It's very difficult to live your life and plan your income when you never know how much you're going to make in a given week.

The Lusty used racial stereotypes in a fetishistic way, and classified us that way. For example, they scheduled in a manner so that there could be three or four white women on stage but only one woman of color. To me, this looked like racism along the lines of "one is exotic, two is a ghetto." It was okay to have one exotic woman but you didn't want to scare the customers by having an overwhelming display of nonwhiteness. It was so racist. It also isolated the women of color from each other so that they could only replace each other on shifts. They never got a chance to dance with each other. They couldn't build support networks with each other and they also couldn't discuss what was going on at work very easily.

You make more money in the Private Pleasures booth than you do on stage, because you make commissions. Managers didn't allow women of color to work there. Not only were they never scheduled—even if they asked—but they were allowed to earn top wage without working Private Pleasures. For the rest of us, there was a rule that you could not get more than eighteen dollars an hour if you didn't work Private Pleasures. Since managers weren't letting the dancers of color into Private Pleasures, simply paying them top wage was a way of keeping them quiet. Management's reasoning was that men would rather pay a quarter to see the dancers of color on stage than the five-dollar minimum fee to see them in the Private Pleasures Booth. It was very racist, but I don't think it was intentional. I'm not saying managers hated the girls. It was about marketing. It was about reading their clientele and making assumptions. I doubt they ever did really good statistics, though. Even if they had, so what? Of course black women are going to make less in Private Pleasures in some ways, or some of them will, because there is a racist world out there. But if you start making your business decisions based on that, then it means you can reintroduce Jim Crow all the way through America because it's more profitable.

Because of the union, management started learning that they didn't have as much power and control as they thought they had. And the union allowed the black dancers some job security to be able to organize. So Siobhan [another dancer] was able to organize an EEOC [Equal Employment Opportunity Commission] suit, which didn't go very far. But in the threat of it, management had to come up with an excuse of why they discriminated against women of color. They were supposedly training the men to find the women of color attractive by making sure that when men went there, there was always a woman of color on stage. Thus their "sprinkle" principle, in which they sprinkled each racial category throughout the schedule. Organizing forced management to come to terms with the fact that their policy was racist.[7] After that, we started seeing women of color on stage in groups. I have occasionally worked with all women of color.

Siobhan is a twenty-six-year-old black woman who identifies as queer. She has been an exotic dancer since 1995. Presently, she is writing a book about people of color in the sex industry. Like Julia, she got involved in the Lusty Lady organizing campaign largely because she disagreed with the way management treated dancers of color. In February 1997, she filed an EEOC suit against the Lusty Lady.[8]

I've been at the Lusty Lady since 1995, and I got involved in the union my second year working there. I got involved because I was and still am one of the few women of color who work there. I was angry that black women were not scheduled frequently in the Private Pleasures booth. On stage, we were always tokenized, and it made me angry because it affected the shifts black women and other women of color were able to get. So I wrote a petition to the general manager at the time, June, about her policy of not scheduling women of color in the booth. There was a fear that the company would lose money because their main clientele in their eyes—white men—wouldn't want to pay five or ten dollars for three minutes to see a black woman or another woman of color when they could see that same woman for twenty-five cents on stage. The four black women who worked there—including myself—held a meeting with June and Josephine, a black show director at the time, to talk about the issue. They of course argued that they weren't racist and that if I wanted more shifts in the booth all I had to do was ask. But we had all asked and there was never really anything that came out of the asking. So it was then decided that they would rotate Black dancers throughout the booth shifts.

Even so, I did file a racial discrimination complaint, which is different than a lawsuit. After I filed it, they hired a plethora of black dancers to try to make up for evidence that might prove that they were racist. Looking back, I don't think my situation was really strong, because they did address the situation once it was brought to their attention. I guess when I filed the complaint I wanted it to be in the company's record—to legally bind them to continue to have racial diversity. Also, at the time I was under the impression that I could probably get damages for past money I had lost because I wasn't being scheduled in the booth. But they ended up coming up with data to screw with my complaint, which I learned is not unusual for companies to do when they're charged with racial discrimination. So my complaint didn't really go anywhere. But the good thing about the complaint was that it is something permanent in their records and it's something that will always be there if people want to investigate. Even with that looming over their head, it's still not perfect. It's something we go back and forth on all the time—what they think is marketable and lucrative in the business. But at least now there are more women of color working at that club than there were ten years ago.

Organizing Sex Workers

As early as the 1970s, sex workers began to organize themselves politically, forming coalitions that adamantly demanded basic human rights for prostitutes. One of the first organizations was COYOTE, Call Off Your Old Tired Ethics, founded in 1973 by ex-prostitute Margo St. James in San Francisco. COYOTE's primary objectives were to advocate for the decriminalization of prostitution and to promote the idea of sex work as a legitimate occupation.

Soon after COYOTE formed, other sex workers' rights organizations began to emerge around the country. The relatively simultaneous development of the sex workers' rights movement and second-wave feminism created a political climate in which debates around prostitution and pornography became polarized. Radical feminists (including many lesbians) believed that the sex entertainment business was a microcosm for women's oppression in the larger society. They claimed that sex work dehumanized, violated, exploited, and enslaved women.[9] These feminists often portrayed sex workers as weak victims incapable of asserting agency.[10] Many women in the sex industry found themselves ostracized from the feminist movement, as historian Gail Pheterson argues: "Feminists who followed the anti-prostitution and anti-pornography line were often viewed by political prostitutes as naïve or self-righteous agents of control and condemnation. Prostitutes were viewed by these same feminists as either victims of abuse or collaborators of male domination."[11]

Even though there was an ideological division between many feminists and sex industry workers, lesbians and sex workers continued to share some commonalities with one another, at least in terms of the organizational structures of their social movements. According to historian Valerie Jenness, "The gay and lesbian movement helped create a socio-political climate more hospitable to prostitutes and their advocates. Not surprisingly . . . the discursive themes of the gay and lesbian movement have been adopted by the prostitutes' rights movement."[12]

COYOTE's groundbreaking work around issues of erotic labor inspired workers in other sectors of the sex industry. Although members of COYOTE worked in diverse areas of the sex business (prostitution, erotic massage, exotic dancing), some dancers felt that they needed to have their own organization to address their specific needs. With the aid of members of COYOTE, Dawn Passar and Johanna Breyer, who worked at San Francisco's Market Street Cinema, founded the Exotic Dancers Alliance in 1993. They were concerned with health and safety violations in San Francisco strip clubs, as well as rising "stage fees" at the Market Street Cinema and other clubs in the city.

Most San Francisco strip joints are of the lap-dancing variety, where workers hustle private dances for tips. Dancers do not receive an hourly wage because the companies consider the women to be independent contractors. Club managers assess a nightly stage fee to the workers for the "rental" of a work space and mandate that they comply with certain rules, like charging set prices for lap dances.[13] Passar and Breyer formed EDA just after the stage fees had risen from ten dollars to twenty-five dollars in only a few months.[14] As the stage fees began to increase, Passar and Breyer filed wage and hour claims with the California Labor Commission. Other dancers followed, and the mounting claims eventually resulted in successful class action lawsuits against the Market Street Cinema. The courts ruled that dancers were employees, not independent contractors; that employers were required to pay at least minimum wage for hours worked; and that requiring dancers to pay stage fees was illegal. The California Labor Commission later reiterated the San Francisco court's ruling, outlawing clubs throughout the state from charging dancers for the right to make a living. Enforcement of these legal decisions is lax, however, and club owners rarely play by the rules.

Although EDA has not attracted a large constituency, a number of motivated women have connected with the group in order to combat poor working conditions in strip clubs across the country. Because EDA is connected with many local health and community services and is a sponsor of the Bay Area Sex Workers' Advocacy Network, it has been instrumental in educating many exotic dancers about their rights in the workplace.[15]

Dancers at the Lusty Lady sought assistance from EDA when they first started organizing. The Lusty Ladies were not the first group of exotic dancers to talk union. Less than a decade after the onset of the topless craze—which began in 1964 when San Francisco local Carol Doda became one of the first dancers to bare her breasts on stage—strippers were considering unionization. In the 1970s, the culinary workers union led an unsuccessful attempt to organize the dancers and waitresses in the clubs along Broadway Street in

San Francisco's North Beach district. More recently, in 1994, workers at the San Diego club, Pacers, voted to unionize. However, support for the union was weak and, as a result, the contract that employees were able to obtain was insubstantial and inadequate. This enabled the club's management to quickly erode organizing efforts by hiring antiunion employees.[16]

What made the Lusty Lady campaign unique was the fact that most of the union activists were lesbians or bisexuals who were already activists around sex work, race, queer, and women's issues. Prior to becoming a labor organizer, Siobhan had been deeply involved in fighting for equal rights for women of color. She views her experiences with other types of activism as related to her labor organizing efforts in the sex industry:

I used to do a lot of race and gender organizing. I was a women's studies major at [San Francisco] State, and I did a lot of outreach. I volunteered at free health clinics, and I worked with black women and other women of color. I wasn't doing anything queer-specific because I didn't feel a need to do that kind of activism at the time.

Being a sex worker is a core part of my identity. Aside from the race stuff, the most activism I've done up to this point is sex industry work. Because I identify more with being a sex worker who happens to be bi as opposed to just being bi, my activism isn't always talking about heterosexism. If I had to describe my activism, I'd say I'm a sex worker activist.

I still work at the Lusty Lady, and I'm on the bargaining committee and I'm a shop steward. I've completed a book of interviews with people of color in the sex industry and I've gone on to lecture at different universities about working rights in the sex industry. With my writing and my lectures, I'm most effective at educating people about issues and demystifying what it means to be a sex worker. I'm also going to grad school to study sociology. What I want to do is research different issues in the sex industry, like the decriminalization of prostitution. I want to get other people who are not in the sex industry to be supportive of us, to make it seem like it's a labor movement and not just something that's affecting sex workers. I recently went to Sacramento to meet with different state legislators about supporting the rights of exotic dancers to be employees and get fair treatment.

One bill that we went to fight against was A.B. 1446, which basically states that an employer could not force an employee to take off his or her clothes. If it passed, it basically would make it a law that exotic dancers could not be employees and that they would stay at the independent contractor status. Independent contractors aren't eligible to be in a union, so the bill is really about keeping dancers from unionizing. We went and met with different legislators at the state capitol. A lot of them are pro-labor Democrats, and pro-union. They don't really think that this bill is going to pass, but we wanted to make sure by educating them.[17]

Decadence also sees connections between being an organizer at the Lusty Lady and her previous activism in identity-based movements. The difference is that her activism at the club combined identity with class politics:

I have been working in the industry for years. I always wondered, "I'm dealing with all these horrid working conditions, yet I'm working with the most rad people. Really smart. Really talented. Why can't we get together and change it?" I thought that pretty much the whole time I have been working. I didn't necessarily think union, but I thought, "God, if we ever got in a room together, all of us, it would be intense."

I had done a lot of political activism before I got involved in the sex industry. Not necessarily around labor issues, more around women's issues, queer issues, and things like that. When I got involved in the sex industry, I got away from that. Not that I wasn't political, I just wasn't active. In a way, this union organizing kicked in an old passion. Back in college and after college, I was involved in Queer Nation. I felt really passionate. I had no interest in going and picketing over some abstract issue, or something where I couldn't actually effect any sort of change.

The Lusty Lady campaign was also something where I could do activist work and actually change something. It was something I was involved in and personally very invested in. It was going to have a direct impact on my life and other people's lives. I definitely thought it was cool that we were the only unionized strip club. Not the first one, but we were the second and are now the only one in existence. I thought it was about fucking time. For years we were taking it and taking it and now we're like, "Fuck that. We're not going to do it anymore."

I have really moved away from identity politics, which I was into when I was younger. In gay activism it was all about focusing on identity, whereas my sex worker activism has not been about, "I'm a sex worker. Respect me." It is focused more on working conditions, and I see it more as labor activism than sex worker activism. I don't do the kind of sex worker activism where I'm like, "Hug a 'ho today. 'Hos are people too." I'm not interested in that. Yeah, there's a stigma to this work, and, yeah, there are people addressing it and that's what they're into and that's cool. But for me, I'm not really interested in addressing the stigma, other than demanding my fair treatment. There are people in all kinds of industries who need to work on their working conditions, not just sex workers.

But still, I see the fight for sex worker rights as totally connected to my activist work in the past. It's the next step. But at the same time I have an understanding of how it all works, the power structure, and what it takes to rise up and fight it. We're workers and we deserve the same rights as anybody else. It's pretty similar—"We're gay so we deserve the same rights as straight people. We're 'hos, we deserve the same rights as people who aren't." I see it as connected. To anybody else in the outside world, we're all the same. We're the sexual deviant outcast, if you're a whore, a sadomasochist, or a fag. They see us all as the same.

Like Decadence, Julia had also been involved in queer activism in the past. She sees many similarities between the sex worker and queer movements. She explores these similarities in *Live Nude Girls Unite!* a documentary film she is making about organizing sex workers.[18]

As far as Lusty Lady organizers go, we all had activism in common. In our generation, the major areas of activism have been around AIDS and gay issues. So we were experienced. And because we were largely gay women, we did not have any fantasy at all of having a man support us in the future. We understood this job to be our sole support and to be the sole support that we would have for a number of years. You just don't have fantasies when you're a lesbian that you are going to meet another lesbian who's going to support you. There's so few of those, and they wear really bad blazers. [Laughter.]

Sex work activism is a much younger movement than gay activism, and we have to do a lot of the stuff now that gay activists had to do in the fifties. We often have to organize secretly, covertly. We have to allow people to be closeted, to come to meetings where they're not going to be identified. We have to help people keep themselves closeted because there's so much risk in being a sex worker. There's risk of stigma. There's risk of having your children taken away. There are many huge issues for us. Things like when you apply for an apartment and the owner wants to know how much money you make and what you do, having to show that you can afford this apartment but not really having any papers to show that you have a job. Also not wanting the manager of your building knowing that you're a stripper because he has a key and he then thinks you're a slut. So we have a lot of issues that people who were gay in San Francisco in the 1950s had. A lot of gay activism was about coming up with demythologizing theories, ideas, justifications, and clarifications. We have to do a lot of that. We need to do the "Ten Most Popular Myths about Strippers" handouts.

I would like to take my documentary and use that as a way to spark a national debate and interest and discussion in understanding sex work as work. I would like to use it to help women and strippers across the country have a way to contact the Exotic Dancers Alliance and become activists themselves.

Maybe the documentary will spark the interest in unionizing. Maybe they didn't know that they could do that. Now they will know that there is a support system. God knows that that has been the only motivation for me doing this much work for three years.

Lesbians in the Sex Industry

Theories postulating that sex workers are likely to be lesbians developed in the late nineteenth century with the rise of positivist science. Medical and psychological researchers asserted that there were strong causal links between female homosexuality and prostitution. The work of psychologists, psychiatrists, and medical doctors like Frank Caprio, Karl Abraham, H. Lichtenstein, and J. Lampi de Groot suggested that prostitutes were not only mentally ill individuals, but also latent homosexuals suffering from either unresolved Oedipal complexes or identity disorders (i.e., inversion—identifying with the masculine). For example, in the 1950s Caprio conducted a study of brothels around the world and reported that he found at least two or more lesbians working in each house of disrepute. From these observations, he concluded that prostitution was:

> a deviant behavior which appealed primarily to women with strong homosexual tendencies; their activities with their customers were a pseudoheterosexual defense against their true desire for lesbian love; eventually, however, many of them lost their inhibitions and turned to open homosexuality. . . . Prostitutes were emotionally sick people whose activities were manifestations of their illness.[19]

Scientists like Caprio tended to group all female sexual "deviants" into the same category. Many argued that nymphomania, or hypersexuality in women, led one to prostitution; and prostitution, in turn, implied lesbianism. It was during these midcentury years that sexual variance in women was constructed into a model of disease.[20] Not until 1974 did the American Psychiatric Association remove homosexuality from its list of mental illnesses.

Nymphomania continues to be considered an illness, but now is addressed under a new name: sexual addiction. The conceptualization and treatment of sexual addiction is modeled after twelve-step programs, like Alcoholics Anonymous, in which excessive sexual impulses are treated as an addiction to a substance like alcohol or drugs. The adherents of sexual addiction claim that one's obsessive sexual behavior may lead one to "compulsive masturbation, compulsive heterosexual and homosexual relationships, pornography, prostitution, exhibitionism, voyeurism, indecent phone calls, child molesting, incest, rape, and violence."[21] In short, correlations continue to be made between sex work, homosexuality, and disease.

In the mid-twentieth century, lesbians and sex workers continued to have a shared history. Elizabeth Lapovsky Kennedy and Madeline D. Davis illustrated this relationship in their study of working-class lesbians in Buffalo, New York, in the 1940s and 1950s. They found that during these years lesbians and prostitutes often patronized the same few bars. "Lesbians and prostitutes became integrated in a complex subculture. Many butches hustled money from straight men who came looking for sexual encounters; many fems supported themselves by turning tricks."[22] Other writers like Joan Nestle and Leslie Feinberg have noted that during this time police often harassed homosexual women and sex workers who were present in the same bars.[23] Since both prostitution and homosexuality were illegal in these years, lesbians and sex workers existed on the margins of society with the other undesirables.

Although the literature on lesbian sex workers is sparse, it has established and maintained a myth that sex workers are predominantly queers. This is illustrated in the 1985 film *Desperately Seeking Susan*.[24] In the movie, the lead character, Roberta, is assumed to be a prostitute. When her sister-in-law hears about this rumor she exclaims, "Oh my God! I have heard that four out of five prostitutes are lesbians!" Although the statistics are used as comedy within the film's script and are, like the movie itself, fictional, they echo the sentiments of the late nineteenth- and early twentieth-century psychologists, perpetuating the notion that sex workers are likely to be sexual deviants.

Certainly, as Decadence, Julia, and Siobhan indicate, some exotic dancers, peepshow performers, erotic masseuses, phone sex operators, porn actresses, escorts, and street prostitutes were and are gay. But because a preponderance of lesbians in the sex industry is debatable and even approximate statistics of workers' sexual orientations are impossible to obtain, looking at "why" and "how many" may be a misdirected line of questioning. The fact is that female homosexuality is intertwined with sex industry work on many different levels—and not only on the level of numbers of queer women in the industry. The business also encourages lesbian acts. It's part of the job to sell to horny male customers the fantasy of the promiscuous and oversexed female—the woman who is willing to engage in any kind of sexual activity no matter what boundaries or cultural taboos she may break. Women who work in the industry often perform sexual acts with other women. These are sometimes referred to as "two girl shows," "girl on girl shows," or "doubles." Most of these performances are just that—performances enacted for the benefit of the male client. Rarely do they simulate the ways in which women actually have sex with one another. Granted, the commodification of female homosexual acts for the benefit of male clients is a distorted view of lesbianism. However, it is an element of the industry, and sex workers, in general, tend to be more open to nonheteronormative sexual practices. Consequently, some activists and theorists consider sex work to be a form of queerness simply by virtue of its transgressive nature.[25]

Furthermore, sex work activists have tended to be very supportive of queer issues, especially in San Francisco, where both movements have a strong presence. They recognize that both queers and sex workers are marginalized because they violate mainstream standards of appropriate sexual conduct.[26] Unfortunately, due to certain veins of feminist thought, lesbians have not always been as supportive of sex workers. Nestle describes the historical process of how this occurred:

> In the bars of the late fifties and early sixties where I learned my lesbian ways, whores were a part of our world. We sat on barstools next to each other, we partied together and we made love together. The vice squad . . . controlled our world, and we knew clearly that there was little difference between whore and queer when a raid was on. This shared territory broke apart, at least for me, when I entered the world of lesbian feminism. Whores, and women who looked like whores, became the enemy or, at best, misguided oppressed women who needed our help.[27]

As links between lesbians and erotic laborers diminished with the rise of feminism, many sex workers began to fight against their increasingly marginalized status by launching their own movement for social justice. All three of the dancers I interviewed understand the nuanced connections between being queers who work in the sex industry and how they are perceived by the larger culture. Julia mainly focuses on the social stigma that erotic laborers face. She explains:

The biggest gay issue for me at the Lusty Lady was that we are all putting on hetero drag. That for the customers we all have to appear to be hetero women who are willing to fuck anything, but of course we would always prefer that a man be there either fucking us or watching us; and that certainly is an act.

I think I'm going to be a sex worker rights activist for a long time. I'm finishing my documentary called Live Nude Girls Unite! *which uses myself as a character and my relationship with my mother to embody the feminist debates about meanings of sexuality, specifically women using their own bodies for pay. So for instance, women in this culture have a lot of emotional abilities. We have the ability to understand emotions because we are trained that way. We don't pathologize therapists for providing emotional support for money. But even though women are also trained to be coquettish or flirtatious or to transfer sexual energy for men, we are pathologized if we do that for money. We're expected to do it for free in a variety of jobs, like being a receptionist, a stewardess, almost any support position job. Women are always in these positions of providing, and yet we're pathologized and criminalized for doing it on the sexual level.*

We need to educate the mental health community about us. We need to educate the legal community about us. So that our children aren't taken away. So that we aren't pathologized by our therapists. So that we aren't locked up, called nymphomaniacs. "Sex addiction" is a term that is applied to us a lot. Also we're pathologized as incest victims. We're presumed to have narratives of trauma that proclaim us as damaged, as not able to take care of ourselves, as not fully adult women making choices for ourselves that are good reasonable choices, that are about self-care. The fact is that we support ourselves, earn fairly good money, are able to support our families and our children, and are able to have lives where we have more time for creative endeavors. We're pathologized for having it. We're pathologized for having it because we provide a sexual service and we don't do it for free. Women who do it for free are treated better than the women who are paid for it. You see that in a lot of movies, where women in the industry are always presented as these harmed little creatures who need to take a lot of baths.

We need to show that we are inclusive of, and not only, incest survivors; that we are inclusive of, and not only, drug addicts. We are also college students; we are also artists; and we are also mothers—every type of person out there.

At the same time, I really oppose the pro-sex essentializing of the sex worker as sexual healer, the woman with more skills doing this because she was born to be this. Or, had we lived in a past mythic culture, we would have been the honored whores or the temple priestesses. That's sort of like the womanist, lesbian feminism of the 1970s where we argued that women were essentially peaceful. Women are not better. And sex workers are not necessarily better at sex. It's just a job. We may have a higher percentage of us who are exhibitionists. We may have a higher percentage of us who are capable of doing splits in high heels. But that doesn't mean that we are women who are more in touch with the sexual energy of our bodies. It doesn't mean that we're better lovers, and it doesn't mean that we're healers. Some of us are and some of us aren't; some secretaries are, some secretaries aren't. Some women who are three hundred pounds have great sex energy. So it's not about being thin, young, and blond.

Decadence explains that although queers in the sex industry generally cater to an exclusively male clientele, they find the industry to be supportive of queer culture.

I don't feel like the lesbian, bi women, or any of the queer employees are treated differently at the Lusty Lady. Even before we unionized, that didn't seem like much of an issue to me. It didn't really come up too much. Definitely there's an antidiscrimination policy. There were a lot of issues of unequal treatment, but I don't think they had much to do with sexual orientation. Managers prefer some people over others, but that was around ideals of beauty. They're definitely going for this blond hair, big tit thing, but I don't see that as "We want you to look straight."

Actually, homosexual behavior is encouraged. Here we have these "Double Troubles," where we're supposed to get it on with one of the other dancers for money. I don't know if it's expected that we're actually into it, but it's definitely encouraged. I've worked in other industries where being queer was definitely a problem. You had to keep it quiet. Before I was in sex work, I was in social work working with teenage girls. I was in this cultural diversity program and I was supposed to be educating these girls about racism and homophobia, but yet I was supposed to keep quiet about my own bisexuality. But I don't feel that it's an issue at all [at the Lusty Lady], especially since almost everybody—well not everybody but it seemed like everybody—was queer to some extent or another. It wasn't like that's something you had to hide. I think there are clubs where that's true, but not in San Francisco and not at the Lusty Lady.

Siobhan agrees that the sex industry promotes lesbian acts, if not identities. It's partly because of that attitude that she views sex work as fundamentally queer.

I've never seen any sort of discriminatory process happen against dancers who were openly queer, but there is a whole issue about what is feminine. One woman I know, a lesbian, had a hard time because one day during a holiday event where we get our bonuses, she dressed up as a man. The managers tried to say that she was already looking too masculine and that the customers weren't into her. Basically that was homophobic because it's not like she looks radically different from anyone else. She looks feminine enough to work in that sort of market. But because she was doing a lot of gender-bending type things it threatened whatever image that they wanted to keep, even on that one day where people were slipping and having fun. But I think a good majority of the women who work there are lesbian and bi, and I never felt that it was really an issue.

I think that sex work falls into queerness for several reasons. Both of those movements—the gay, lesbian, bisexual, transgender movement and the sex worker movement—deal with sex and having the right to do what you want with your body, whether that's changing your sex, or sleeping with the same gender, or commodifying yourself to make money off of your body. I feel like my being bisexual is very much linked to my fight for sex workers to have equal working rights, just as I would fight to have the right to love whoever I choose in terms of gender. Those two issues are definitely interconnected, and I think more and more we're beginning to realize that. Unfortunately there's always a schism. Some lesbians don't like sex workers, and some people in the gay community think sex workers are making them look bad because of the AIDS epidemic. All of this stems from the same thing: repression of sex and sexuality by the patriarchy.

In terms of management, they're supportive of queerness because they see it as just another cute marketing thing to put out there. The customers, on the other hand, they're really supportive of the bisexual girl fantasy. But for the most part, I think they are homophobic when it comes to other men being queer.

Theories abound as to why so many lesbians and bisexual women apparently work in the sex industry. The nineteenth-century claim that sex workers are often lesbians continues to circulate. But numbers and statistics are irrelevant. The important issue at hand is that lesbian and bisexual women are present in the sex industry. And it is queer women like Julia, Decadence, and Siobhan who are leading the way in the fight for fair working conditions in this business.

The Lusty Lady's success has motivated dancers all over the country to start to organize. Attempts have been made at clubs in Alaska and Philadelphia, and at another club in San Francisco. None have been completely successful, but it is obvious that strippers are becoming more aware of their rights and are combating exploitative employers and unfair working conditions. However, it is unclear how much support they will obtain from the labor movement and whether the workers' rights movement will embrace them. When the employees at the Alaska and Philadelphia clubs began to organize, they originally joined up with the Teamsters, but were quickly dropped for "unknown" reasons. As Decadence explains, many unions still seem to focus only on the *sex* part of *sex worker*:

I'm still working at the Lusty Lady. I'm a shop steward. If a worker wants to bring a grievance, I'm one of the persons who handles the case.

We've had clubs from all over the country call us up and ask us how to organize. We've gone to a few different clubs to talk to them, but so far we're still the only one. I think that we're a role model for all other sex workers who want to organize, although we had a unique situation because things were already a lot better at the Lusty than at some of the other clubs, especially here in San Francisco. I can't imagine trying to organize at any of the other clubs. Still, we ran a great campaign and we can give advice.

We also have other chapters of our union in other industries looking to us for advice. Our campaign was about a worker issue, rather than a sex worker issue, so I see that people in other industries can look to us. The problem that comes in is the stigma. People don't want to see that we're just like them. They're on an assembly line and we're in a peepshow. But it's just basic labor issues.

I went to an Organizing Institute run by the AFL-CIO, and we were talking about how to organize. I felt that their strategy was really limited. Having just been through this campaign, I was bringing up points about different types of strategies you could use. I found that they were totally condescending and dismissive of the work we had done—just because it was around sex. Our campaign wasn't really that much different as far as how to organize strategically. We could be helping a lot more people, but they see us as different from them because it's involving sex. That's too bad, because we rock.

Notes

1. See Vern L. Bullough, "Prostitution, Psychiatry and History," in *The Frontiers of Sex Research*, ed. Vern L. Bullough (Buffalo: Prometheus Books, 1979); Carol Groneman, "Nymphomania: The Historical Construction of Female Sexuality," in *Deviant Bodies*, ed. Jennifer Terry and Jacqueline Urla (Bloomington: Indiana University Press, 1995); Joan Nestle, "Lesbians and Prostitutes: A Historical Sisterhood," in *Sex Work: Writings by Women in the Sex Industry*, ed. Frederique Delacoste and Priscilla Alexander (San Francisco: Cleis Press, 1987).
2. Most strip clubs are notorious for their misogynistic and pimpish management. Thus the Lusty Lady was unique in its claims to be "woman-friendly."
3. Jane, *No Justice, No Piece! A Working Girl's Guide to Labor Organizing in the Sex Industry* (Distributed by the Exotic Dancers Union, 1999).
4. From an interview conducted by the author with Decadence on April 21, 1999, in San Francisco. Like the other dancers I interviewed for this essay, Decadence asked that I not use her real name.
5. The process of implementing a union into the workplace involves several steps. First, the majority of the employees need to sign union cards. Once the cards are signed, the organizers usually ask the company to recognize the union. If the company refuses to do so, which they usually do, the organizers will then request a National Labor Relations

Board election, in which the employees vote on whether or not they want to have a union. The NLRB will then conduct a series of hearings, most commonly to ascertain which employees will be able to vote in the election.

6. From an interview conducted by the author with Julia on April 15, 1999, in San Francisco.
7. Racial classifications such as this are illegal. The management at the Lusty Lady eventually dropped their racial classification system after the EEOC complaint and several grievances were filed.
8. From an interview conducted by the author with Siobhan on April 28, 1999, in San Francisco.
9. See Kathleen Barry, *Female Sexual Slavery* (New York: University Press, 1979); Andrea Dworkin, *Intercourse* (New York: The Free Press, 1987); Catharine A. MacKinnon, *Towards a Feminist Theory of the State* (Cambridge: Harvard University Press, 1989).
10. For further discussion of this idea, see Shannon Bell, *Reading, Writing, and Rewriting the Prostitute Body* (Bloomington: Indiana University Press, 1994).
11. Gail Pheterson, "Not Repeating History," in *A Vindication of the Rights of Whores*, ed. Gail Pheterson (Seattle: The Seal Press, 1989).
12. Valerie Jenness, *Making It Work: The Prostitutes' Rights Movement in Perspective* (New York: Aldine de Gruyter, 1993), 21.
13. According to legal definitions, an independent contractor is not bound to follow any rules or regulations set forth by an employer, 29 Cal Jur 3d (Rev), Employer and Employee, sections 9, 12.
14. Over the years, stage fees have risen dramatically. As of this writing—July 1999—they are presently well over two hundred dollars per night in several clubs.
15. I obtained this and all information on the Exotic Dancers Alliance from personal conversations with members, archived materials, and the group's website: www.bayswan.org/EDAindex.html.
16. The information on Pacers was acquired from the EDA's archived materials.
17. A.B. 1446 ultimately died in the California Assembly Labor Committee.
18. *Live Nude Girls Unite!* had its national premiere in October 2000.
19. Bullough, "Prostitution, Psychiatry and History," 88.
20. For further discussion of the relationships between female homosexuality, prostitution, and disease, see Bullough, "Prostitution, Psychiatry and History"; Carol Groneman, "Nymphomania"; Joan Nestle, "Lesbians and Prostitutes."
21. "Sexual Addiction" brochure of the Golden Valley Health Center, cited by Janice M. Irvine, "Regulated Passions: The Invention of Inhibited Sexual Desire and Sexual Addiction," in *Deviant Bodies*, 324.
22. Elizabeth Lapovsky Kennedy and Madeline D. Davis, *Boots of Leather, Slippers of Gold: The History of a Lesbian Community* (New York: Routledge, 1993), 96.
23. Nestle, "Lesbians and Prostitutes"; Leslie Feinberg, *Stone Butch Blues* (Ithaca: Firebrand Books, 1993).
24. Susan Seidelman, *Desperately Seeking Susan*, 1985.
25. See Eva Pendleton, "Love for Sale: Queering Heterosexuality," in *Whores and Other Feminists*, ed. Jill Nagle (New York: Routledge, 1997).
26. See Bell, *Reading, Writing, and Rewriting the Prostitute Body*.
27. Joan Nestle, "Lesbians and Prostitutes," 232.

Being a Lesbian Trade Unionist:
The Intersection of Movements

Teresa Conrow

Ten Percent Is Not Enough

I first heard the chant "10 Percent Is Not Enough . . . Recruit . . . Recruit . . . Recruit" at a dyke march. The chant does a great job of making light of straight people's fears that lesbians will negatively influence straight women. This chant in particular, for me, was a piece of culture with the potential to transcend some of the divisions within my life and between the lesbian and labor movements.

Both the lesbian and labor movements are used to chanting at demonstrations and on the picket line. In the labor movement, the "10 Percent" chant can be used to poke some fun at our focus on numbers and our need to grow. At present, labor unions in the United States are in the middle of a huge effort to reverse a massive, thirty-year decline in union membership. Currently only 9.4 percent of private-sector workers are union members.[1]

Unlike the often subtle humor of the lesbian and gay movements, labor movement chants usually are more direct—"Two, four, six, eight . . . We Want to Negotiate," for example. But the very loss of ironic nuance that occurs when the "10 Percent" chant is translated from a dyke march to a labor rally gives the chant a subtle underground edge that makes the link between the two movements even more perfect. At a union demonstration people might think the chant was "purely union," but for any lesbian union activists present it is a strong affirmation of the presence of both our movements.

Out and About in the Labor Movement

In this essay, I want to address the ways in which I, as a lesbian trade unionist, live in the midst of the intersections of movements. My focus will be on the intersection of sexuality with class, as well as the intrinsic intertwining of race and gender with sexuality and class.

I will first look at the shared histories of the lesbian and labor movements, then the intersections between the movements, and finally at how we build spaces at these intersections. Throughout the article, I use the words *lesbian, gay, dyke, lesbian/gay/bisexual/transgender,* and *queer* to represent the various facets of the lesbian and gay movements. The emphasis is on the lesbian movement because it is the movement I identify with.

I have worked for the labor movement for over fifteen years. My first strike was as a rank-and-file worker in a bread factory. By the time I was involved in my second strike, I was a full-time labor representative working for the Red Cross nurses union in Los Angeles. We won the strike. I continued to work as a labor representative and organizer mostly for service-sector unions through the 1980s and early 1990s. I came out as a lesbian while I was a labor representative for a health-care workers union. I was fortunate to be able to learn from a gay chief steward who helped model for me how to be very out and active in the union and workplace.

In 1994, I began teaching part time at the labor center of a community college. I now teach organizing and campaign skills to unions in the United States and around the world. I was raised in Canada and I believe the Canadian culture and identity I have retained from my childhood have helped give some perspective to my international union work. I feel very fortunate now that my work allows me to travel and write and learn and think and organize.

Like all activists, my work bridges many intersections of social movements. My work is framed by the labor movement and class (my first "professional" job was as an organizer); being a lesbian (providing an understanding of and interest in lesbian and feminist issues); my whiteness (giving me racial privilege I share with a number of white labor leaders); and my Americanness (which gives me international privilege, rights, and access).

As an organizer, I attempt to use my particular space at the intersections to further social movements. My presence as an out lesbian and as a woman can be used to break through oppressions of gender and sexuality and help create more room for lesbians and women. This same presence can also erase the voices of those who share my gender and/or sexuality but not my whiteness, "Americanness," or class privilege. It gives my listening and organizing skills a workout.

This continual struggle for consciousness about my position in relation to all the various social movements is absolutely essential. If all workers are truly included in the labor movement, and all lesbians in the lesbian movement, our movements do not just become larger, but their goals change dramatically. Representation and inclusion are crucial not simply because we need to be big and powerful enough to win improvements in the lives of workers and lesbians, but because without true representation—without all workers, all lesbians, all people present—the souls of our movements become endangered. As activists, we end up eventually fighting against the very movements we are working to build because our movements do not represent us and our humanity.

Movement Histories: Shared Struggles

Despite their differences, the labor movement and the queer movement share a great deal. First, both movements have historically stood for far more than their tallied membership might show. At its heart, the labor movement represents all workers, not just the 10 percent who are unionized. Among other things, unions have brought us the weekend, the eight-hour day, higher wages, collective bargaining, and nondiscrimination clauses.

Likewise, the queer movement represents not just the 10 percent of the population who are lesbian and gay, but the freedom to explore the totality of the gender identities within each of us—gay/straight/bisexual/transgender. The fight for freedom from harassment and violence in the workplace and on the streets benefits nongay people as well as gay people. The gay and lesbian movement has also helped us reexamine the totality of what families and communities look like. Even domestic-partner benefits, usually identified as a gay issue, in practice often help more nonmarried straight couples than gay ones.

The labor and gay movements have a long history together. Many lesbian/gay/bisexual/transgender activists don't realize that clauses prohibiting discrimination based on sexual orientation have been in union contracts for years—long before laws against workplace discrimination were passed. In fact, in places where state and local nondiscrimination laws still do not cover gays and lesbians, the only protection workers have from homophobia on the job is through union representation. Unfortunately, the labor movement has not had a history of publicizing these benefits in the queer community and instead has often actively distanced itself from and fought against lesbian and gay movements.

It is important to remember, however, that the labor movement also has a history of accepting lesbians and gays. In Los Angeles, in the early 1980s, a contingent of gay men attended a demonstration against U.S. intervention in El Salvador. They wore what might be called political drag (dresses, but no makeup). During the march they were told loudly and publicly that they should not be present because they gave the march a bad image. It took a union leader to welcome their participation. He made a point of telling them, "Your people have great clothes and great chants." In my experience, straight trade unionists are often able to rely on their understanding of discrimination, difference, and solidarity to form alliances with lesbians and gays.

Lost Stories

The shared history of the lesbian and labor movements can be found in the tremendous number of people who bridge the intersections between these movements. Most of their histories and stories have been stolen from us. Cheryl Dunye's film *Watermelon Women* tells the story of a black lesbian filmmaker's search for the names and lives of black lesbian actresses and filmmakers who came before her.[2] We have our own particularized search for the "Watermelon Women" of the labor and lesbian movements.

We know working-class lesbians have been with us for a long time, often concentrated in either traditionally female or traditionally nonfemale work, but usually we do not have access to their names or stories unless someone has dug through layers of cultural biases and barriers to find them. The stories that are most hidden are those involving working-class lesbians of color.

We need to remember that the lesbian and gay labor movement is not new, not white, and not middle class. One lesbian who used to drive a truck delivering auto parts tells of finding out that her job had once been done by two women who passed as men. In the 1950s, this couple—one black, one white—had created a work space that benefited the lesbian who followed them twenty years later in the same job.[3]

Even when we don't know much about the working-class lesbians who came before us, the knowledge that they existed makes our own lives easier. However, more and more of our history is being lost every day. Those of us who bridge intersections must encourage each other to protect the stories of our lives and tell them to others, or we will lose them—particularly the stories of lesbians who for whatever reason do not fit our current media image of white, middle-class, physically unchallenged American lesbians.

Out of the Dark—Lesbian and Gay Visibility in Unions

It was another lesbian trade unionist who told me about the first meeting of lesbians and gays at a Service Employees International Union (SEIU) convention. It was literally held in the dark—in an unlit room. It was too dangerous for people to be out, but they wanted to connect and talk to each other. You could only come by special invitation, and no one knew who else was in the room. Only a few felt comfortable speaking, even to each other. Many were both silent and faceless.

In the 1980s, John Sweeney, then president of SEIU, now president of the AFL-CIO, first spoke the words "lesbian/gay/bisexual/transgender" from the podium at an SEIU conference. I sat at a table with a small group of out lesbians, gay men, and bisexual people. We wanted to share the moment together. It was an important historical event for all of us, but despite how far we had come, we knew we had a long way to go.

It was not until 1998 that Pride at Work, a national group representing lesbian/gay/bisexual/transgender union members, was legitimated as an official constituency group of the AFL-CIO.[4] The words *lesbians, gays, bisexuals,* and *transgender* now show up at union conferences, on posters and sometimes even in workplace surveys and leaflets. The labor movement now has a record of joining publicly with gay communities to fight for gay rights and against right-wing homophobic initiatives in Hawaii, Alaska, Oregon, North Carolina, and Colorado.

Unions have been able to prove that taking on issues relating to homophobia at work has built union strength, not weakened it. In one SEIU local in Oregon, the union leadership provided special training for all stewards in the state on how to combat homophobia in the workplace. Only one steward resigned over the increased visibility of lesbian and gay issues in the union, but the union recruited many additional stewards in the process.[5]

There are incredible potentials, as well as serious threats, to Pride at Work. Unlike many national AFL-CIO structures, a vast majority of its members and top leadership are rank-and-file union activists, not union staff or elected officers. This has given Pride at Work tremendous importance, potential, and heart in a labor movement that is fighting its own bureaucratization.

The biggest danger to the organization lies in the replication of the gender and race hierarchies of oppressions within the organization. In some places, such as District 37 of the American Federation of State, County and Municipal Employees (AFSCME) in New York City, race and gender representation has been organized into the lesbian and gay union structures from the beginning. In other places, like Los Angeles, tremendous leadership commitments are being made by Pride at Work activists to change the predominately gay white male organizational culture that has already been established.

Building Pride at Work without full representation and inclusion is analogous to moving an organizing committee to action when there are still huge parts of the workforce absent from the committee—once you start off without people, the organization is moving in a direction that is hard to correct. New leadership from the national 1999 Pride at Work convention has brought more gender equity and some more color to the top leadership, but the struggle remains.

Intersections between Movements: Intersection Connections

Lesbian trade unionism is not an intersection of two social movements, but the intersection of many movements and oppressions. Race, class, gender, age, language, physical disability, ethnicity, and other oppressions are not separate and divided.[6] They won't come to our movements as two or even three oppressions to be added to our work, one at a time and neatly packaged.

Oppression comes like people do, in a huge variety and assortment that will defy classification. Looking at the intersection between two movements means looking at the intersections between many movements.

If we are talking about building and strengthening social movements, these intersections and connections between people are powerful. The connections can be bigger than words. I remember one Brazilian trade unionist who hugged me when I was talking about how happy I was that a young friend of mine was bending the gender "straightjacket." Given the language, racial, and North-South difference, I don't know a lot about this labor leader, but I know we connected. I, in particular, need these connections to be able to think and act outside of the prevailing oppressing culture. I sometimes feel a bit sorry for straight trade unionists who can't envision the doubly strong connections of solidarity and struggle that we lesbian and gay union people can access.

In the workplace, the connections between lesbian/gay/bisexual/transgender people can be very powerful and important to union organizing. Our presence in the union brings some more of the heart, soul, and humor that our labor movement needs. In the 1980s, I worked as a labor representative in a hospital where an out gay, out HIV-positive man was the main activist and leader. In a matter of months, we raised union membership from less than 5 percent of workers to over 40 percent. Much of the growth was due to the relationships and organizing work of this gay activist, who was able to make inroads into new areas of the hospital, pulling together workers who respected and trusted his honesty and openness. He was the person who helped me see how to come out and be out in a union environment.

One of the key issues in any organizing campaign is to know when to keep committee and work site issues underground and when the campaign should surface strategically. There is no one more experienced in the subtleties and issues of "outing" than the lesbian/gay/bisexual/transgender communities.

Hierarchies within Our Movements

The labor and gay movements have both had long histories of weakness and dysfunction around issues of oppression outside a narrow definition of either class or sexuality. From this weakness we get what we basically have now—a labor movement unable to fully take on homophobia at the workplace and a lesbian movement that for the most part ignores the fight for improvements in lesbian lives at the workplace. Neither of the two movements are able to cope with issues of race, ethnicity, age, and gender. Both movements represent many people who face oppression on fronts in addition to class and homophobia. If the gay movement and the labor movements really fight for justice for all workers and gays, then issues of importance to people of color, women, young and old people, immigrants, and the disabled will, by necessity, form a large part of both movements' struggles.[7]

The 10 percent of the workers in this country who are gay are a huge number for the labor movement to write off. The lesbian and gay movements need the resources and strategic power of the labor movement. However, because they refuse to intersect, the two movements lose even more than numbers and money. This inability to intersect on issues of race and gender as well as class and sexuality means that our movements lose the ability to fight for economic and social justice, and as a result perpetuate injustice. The labor movement focuses on narrowly defined economic issues in fear of dividing the workers along gender or race lines. The lesbian and gay movement hypes itself as part of the striving-to-be "normal white middle class."[8]

One of the most disturbing things about life at the intersections is the way in which those who are visibly promoted in our organizations and cultures are those who are at the top of other oppressions. Each movement's particular hierarchies of oppression are clear and visible. For the most part, white middle-class lesbians lead the lesbian movement, and straight, white, working-class men lead the labor movement. When our movements do try to work together organizationally, it is no wonder they have difficulties. The very people who bridge the gaps between labor and queerness on a daily basis are not present when the top of one movement meets the top of the other. The similarities in the race and age of the top leaders can result in cultural bondings that further oppressions within our movements.

There are exceptions, but at this time in our history the exceptions sometimes reinforce the rule. Women, for example, have recently moved to more positions of power in both the gay and labor movements. This has benefited both movements tremendously. The problem is that these women are likely to be straight, white and/or middle class. The movements' cultures and organizational structures pressure them into tokenized positions. They may even find themselves "in drag" as organizational forces push them to act more like men than the men. Despite these constraints, women and other underrepresented groups holding positions of power within movements have helped build a more inclusive agenda and a change in organizational culture and goals.

Self-consciousness about our simultaneous placement of both benefit and exclusion is important. I struggle to place myself against the privilege that makes my presence on a committee or at the front of the room part of the historical oppression of white women once again representing lesbians. In the very act of being asked to speak about being a lesbian trade unionist, I am allowed to join in publicly ignoring race.

Fortunately, as we live our lives, we are able to find our own spaces at the intersections, regardless of what our movements and cultures lay out for us. None of us lives inside a paradigm that only focuses on economics or sexuality. We do not and will never really fit our movements if they are divided in this way.

Only One Lesbian Is Not Enough

It is sometimes tempting to imagine what the space at the intersections looks like—or should look like. For a time, I was the only full-time out lesbian staff organizer in the Los Angeles labor movement. I was frustrated being an interpreter of the entire range of lesbian cultures. At one point, I jokingly instructed a straight coworker who had been peppering me with questions about lesbians to be careful in his use of words concerning the lesbian and gay movement. I explained to him that we always put the word "lesbian" before the word "gay" in deference to the specific additional oppression of women. It wasn't until months later that he came and questioned me about why, if that were true, the Los Angeles Gay and Lesbian Center was called the Los Angeles Gay and Lesbian Center.

After I admitted to my deceptiveness and wishful thinking regarding the sexism within gay culture, we talked about the dangers of the "token" experience of interpreting culture. It is dangerous to take just one lesbian's word to represent all the various lesbian communities. Even if the token lesbian union activist is not deliberately steering you wrong, you do not know what she can and can't see, which working-class, union, lesbian experiences she knows and doesn't know, and which experiences she may find problematic or difficult.

Representing the Intersections

Many years after I first heard the "10 percent is not enough" chant, I was able to use it openly with all of its full dyke power as part of a speech at a labor event. It worked spectacularly, bringing together the forces of laughter and justice. There were only four out gays and lesbians in the audience of four hundred, but you wouldn't have known it from the sound of the crowd. They warmed up with "10 percent is not enough," did a gay-created picket line rendition of "Stop in the Name of Love" with all the hand movements, and ended by chanting, "We're here, we're queer, get used to it." It was one of those grand and monumental times.

The union people got to see one view from a particular lesbian who had been given the public opportunity to help bridge two movements. This privilege and power to interpret and represent the lesbian trade union movement is very much a product of how my class and race intersect with my sexuality. It was a white, middle-class lesbian who was given the privilege of being part of a panel about diversity. The panel took place at a conference of labor educators, most of whom worked in an academic setting. There were five trade unionists on the panel: a black woman, a Latino man, an Asian man, another white woman, and me. We were each to speak about issues of diversity within the labor movement. As far as I know, all of the others were straight. It wasn't until long after the conference that I really thought about just who was present to represent whom on the panel.

At the time, it did not occur to me to use my time on the panel to speak specifically and directly about the women's movement, or race, or class. What made it worse, of course, was that this was not the first time that the lesbian and gay labor movement had been represented and interpreted by white middle-class lesbians and gays. It was not surprising that the majority of the four people in the audience who identified as out lesbians and gays were white and, due to the nature of the event, most likely were currently middle class.

We can only make more space at the intersections of the labor and lesbian movements by including all lesbian and labor experiences. Because of the ways race intersects with class in our society, working-class and poor lesbians are more likely to be women of color than the lesbian population in general. Both the labor and lesbian movements represent huge racial, class, and gender identities that must be big, visualized, particularized, and present if the movements are to intersect on more than narrow issues and viewpoints.

Building Space at the Intersections: Working to Be Visible

Sometimes being both a lesbian and a union activist means being invisible to the point of near nonexistence. In 1998, I stayed at a gay hotel when I was working with unions in Melbourne, Australia. I was down at the harbor many nights at the dockworker protests, one of the biggest union battles of Australia's recent history. I don't know who was more surprised when one of the gay guys who worked at the hotel thought I was the nicest straight woman he had met. It was embarrassing and uncomfortable for us both. Had I not been gay enough? Did I not fit his stereotype of what a union dyke would look like? Where was my space? What made it impossible for him to see me as an out lesbian union person?

Trade unionists often expect lesbians to cross over into union space, not vice versa. Union leaders are often afraid of us—afraid to be seen with us, to talk, to listen, and to ask questions. Working-class lesbians, on the other hand, are more likely to choose a certain level of participation in a union or workplace and frame their level of being out through a studied determination of how much safe space exists there.

In 1998, Victor Reuther, the famous leader of the United Auto Workers, and his granddaughter, Valerie Reuther, were brought to a gathering of labor and community organizers to speak about their relationship to each other in both their personal and political lives. It was an extraordinary event. The two of them were clearly very proud of each other and each other's experiences of organizing. I was honored to be asked to introduce them, and I briefly interviewed each of them before the event.

One of the things that struck me was how easily Valerie had entered into her grandfather's movement. She had been attending union marches and rallies since she was a child. Victor, on the other hand, as enthusiastic and supportive as he was of his granddaughter's lesbian activism, had only been to one gay demonstration with her. When I asked him about this he paused for a moment. I could see the disappointment in his eyes. His recognition of the difficulty of going into her organizing space and movement was powerful. Victor Reuther is not the only one. Some day I would love to see union leaders enthusiastically and easily recruiting union members to attend a lesbian-led demonstration against the right wing, or including *Stone Butch Blues*, a union-positive novel about a transgender auto worker, on their reading lists.[9]

A few years ago, lesbians started appearing on the front page of national straight magazines for the first time. k.d. lang was on the cover of *Vanity Fair* and two other white lesbians were on the cover of *Newsweek*.[10] A speak-out on lesbian visibility was organized in West Hollywood. The advertisement for the event in the *Lesbian News* showed the *Newsweek* lesbian cover page. When we got to the event itself, it was a study in whiteness. The cover pages of the magazines had been enlarged and posted on the front of the stage. Four of the five panelists were white. The only black panelist, Alycee Lane, spoke about the importance of analyzing who was being represented in this new visibility and who was not.[11] The audience reaction was intense. Lane was accused of trying to destroy this moment of celebration of the "new lesbian visibility." One person rose to his feet and declared that he was not racist, even though no one had accused him of such. It was one of the more fascinating lesbian events I have ever attended. It was very discouraging to be reminded of how little space there is in the lesbian community, but it was invigorating and good to see so public a skirmish in the war to create more space.

Making issues of class more visible in the United States is difficult. We seem incapable of talking about class in anything other than coded language, even though we know exactly where we and others stand in terms of class status—including our current class position, our class position at birth, the class we aspire to, and our ability to deceive others about our class status. This lack of language and consciousness has had an impact on the U.S. labor movement's ability to confront and organize class clearly.

Working outside of the United States in places where there is more awareness of class issues has helped make class more visible to me. When I was in Australia in 1998, I was walking out of the central union building with one of the top elected labor leaders in the city on our way to a press conference. Construction work was being done on the outside of the building. As we crossed into the parking lot a worker pulled the union official aside and said, "Hey, did you see the business section of today's paper? Make sure you mention the effects of the companies' planned merger in your talk today." The labor leader thanked him, and they discussed some economic points. The ease of interaction between the two of them forced me to confront my own thinking. From my position, I had not seen the building worker at all, let alone been prepared to have eye contact and a conversation with him.

This lack of awareness of class results in the public invisibility of working-class lesbians in the lesbian movements. Within the labor movement, our inability to talk about class blinds us to the particular ways in which the voices of rank-and-file workers can be obliterated by the currently middle-class union voices who are speaking for them. Within the lesbian trade-union movement, the historical role that women in the trades have played in creating lesbian union space can be ignored by the emphasis on lesbians in the service industries.

Race and Class and Gender . . . Oh My!

The fear of confronting race, class, gender, and all the divisions that could unite us is big. It is bigger than the threat from any of the lions and tigers and bears imagined down the yellow brick road. When the spaces between the movements do become larger and more visible, there is social discomfort. Sometimes we become fifth graders, unable to contain our giggling and wiggling. Other times pain and anger silence discussion. We make constant choices about how much to speak about race and class and gender, how much to write about it, how much discussion time to spend on it, and how aware and active to be in our lives.

The laughter and unease can be fun. I once took part in an introductory exercise at a session on popular education in the labor movement. The group was asked both silly and somewhat serious questions to identify who was in the room. Whoever fit the description given was to stand up. Someone asked who were "friends of Dorothy," an old phrase from the 1970s that was used to identify whether people were gay or lesbian. A whole lot of people moved to the front of the room. I was momentarily stunned at the ratio of lesbians and gays to straights in the room, until we figured out that they were all standing up because they were friends of a labor educator named Dorothy.

When someone does confront issues of difference and oppression publicly and directly, there is often either a panic of fear and social discomfort or a sense of relief, depending on where one sits in terms of privilege. After a moment of complete silence or an intake of breath, some people will often start defending or opposing the individuals or the organizations involved instead of setting about solving whatever problems may have arisen. In many of our organizations, we know that the emperor is not wearing any clothes around these issues but we can't then talk about it. Without the power and space to even discuss the problem, we will never get any clothes on the man—let alone decide whether he should be dressed first in a hard hat or a yarmulke, an Armani suit or kente cloth, bald or wigged out in full drag.

During a recent union organizing class, I was leading a discussion on how we might involve underrepresented groups in organizing campaigns. It was a great class of about forty organizers and rank-and-file leaders, and they were eager to get into a topic so central to their organizing lives and experiences. The class first made a list of all the various groups that were not represented in their union organizational structures equal to their representation in the workforce. The list was obviously a long one, reflective of the diversity of the Los Angeles labor movement. Rather than try and deal with the whole list—and thereby not getting into the reality of the experiences of any one group—I asked the group to choose which of the underrepresented groups they would like to spend more time discussing.

The group chose to focus on young lesbians, combining the youth, women, and gay categories from their original list. We looked at the advantages and disadvantages to young lesbians of becoming more involved in the union. The jokes and laughing started. When we began listing the advantages and disadvantages from the union's point of view of involving more lesbians, I actually had to stop the class and challenge them to see if we could discuss the topic for at least five minutes without laughing. They were joking about the fears some union leaders (including themselves) might have of lesbian issues taking over the agenda of the labor movement. The laughter was a way to release some of the tension around the topic. We laughed about our laughter.

We did come up with some good insights on the issues, and we congratulated ourselves for having what was probably the longest public discussion about the topic in the history of the Los Angeles labor movement. We then discussed ways the union could increase the involvement of young lesbians in union structures. The group wanted to encourage union leaders to attend and support fun lesbian events and came up with concrete ways the union could make it widely known it was organizing to protect lesbians in the workplace.

I have used this same exercise in different variations with many unions in the United States and other countries. There is usually an initial awkwardness as we make the list of underrepresented groups and analyze why they are underrepresented. We try to make sure we have not left anyone out, and we struggle to name groups when our language is often so limited. Discussions about race and ethnicity seem to result in painful and fearful silences rather than laughter; and sometimes they give a more immediate public voice to some of the anger in the room. In the union context, the level of emotional reaction lessens when the group discusses a section of the workforce that may be underrepresented, such as the cafeteria workers, even though they have identified that this underrepresentation is obviously linked to race and gender. A lot of the lists and reactions vary, of course, depending on which underrepresented groups are present in or absent from the room and what country and union culture we are working in.

All of these discussions are framed by my own racial, class, and cultural identities, which in turn are magnified by the power I have as the facilitator. I have found popular education methods (and the group problem-solving methods of Augusto Boal, in particular) to be crucial. Participants most knowledgeable and involved in the issues frame the discussions, identify the relevant issues and problems, and develop ways to organize around these problems.[12] We do not always get it right. Some groups have left lesbian and gay people off the list of underrepresented groups entirely. Other times, we have had to work through the particulars of whole groups of people that were hidden under large group labels, such as "people of color" or "Asians." In almost every group, people seem at first to miss the idea that there are groups of people that come from more than one group—lesbian Filipino nurses, for example. When we can, the group catches the mistakes. We honor our efforts and hopefully remember the lessons more because they were based on our mistakes.

When people at the top of a hierarchy of oppressions work to confront oppression, they are often given a level of credit above what others receive. When I first started learning Spanish, I found many of the Spanish speakers in our union hall extremely helpful. It makes a big difference in the learning process if you are able to find native speakers who are patient enough to listen to your initial one- and two-word sentences, mispronounced words, and missing verbs, and help you practice. Both the native English and native Spanish speakers thought it was great that I was taking time out of my busy life to learn Spanish. When Spanish-speaking union members practiced their English, the encouraging words were much fewer and farther between.

I learned a lot about helping to make more room at the intersections in 1993 when I was on the first steering committee of the National Organizers Alliance. The goal of the newly founded organization was to create safe spaces and support for people who dedicated their working lives to organizing. The bylaws of the organization required a steering committee that was at least half women, half people of color, and that included young people and members of the lesbian/gay/bisexual/transgender community. In preparation for the first national gathering of organizers, we analyzed the potential representation issues and determined that the most underrepresented group was likely to be people of color. We then made a list of all the organizers of color that our already diverse steering committee could identify and assigned each of them to be contacted and visited by one of us to discuss their involvement in the formation of the gathering. It was an organizing process familiar to any union organizer who has had to build an organizing committee in a workplace. However, despite years of community and union organizing experience, this was the first time I had seen these organizing skills fully and methodically applied to internal issues of gender and race representation prior to an organization's formation. The encoding of representation into the organization's bylaws strengthened the group's ability to deal with issues of representation and inclusion in the future.

Creating more space and power at the intersections of queerness and labor does not blur the differences of race, gender, age (or any of the other oppressions that keep us unequal and "less than") but instead draws on these differences. The problem with a focus on class or sexuality alone is that such a focus can lessen the differences between us.[13] We need these differences.

In its tentative efforts to reach into the lesbian community, the labor movement has begun hiring more out lesbian organizers. However, some unions are telling these organizers that they should not stay involved in lesbian activist organizations because they will need all of their time and energy for the union—an interesting way to disconnect the organizers from the very communities they were hired to link with. The only way to answer the question of which is more important, being a unionist or a lesbian activist, is to demand the space and power to refuse to separate the two.

It is clear that fighting for social and economic justice means fighting at all levels of oppression at the same time. While some of us may hesitate because it looks like it would be harder to take it all on at once, we know it is in fact easier. It is easier because as individuals we already live with all of it, and we are already dealing with all of it. It is to our credit as human beings that we are able to find ways to negotiate around the spoken and unspoken boundaries, making spaces for friendship and desired spaces at the intersections.

Speaking the Language—Finding the Purse

Often, there is not a sufficient range of language and vocabulary to describe the boundary areas of race, gender, and class intersections. You can tell you are in the borderlands if it takes more than one or two words to describe you. "Lesbian trade unionist" is three. And then there is the four-word person, "black lesbian trade unionist," or five-word person, "young black lesbian trade unionist." The longer the phrase, the less it seems like a real person and the more of a label it becomes. Language and naming is key to identity and consciousness. The pain of inadequate words can be intense. Fortunately, though, language can grow and change as movements grow in power.

The expansion of language can be powerful. In 1998, thousands of demonstrators blocked the wharves during the Maritime Union of Australia (MUA) dispute on the Australian docks. The demonstrations went on for weeks. There were MUA members, Maori construction workers, vegetarian punk rock activists, homeless permanent campers, techno rock DJs, activists from the Aboriginal movement, seventy-year-old white women engaging in civil disobedience, and politicians in suits—all protesting together. The range and numbers of the activists were astounding.

The vocabulary of the union leaders expanded greatly to meet the cultures and peoples of Melbourne. At one point, one of the top leaders from the MUA got on the mike and announced that "a lady's purse had been found." A few seconds later he came back on, matter-of-factly stating that "if anyone was missing the woman's purse, they could come to the picket captain's trailer for it." A few more minutes passed before he gave us the final rendition. "A purse has been found. Not necessarily a woman's purse. Please go to the picket captain's trailer if you have lost a purse." You just wanted to hug him.

Stop in the Name of Love

The power that the lesbian/gay/bisexual/transgender movements can bring to labor is underestimated and underutilized. This became visible during the 1988 Melbourne dockworkers' dispute. There were weeks when we had to block the movement of any shipments from the docks. Despite my years of experience with civil disobedience in the U.S. labor movement, the militancy of the MUA picket line was the strongest I had ever seen. If we were to win, the human barrier of protesters preventing the shipment of goods could not be broken.

We had already turned back the police once by surrounding them with thousands of workers. Our fear was that the police would come when we were the weakest—in the middle of the night or when people were most tired of the twenty-four-hour full-stop nature of the protest. Given the tremendous organizational strength of the unions in Melbourne, we knew that if we could hold the line for even twenty minutes we could bring in enough protesters to surround the police again with sheer numbers and they would leave us alone. We had access to tremendous resources—a radio station to announce events, a gigantic citywide telephone tree, a great sound system at the actual picket site, and the ability to pull hundreds of workers in the middle of the night if we needed them.

The labor leaders had already agreed that in the event of a police confrontation, the demonstrators would be surrounded at least one level deep by the strongest, most muscle-bound people in Melbourne to prevent any breaches in the line. Any demonstrators and politicians that wanted to be arrested publicly would be placed in front of them, with everyone else in the middle.

It was in this context that a group of us developed a "plan," which drew heavily on gay male culture. We loved the plan, even though we knew it would be too much of a cultural leap for our movement to handle. It had the potential both to give us the extra twenty minutes we needed to win a confrontation with the police and to create a bigger space for who we were as a labor movement.

Our plan was supposed to kick in at the moment the police were poised to take on the strong blokes at the front. The sound system would begin blasting, "Stop in the Name of Love . . . Before You Break My Head . . . Think It Over . . . Think It Over." A whole second line of people in full red satin and glitter drag would come out from under the arms of the frontline protesters and lead the group in singing and hand motions.

There was no question that it was a good plan, but we never really seriously discussed its implementation. We knew it was too over-the-top for its time. Maybe, sometime in the future, our plan will no longer seem unusual. In the end, the dispute was won with additional struggle and protest, but without another major police confrontation.

Some day, I hope to be part of a labor movement that can utilize all the power that resides in the intersections of movements—that will be a labor movement I can be fully proud of. Meanwhile, we face the challenging and invigorating task of getting to know more and more about ourselves and each other with all of our differences honored. Social justice is not possible without social justice. So simple and so complex, but that is who we are as people and as movements—intensely simple and intensely complex.

Notes

I would like to thank Alana Bowman, Alycee Lane, Carmen Figueroa, Gilda Zwerman, Linda Delp, Sally McMannus, and Yutian Wong for their assistance and thoughts at various stages of this project.

1. The AFL-CIO reported in January 2000 that its two-decade-long drop in membership finally leveled off in 1999. With 16.5 million members, the AFL-CIO represents 13.9 percent of the total workforce. This breaks down further to representation of 37.3 percent of public-sector employees and 9.4 percent of private-sector employees. See Steven Greenhouse, "Growth in Unions' Membership in 1999 Was Best in Two Decades," *New York Times*, January 20, 2000, p. A13.
2. Cheryl Dunye, *Watermelon Women* (First Run Features, 1997).
3. This story comes from Gilda Zwerman, a lesbian scholar from New York City.
4. AFL-CIO constituency groups are officially sanctioned national organizations of AFL-CIO union members that promote a national union voice for women and people of color, as well as lesbian/gay/bisexual/transgender people. There are currently six constituency groups: the Coalition of Labor Union Women, the A. Phillip Randolph Institute, the Labor Council for Latin American Advancement, the Asian Pacific American Labor Alliance, the Coalition of Black Trade Unionists, and Pride at Work.
5. See Ann Montague, "We Are Union Builders Too," *Labor Research Review* 12, no. 1 (spring/summer 1993): 79–83.
6. For more on the theory of intersectionality, see Kimberlé Crenshaw et al., eds. *Critical Race Theory: The Key Writings That Formed the Movement* (New York: The New Press, 1995); Gloria Anzaldúa, *Borderlands/La Frontera: The New Mestiza* (San Francisco: Aunt Lute Books, 1987); and Cherríe Moraga and Gloria Anzaldúa, eds., *This Bridge Called My Back: Writings by Radical Women of Color* (New York: Kitchen Table Press, 1984).
7. In this article, I refer to race and gender intersections as a way of representing this list without repeatedly recreating it.
8. I use the words "middle class" to refer to the upper pay ranges of the working class, as opposed to the rich, who have enough wealth to not work.
9. Leslie Feinberg, *Stone Butch Blues* (Ithaca, N.Y.: Firebrand Books, 1993). Feinberg describes union life as part of transgendered life experiences in the United States from the 1950s to the 1970s.
10. *Newsweek*, June 21, 1993; *Vanity Fair*, August 1993.
11. Alycee Lane is author of "Black Bodies/Gay Bodies—The Politics of Race in the Gay/Military Battle," *Callaloo* 17, no. 4 (1994).
12. For more information about problem-solving interventions, see Teresa Conrow and Linda Delp, "Teaching Organizing through Workers' Experiences," *Labor Studies Journal* (spring 1999): 42–57.
13. See Crenshaw et al.

Making Out at Work

Tami Gold

The Background

In June 1992, Kelly Anderson and I videotaped a conference on gay and lesbian workplace rights that was sponsored by LAGIC, the Lesbian and Gay Issues Committee of District Council 37. D.C. 37 is one of the largest units in the American Federation of State, County and Municipal Employees, and the conference was held at its headquarters in Manhattan.[1] What made this labor event different from hundreds I had been to in the past was that everyone here was queer. The first regional conference of its kind, it drew gays and lesbians from several unions and many different workplaces across the Northeast.

Kelly and I were there to get interviews for *Labor at the Crossroads*, known as *Labor X*, a monthly public access television show we produced. We set up a camera and lights in the lobby of the building and invited participants to be interviewed about their own experiences, in and out of the workplace closet. Before we knew it, a line of people were waiting to testify about what they encountered as gay men or lesbians on the job.

"Am I out? I was never in. I'm out, way out!" a young African American woman declared. She was wearing a tie and pushed her hand as if to break an imaginary box. Laughing and self-confident, she said, "I advise all the men on my job what ties to buy and how to dress fine." A white woman in her late thirties spoke hesitantly, explaining that she lost her job with the Board of Education and was trying to prove that it was because she was a lesbian. Before she finished her story, a middle-aged Puerto Rican man jumped into the lights. Looking straight into the camera, he told us how his coworkers in the Department of Public Works swung their hips and limped their wrists when they passed him at work. His shop steward kept saying, "That's your problem." We walked up to a Latina who was listening. "Yes, you can interview me, but you can't show my face," she said. "I'm an electrician. I'm not out, and I'm scared for my life. I'm the only woman on the construction site and I have to first prove myself and get into the union before . . . who knows if it'll ever change?"

It was at this conference that we met Nat Keitt, an African American library clerk who works in the Bronx. When we asked him if he was out on

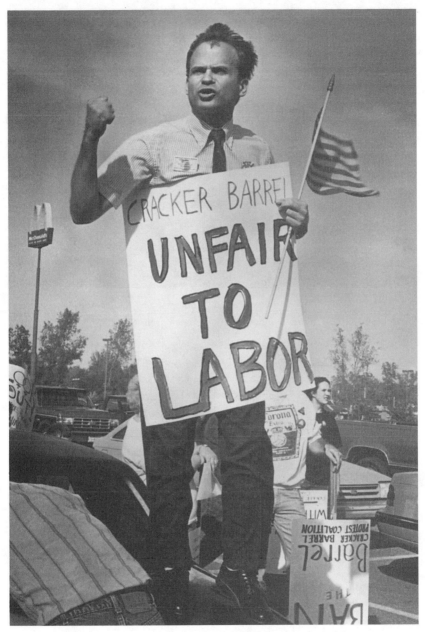

Ron Woods, All-American. Photograph by Bob McKeown for ANDERSONGOLD Films. Reprinted with permission from ANDERSONGOLD Films.

Nat Keitt: "I'm out on my job. I was never in." Photograph by Andrea Ades Vasquez for
ANDERSONGOLD Films. Reprinted with permission from ANDERSONGOLD Films.

the job he smiled and looked as if he was about to sing. "I'm out on my job.
I was never in! I happen to be fortunate to work for the New York Public
Library and have D.C. 37 and Local 1930 behind me. They take care of all
those silly problems that are major in other parts of the workforce. Our
union makes sure we, as gays and lesbians, have rights and are protected.
They have it all in the contract."

As the conference closed, Regina Shavers, an African American woman
in her fifties, took the podium. Shavers worked as a 911 operator and was a
cofounder of LAGIC. Her deep sing-song voice was both self-confident and
determined. "You have started something now! So many people have come
up to me this weekend and asked how to start an organization in their workplace. Last week we told them we are everywhere, now we are telling them
'We work!'"

This conference, we felt, must be a milestone in the young history of a
movement for gay and lesbian workplace rights. Instead of editing these interviews into a single *Labor X* episode, Kelly and I went with our gut reaction and followed the story we saw developing at the conference. Although
we didn't know it then, our filming that weekend in 1992 would result in
two documentaries that challenge traditional notions of class and sexual
identity. The first was *Out at Work: Lesbians and Gay Men on the Job*, which

was completed in January 1997 and premiered at the Sundance Film Festival. The second was *Out at Work: America Undercover*, a made-for-television documentary commissioned by HBO. It premiered on television in January 1999. Kelly and I were the coproducers and codirectors of both films. While connections between class and sexual identity are visible in both documentaries, they are thematically explicit in the first, which focuses on the shop floor and the union movement. The second is directed at passage of the Employment Non-Discrimination Act (ENDA), a piece of federal legislation pending in Congress that would prohibit discrimination against workers in all fifty states on the basis of sexual orientation.

When we began filming, Kelly and I didn't have a clear idea of what the completed project would look like. However, we continued to interview LAGIC members and traveled around the country to cover events involving other gay and lesbian trade unionists.

In 1993, we went to Washington, D.C., to cover the March on Washington, a national gay rights rally that included a sizable labor contingent. There, we met Howard Wallace, a lead organizer of a San Francisco boycott against the Coors brewery company that began in 1973 and lasted several years. Howard was one of the first activists to come out and fight publicly for gay rights in the U.S. labor movement. A peace activist in the 1960s, he also helped found the Lesbian/Gay Labor Alliance in San Francisco, the first organization of its kind in the country. Through the Alliance, Howard became involved in the Coors boycott.

This boycott was one of the very few struggles that united African Americans, Latino, labor, and gay workers in a common cause. According to Wallace, the boycott had been initiated by the Latino community to protest Coors' discriminatory hiring practices. Coors not only discriminated against people of color, Wallace said, but it was also known for its homophobic employment policies and antiunionism.

Though we had heard about this boycott, neither Kelly nor I knew the details. We had not known, for example, that San Francisco Supervisor Harvey Milk actively campaigned against Coors before he was assassinated in 1978. With Milk's help, the boycott spread by word-of-mouth through San Francisco's Castro District—the city's premier gay neighborhood. After hearing this story, Kelly and I realized that this joint effort was perhaps one of the first major public demonstrations of the links between class and sexual identity.

At this point, we began to think that we should document the history of gay–labor activism, and we developed funding proposals for a film based on this broad conception. We anticipated that the documentary would cost

$168,000. Over the course of four years, we sent out more than thirty funding proposals and raised a total of $65,000. We didn't pay ourselves, and the equipment was an in-kind contribution.

Both progay and prolabor, our project was not an easy package to sell. So we went to our friends first. We got money from the UAW and the Women's Committee of the United Steel Workers of America. Small donations trickled in from other unions. The International Ladies' Garment Workers' Union gave us $1,000, but only as a measure of their respect for our work. They didn't think this particular film would be of much use to them. As one officer of the union told us, "Our members are not gay; they're Chinese."

Despite the generosity of our supporters, however, Kelly and I weren't raising enough money from unions or foundations. We began 1996 by reviewing over seventy hours of footage we had shot in the past three years. We had clearly documented the formation of a diverse working-class gay and lesbian movement. In addition, we had encountered many people who had powerful personal stories to tell. We had already met Nat Keitt at the LAGIC conference three years earlier. In Washington, we met Ron Woods, a UAW member at Chrysler in Michigan. Not long after that, we met Cheryl Summerville, a nonunion worker at a Cracker Barrel restaurant in Bremen, Georgia. Their stories began to emerge as the strongest material we had.

As we were in the final stage of logging and transcribing our footage, we received a $20,000 grant from the American Film Institute's Independent Filmmaking Fund, which was supported by the National Endowment for the Arts. It was a bittersweet moment—the last time the American Film Institute would receive money from the NEA for projects of this kind and the end of an era of support for truly independent filmmaking. This grant would enable us to complete the film within the year, if we omitted the history and focused exclusively on Cheryl, Nat, and Ron. To some extent, our eventual decision to focus on them was a practical matter: we simply hadn't raised enough money to make a sweeping historical documentary.

In abandoning the idea of a history, we lost the opportunity to document the growth of a movement that was little appreciated or understood by the general public at the time. Nor could we document the emergence of ideological struggles within a diverse movement of working-class queers. On the other hand, our decision to focus on individuals allowed us to pull people in emotionally. It also gave us the chance to examine—close-up—how class and sexuality intersect in the workaday lives of lesbians and gay men.

Once the film was completed, we had to deal with its distribution. *Out at Work* premiered at the 1997 Sundance Film Festival and was a contender for the PBS series, *Point of View (POV)*. Though only $13,000 of our funding had come from labor unions, PBS concluded that—as a percentage of our total budget of $65,000—this amount exceeded their underwriting guidelines, and the film was never shown on *POV.* Though our spirits were buoyed somewhat by a flurry of public controversy surrounding PBS's decision, we were angry and discouraged.

Just when we were most depressed by it all, HBO officials contacted us to say they loved the film and wanted to discuss alternatives for airing *Out at Work* on HBO. What resulted was a second version of the film, which has already reached an HBO audience of approximately forty million households.

To me, this brief history of our project is only a surface account. In writing about the making of *Out at Work*, I want to talk about the interior workings of the film. I want to reflect upon the deep personal, political, and professional connections between a filmmaker and her subjects. In writing this essay, I have chosen to interweave some personal memories from my twenties, when I held many jobs in factories and kitchens throughout northern New Jersey and when I kept my identity as a lesbian secret from most of my coworkers and sometimes even from myself. I have incorporated these memories because, on reflection, many of the people interviewed for this film shared experiences that resonated with my own life. It is my way of illustrating that lesbians and gay men have always worked in factories, in fields, in kitchens, in coal mines.

By focusing on individuals in the films and in this essay, I hope to make clear that the struggle for lesbian and gay rights in the workplace continues on many fronts. It continues on the political level, where activists and friendly legislators attempt to pass laws banning discrimination against lesbian and gay workers. It continues in the labor movement, where workers and union activists work together to win rights and end abuses. And, most importantly, the struggle continues at the individual level, where gay people and their straight coworkers confront their own desires, fears, and doubts about sexuality and rights.

The Filmmaker

Although it is not autobiographical, *Out at Work* is indirectly about me. I entered the creative world through an unusual door—as a recovering high school dropout. When I grew up there were no words or diagnoses for learning disabilities. At thirteen, I could barely read and was silenced by speech impediments. I used painting and every imaginable creative means to tell my teachers, my friends, and my classmates that I was not stupid. I used the paint brush, the hallway bulletin boards, the school yearbook—anything with a surface—to communicate, to tell stories. My filmmaking grew directly out of my personal disabilities. I have used the moving image—words and sounds—to resist my own silence and to tell the stories of other people whose voices are too often silenced.

My work is consciously small. I take a little piece of a problem in a person's life and use my camera as the microscope. It is through the lens, the projected image on a huge screen, that this examination illustrates larger political concerns. I am always conscious of the ethical issues involved in documentary filmmaking because the seamless process of editing is sometimes a temptation to manipulate truth. As an artist driven by accountability to those who share their lives with me, I am concerned about how to tell a complicated story, with many twists and turns, in a short amount of time. How can I take fifty hours from a person's life and reduce it to thirty minutes? What do I leave in? What don't I tell?

The common thread in my work is that the "political is personal" and that "silence = suicide." These two themes are the literal subjects of both versions of *Out at Work*. At their most fundamental, these films are about coming out in the workplace—about gay men and lesbians who break the silence surrounding their sexual orientation and who liberate themselves personally and politically in the process. These films are also about personal and civil rights that are basic, yet revolutionary. Revolutionary, because the inequities in our society would be radically redressed if all people—in their full diversity of identities—had fundamental personal and civil rights.

Out at Work Story: Nat and David

After meeting Nat Keitt at the LAGIC conference, Kelly and I saw him at most of the gay–labor events we attended. At first sight, many people take Nat for a woman. His hair is long and lustrous; his voice is high and lilting. A conspicuously effeminate man, Nat is also a strong and proud trade unionist. A member of his local's executive board, he cares as much about the bread-and-butter concerns of every worker as he does about the issues that are of special concern to gay and lesbian workers. "What the union does," Nat said, "is give you dignity. It helps you to go about your business of living in a dignified and proud way."

At a union holiday party, we met David Sanabria, Nat's lover of ten years. David had done heavy industrial work most of his life. He was a tall, thin Puerto Rican man who unapologetically passed as straight on his job. "A person who has to hide the fact that he is gay and go to work doesn't socialize because of this," he said. "There are comments constantly made and work becomes very stressful. And a lot of people have this great fear that if their coworkers find out, these coworkers are going to wind up either bashing or constantly harassing them."

Kelly asked David if this had ever happened to him.

"Well," he said, "fortunately they have never found out that I was gay."

What David said made me very sad. Even though the labor movement started decades before I was born, and the gay liberation movement started in the early 1970s, most of us in the 1990s are still hidden in factories, in schools, and in our families.

Hoboken, New Jersey, 1972—I was working at a Maxwell House Coffee production factory. It was at the height of second-wave feminism. The opening of "nontraditional jobs" to women created new opportunities for many of us. I was hired to work in a traditionally male job, "Mixing, Roasting, and Grinding," alongside the huge roasting ovens that transformed the green beans imported from Colombia to dark brown coffee.

I had been living with a woman for over a year. She wasn't my first female lover, but I did not identify as a "lesbian." When pushed, I might have used the word "gay," which to my twenty-three-year-old ear had a softer ring than "lesbian." It sounded less certain, less confrontational. To me, "lesbian" connoted militance, not to mention a singular identity I wasn't ready to accept.

Imagine this: It's dark, the second shift—3 P.M. to midnight. Maxwell House juts out into the Hudson River. Two sides of this huge industrial structure are glass. There are around twenty of us working with masks and earplugs, dumping ground coffee beans into huge vats. We joke about brown lung disease. Words and phrases like "faggot," "homo," and "he takes it in the ass" are common, everyday language—and they are usually directed at one worker in particular. During break time, I wash the brown powder from my face, reapply lipstick, and lie on the plastic couch in the ladies' locker room with coworkers. We sing Joni Mitchell songs as loud as we can. Then back to the assembly line, where it starts all over again: "faggot," "homo," "he takes it in the ass."

After two years, I finally defended the guy who took most of this abuse, and my world at Maxwell House turned upside down. This guy never actually said he was gay. He might not have been, but he was slight, soft-spoken, and a bit shy. That's all it takes in a factory. My words were simple: "Leave him alone, nothing is wrong with gay people or being gay!" I might as well have come out. For a few months there were whispers and stares throughout the ladies' locker room and on the assembly line. In other words, Tami must be queer. I was ostracized by union activists. I was called dyke, homo-lover, white nigger, and even physically threatened. My foreman gave all the girls in "non-traditional jobs" gift-wrapped dildos for Christmas. I stopped hanging out on the couch in the locker room and never sang at work again. Yet I remained successfully closeted for three years. I told no one that I had a female lover, and, by the end of the following year, my lover and I split up. At the time, I thought my closetedness was an accomplishment. Only years later did I begin to understand what I had actually contributed to.

Kelly and I spent time with Nat and David in their home in Middletown, New York. On one visit, we videotaped them preparing dinner. Nat was criticizing gay people who remained closeted at work, and suddenly David became angry. He didn't think being out on his job would have helped his situation, so he had stayed in the closet, even though it meant lying about his relationship with Nat. He was convinced that Nat was just lucky because library work had historically accepted lesbian and gay employees. In fact, Nat was doubly lucky: his union was one of the first to fight for its queer members. In contrast, David called his union the "good old boys club." To make matters worse, David's family had never accepted his homosexuality, while Nat's family was warm and embraced them as a couple. As Nat put it: "My father knew from day one. My mother told my father, 'You have another son, sweetheart.' And he said, 'We have a girl.' He was looking at me, and he knew! He says he knew from day one."

At first we did not know that David was HIV-positive and had had to stop working. Their friends, their minister, Nat's coworkers, and his union president all knew the nature of David's illness, but it was not discussed. At first, David received disability benefits from his employer, but the clock was ticking and his benefits were running out. David was alone most of the day and night, and he was getting sicker. Union activism added to Nat's time away from home, yet Nat's union work was extremely important to both of them. D.C. 37 was lobbying the administration of New York City Mayor David Dinkins for domestic-partner benefits. If the campaign was successful, these benefits would be granted to all New York City employees, including gay workers like David and Nat. David wanted desperately to be registered as Nat's domestic partner, which would entitle him to Nat's union health benefits. It also meant a lot to David in terms of personal commitment. "Domestic partnership means very much to me because it says that we are together," he said. "We are recognized by the city that we are living together and we are responsible for each other and willing to take that road together. That's what it means."

Out at Work Story: Ron Woods

In early April 1993, Kelly and I learned that the AFL-CIO was planning to host a reception for union members attending the national gay, lesbian, and bisexual March on Washington to be held later that month. We filmed this event because we thought it could illustrate changes in labor policy at the national level.

Among the emcees for the reception was Susan Moir, a former school bus driver from Boston and an activist in the Gay and Lesbian Labor Action Network (GALLAN), one of the oldest queer labor groups in the country. Kelly and I had met her a year earlier at the LAGIC conference. Back then, when we asked her about her job, she explained, "I've had my tires slashed and I've been threatened with rape." How had she dealt with this? we asked. "I killed him!" she replied. There was a long pause. "Only kidding!"

As the AFL-CIO event came to a close, Susan reminded the crowd why we were marching in Washington, D.C. Her words sounded like a poem.

> It doesn't matter if we call it the revolution,
> it doesn't matter whether we call it decency,
> it doesn't matter if we call it fairness.
> It is all the same fight.
> In the fight for universal health care,
> in the fight for a fair and decent workplace,
> in the fight to end discrimination and oppression,
> and for liberation for all of us,
> there is no stronger coalition than Queers and Workers!
> And we are that!

The reception was a lot for me to take in—to imagine a labor movement with working-class queers at the helm. Most of the high-ranking labor leaders we saw there were white, straight men, but we could not stereotype them or assume they would ignore the concerns of gay and lesbian workers. The contrary proved true. John Sweeney, then president of the Service Employees International Union (SEIU), and Gerald McEntee, president of AFSCME, spoke strongly in support of gay rights. Nevertheless, when we interviewed these men later, they revealed some personal discomfort. Sweeney insisted on being interviewed with his wife at his side. McEntee repeatedly looked around anxiously and asked, "Where's my wife?"

Hoboken, New Jersey, 1975—After I gave birth to my first child, I worked as a cook in a day-care center. It was a part-time, minimum-wage gig, but it was a way to get free child care for my daughter, Amilca. There were four of us working in the kitchen: an older married woman, an extremely stylish young white woman who had never lived outside Hoboken, a young African American woman from Jersey City, and me.

After months of working and sweating in this tiny kitchen, the three younger women secretly confessed to each other that we had sex with women. The Hobokenite introduced us to her aunt's bar, called My Way, which was hidden near the railroads and factories. It was the first lesbian bar I had ever entered, and many of the women who hung out there worked at the local factories. I recognized some of the women who brought their kids to my daughter's day-care center. We'd make eye contact, acknowledging caution. They looked like everyday Hudson County women in the 1970s—teased out platinum hair, tight pants, and red lips. I dressed like them, but my hair was dyed blue-black.

Kelly and I met Ron Woods at the AFL-CIO reception. A member of the UAW, Ron had been an auto plant electrician at Chrysler for seven years. His name was familiar because his "coming-out" story had been featured in *Solidarity*, the national magazine of the UAW. Recounting that story to the crowd, Ron described how he had helped to organize a protest demonstration when Cracker Barrel, a restaurant chain with an antigay employment policy, opened its first branch in Michigan. He was outed the next day when his picture appeared on the front page of *The Detroit News and Free Press*. He walked into the engine plant where he worked to find this picture plastered on the wall, announcing to his three thousand coworkers that he was gay.

"My life became a living hell,' Ron said. "There was even a magazine article about Cracker Barrel, and it said there are no laws to protect homosexuals in the work environment in Michigan. Someone underlined it and hung it up at Chrysler, and they wrote beside it, 'So FUCK Woods.' That's what it said, 'So get Woods!' . . . If it wasn't for my union, I would not have a job right now."

On the morning of the gay pride march, Kelly and I interviewed Ron in his hotel room. It was his first interview for a film, and he seemed excited. It was also his first pride march and the first time he was in Washington, D.C. While we were setting up the equipment, Ron laid out different T-shirts on the bed. He wanted to wear the shirt that best represented him. One shirt had his union logo, another had a rainbow triangle, and the third had the name of his home state, Michigan, in large letters. He put on the Michigan shirt and explained that it best described who he really was—just a regular guy from the Midwest. I was surprised that he wanted to be identified as

"Michigan" over "gay" or "union." I could not imagine choosing to wear a shirt with "New Jersey" emblazoned across my chest.

What follows is an excerpt of the interview we did with Ron that day.

KELLY: What's it like working in a large auto factory?

RON: There are thousands of people where I work who have intense hatred and disgust for homosexuals, dozens actively want to attack you. I swear, four people did, and it's traumatic because you don't know when it's going to happen—in the locker room, while taking a shower, or on my way to my car. I would hear people, even union officials, say things like "We have to be real careful in the showers now."

KELLY: Did anyone actually hit you?

RON: Oh yes. I was attacked three times since the Cracker Barrel article. I was pushed off of a cart. And everyone was always saying, "I'll meet you after work." I'm not an activist at work. I believe in totally separating my work and my activism. I don't feel I should go to work and start conversations with people, "Don't you think this is great, these new things, gay rights," and all that. I've never done that, except with Cracker Barrel. I spoke with three union officials, and I tried to get the union to come out publicly against Cracker Barrel's antigay policies. I thought that was very legitimate, to speak with elected officials and the editor of the magazine. I mean . . . it's reasonable to discuss things that involve the work environment.

TAMI: How did your work environment change after coworkers found out you were gay?

RON: It was very important to me to just be a good employee, stay to myself, be quiet. I never once would sit with anyone [in the cafeteria]. I didn't want to embarrass anyone. I didn't want to be attacked. Someone might feel they had to throw something at me so people would know how straight they are or how macho they are. So I always sat alone. I would always sit in a corner with my back against the wall. I would walk by this table with eight people. And I'm not that big, and these are all big brawny guys. I would walk by, and they would be saying things, all kinds of things.

KELLY: Like what?

RON: "There he goes," and swearing. I hate to say the words. The word "faggot," I would always hear the word "faggot."

TAMI: How did it feel, emotionally?

RON: I was very alone, very isolated. In the middle of winter, which is a very depressing time for me, my mother asked me to change and started crying. And I started crying. I lost everyone. But I wouldn't give up. I would not give up. I told myself, "You go in there every day. You will never miss a day un-excused." And I never have. And I haven't been late on record for about two years and eight months. And I said, "I don't care if you have a cold, if you have a flu, it doesn't matter what. You're going to be the best employee they ever had. And they're going to live with me, just like I have to live with them." And I went in there all the time and did the best I could, and I real-ized it wasn't going to work, that until the day I retire and the day I die, that I would always be that faggot people hated.

After the interview, Ron seemed upset and said he wanted a few min-utes to himself. We packed up and told him we'd meet him in the hotel lobby. But, unintentionally, we had left the wireless microphone on him. While we were waiting for the elevator, we could heard him through the headset. He was crying softly and scolding himself for revealing so much personal pain to strangers.

Ron came to the demonstration with us. We joined the labor contingent and marched under the banner "OUT, PROUD & UNION." It seemed as though everyone had suddenly realized that gays and lesbians were every-where—even in factories and unions.

Hoboken, New Jersey, 1976—I was working at the Levolor venetian-blind plant, located behind Jefferson Street. The plant was very noisy and the only time the women who worked the line could speak to each other was when there was a breakdown and the machinery was turned off. I worked with a young white woman from Jersey City Heights named Maryanne. We worked on a machine that fed the long-thin plastic material into the thread-like skeleton nets. Maryanne was a skinny, quiet woman in her early twenties with blonde wiry hair, ashy skin, and heavy eyelids. In time, I learned that she lived with her friend and son on the same block as her parents. Little by little, she shared more about her life. Maryanne's housemate was a child-hood friend whom she referred to as her "husband," though she said they were never married. This friend rescued Maryanne when she was pregnant and unwed and her father had thrown her out of the family. The two friends had been together ever since.

Between all the noise and motion of this assembly line, we shared photos of our children. One photo was of Maryanne's son and her housemate—her husband—only her "husband" was a woman. Maryanne watched me very closely as I examined this photo. Suddenly she was animated and explained that she lived on the same block as her parents—especially, to rub it in her father's face that she's a dyke, a bull dagger, a woman who had been saved by another woman.

Out at Work Story: Cheryl and Sandy

In the spring of 1994, Kelly and I traveled to Georgia to meet Cheryl Summerville, a former cook at a Cracker Barrel restaurant outside Bremen. She was fired in 1991 under a new company policy that prohibited the employment of homosexuals. On her day off, Cheryl had learned that the company was firing gay employees. When she returned to work, she asked a supervisor about the new policy. "He told me to go back to work," Cheryl said. "They actually were targeting effeminate men on the floor. I told him that we were one and the same and that if it applied to them, it applied to me, too. 'You know I'm a lesbian. Are you going to fire me?'" Later that morning Cheryl received a termination paper stating she was being fired for "failing

Cheryl Summerville: Fighting Cracker Barrel from the outside. From ANDERSONGOLD film footage. Reprinted with permission from ANDERSONGOLD Films.

to comply with normal heterosexual values." On this termination paper, the supervisor had written, "Reason for termination: Employee is gay."

The following day, Cheryl called the American Civil Liberties Union to inquire about filing a lawsuit, only to be told it wouldn't stand a chance. "They told me there was absolutely nothing we could do about it; what they [Cracker Barrel] had done was perfectly legal. And I was shocked. I really and truly thought I had protection, and I didn't."

Kelly and I were also shocked to learn that in 1994 it was legal in forty-two U.S. states to fire someone for being a homosexual.[2] If the ACLU couldn't help, Cheryl wanted to find some other organization that could. Encouraged by Sandy Reilly, her lover of thirteen years, Cheryl approached the Atlanta chapter of Queer Nation. The codirector of this chapter was Lynn Cothren, a man who had been Coretta Scott King's personal assistant at the Martin Luther King, Jr., Center in Atlanta. We interviewed Cothren, who said, "The King Center gave me the training to do the kind of activism that I believe in, which is nonviolent action." Sometimes against opposition, he insisted that Queer Nation follow a strategy of nonviolent, civil disobedience. Lynn hoped Queer Nation could build a strong coalition of gay men, lesbians, and straight folks, along with women's organizations, unions, and churches. The group's motto was "Straight not Narrow." At the height of the Cracker Barrel struggle, the group was the South's largest coalition organized around a lesbian and gay issue.

Our meeting with Cheryl took place at Lynn's home. Sandy was also there with the couple's one-year-old daughter, Devin, and Cheryl's teenage son, Chris. We sat around a beautifully set dining-room table as Lynn recalled his first meeting with Cheryl. "Cheryl knew instinctively that this was morally wrong and she couldn't stand for it. If they were going to fire gay men, they would have to fire her. She felt the relationship that she had [with Sandy] would not be valid. That was her spirit. It was like, 'If I go back in the kitchen and don't acknowledge my lifestyle, and I allow them to do this, then my relationship is not valid.'"

Cheryl recalled the civil disobedience training she received through Queer Nation. "We saw a lot of movies, read books, had teachers come in. We studied, especially on the civil rights movement, and of course they did sit-ins. We were taught not to resist whatsoever. It worked. The first time we were arrested, they never once had to handcuff any of us. The next day, the first thing we saw in the newspapers [were editorials saying], 'Don't arrest them! Change the policy!'

"My son was fifteen years old when I was fired," Cheryl continued. "He had problems in school and I had to take him out of school, had to change schools because they told me they couldn't ensure his safety. They wrote slogans on the gym wall that said, 'Chris' mother's a fag and so is he.' He was threatened. I would take him to school and watch him walk in the building, and I'd tell him not to come out until after I was there. When I think about it affecting Chris . . . I get more angry; that's when I lose my temper. A bunch of us from different organizations went to the Southern Baptist convention and protested. The Baptists were coming out and shielding their children from us, and Chris was with us. A man pushed my son, and when he did, I lost it. That's the only time at a protest I ever lost my temper. I'd about killed him, right there."

Jersey City, New Jersey, 1978—It was my first day working as a pipe fitter at New Jersey Public Service Electric and Gas. I had aced my two weeks of training and now it was the real thing. I would be making the highest hourly wage I had ever earned and was determined to hang in no matter what. When I arrived at the PSE&G yard, I couldn't find any women in the sea of two hundred men in dark blue uniforms. I was given a uniform and told to change. There was no locker room for "LADIES," so I just stood there among all these men. The guys started to chant, "Jackie, Jackie! Paging Jackie!" Out of the blue walked a heavy-set, muscular, African American woman with closely cropped hair. With her hard hat on, Jackie looked like a man. It was only when she took the hat off that her small, soft features stood out.

Management sent Jackie and me to a construction site where I had to use a jackhammer. With no previous training, I couldn't control the jackhammer for a second. Carefully, methodically, and in a whisper, Jackie explained that it was do or die and that she would stay by my side but that I had to do it— I had to prove myself.

Jackie stayed by me for a little less than a year, and we became close friends. She didn't know many Jews and took a real liking to me. In the yard she was one of the men and—like the rest of them—she gave me a hard time with the whistling and ass-grabbing. But alone, she was real soft and warned me not to let anyone know that I had a child, because then they would know I slept with men, and it would be all over for me.

Out at Work, I

Kelly and I followed Cheryl, Ron, and Nat for more than four years, during which we decided they would be the subjects of our film. During those years, as David became sicker, Nat helped to organize a coalition of gay and lesbian city workers that won health benefits for domestic partners in New

York City. In Georgia, Cheryl became the cochair of Queer Nation in Atlanta and a leader in a national campaign to get Cracker Barrel to change its policy. In Detroit, Ron found himself unable to continue working under tremendous pressure and asked the union for a transfer. His steward, Mike Harrald, was the first African American to work in skilled trades at the Chrysler plant. Remembering the brutal harassment he had faced twenty-five years earlier, Mike understood exactly what Ron was going through and helped him transfer to the Chrysler Technology Center. Once there, however, Ron experienced harassment again as rumors about his homosexuality spread through the plant. Yet a few coworkers befriended him and found themselves changing some of their own preconceptions. In our film, Ron's story ends on a high note, as the same coworkers who once abused him elect him to be a delegate to the 1996 UAW convention.

At the conclusion of the first *Out at Work*, our characters faced mixed realities. Having won domestic-partner benefits, Nat has to come to terms with David's death. Cracker Barrel never changed its policy, but Cheryl and the Queer Nation coalition educate thousands of people across the country about how most gay and lesbian workers lack basic rights. At the UAW's convention, Ron speaks in favor of a resolution that would prohibit discrimination against gays and lesbians covered by UAW contracts. The resolution passes unanimously, but, in negotiations with Chrysler the same year, a demand based on this resolution is dropped when the union recognizes it cannot win a national strike over the issue of gay rights.[3]

Jersey City, New Jersey, 1977—My husband worked at the New Jersey Bulk Facility of the U.S. Postal Service and introduced me to his coworker Frankie. Frankie was a thin and flexible, rubber band–like, African American man in his early twenties with sandy brown hair. He was one of the first people I ever met who identified as "gay." It was, as he put it, who he was—as much a part of his identity as his blackness.

Frankie was a great storyteller. He would speak slowly and deliberately. We were in a run-down bar outside the bulk facility when he told me how he was introduced to homosexuality. The pastor of his church in the Greenville section of Jersey City had sexually propositioned him when he was about twelve years old. As he detailed his early sexual experiences, he never said or implied that he was forced, violated, or raped. It just happened and it went on for years. Frankie's family was poor and money wasn't easy to come by. Before he realized it, the pastor was giving him a few dollars here and there. As Frankie got older, he learned how to use the secrecy of homosexual desire as a way to make money. Frankie sold his sexual services throughout Jersey

City, but never on the streets. Always to paying professionals—ministers, local politicians, management, and even a union official at the bulk facility. The way Frankie explained it, as long as it was (in his words) illegal, he could sell it. As long as homosexual lust had to be hidden, he had a product to sell.

The Aftermath

Two days before Thanksgiving in 1996, Kelly and I got a phone message from a member of the Sundance festival advisory board: *Out at Work* had been accepted. We went to Utah for the occasion. On a cold and snowy evening, documentary filmmakers from different parts of the country were partying at a condo overlooking a magical Utah nightscape. Many of them knew that Kelly and I were waiting anxiously to hear if our film had been accepted into the lineup of the PBS series, *Point of View*. The room fell silent when the two directors of *POV* arrived at the party. Then, suddenly, there was collective chatter about *Out of Work*—what a wonderful film; a must for public television.

It was not to be. In March 1997, we learned that PBS had overruled *POV*'s decision to broadcast the documentary. PBS officials said they admired the film on its merits, but they refused to distribute it because "it fails to comport with our normal underwriting guidelines." Specifically, PBS objected to grants we had received from, among others, the UAW, the Astraea National Lesbian Action Foundation, and D.C. 37. In calculating our total production budget, PBS would not consider that Kelly and I had donated our own time as an in-kind contribution. By omitting this, our production budget appeared to be much lower than it actually was and, consequently, the percentage of money we received from unions appeared to be higher.

After years of rejection letters from public and private foundations, and little success at grassroots fund-raising, Kelly and I felt like we were being punished for our commitment to an issue not often discussed in mainstream media and less often funded. Fortunately, we were not alone in our outrage. Family, friends, and even strangers cut off their public television memberships. Kelly and I were guests on radio talk shows. Ron Woods joined in on what was becoming a campaign, using his elaborate E-mail list to get the message into cyberspace: "Urgent—PBS censors pro-union gays and lesbians!" Together with the *Nation* magazine, the City University of New York, and several gay and lesbian labor groups, students in the American Studies program of New York University organized a conference to discuss "*Out at Work*: The Documentary PBS Refused to Air!" At the last moment, a representative of PBS agreed to attend this conference, and she was visibly shaken by the vehemence of anti-PBS sentiment audience members expressed.

In the middle of this flap, a senior HBO producer called us. She had just screened the film and loved it. HBO wanted to acquire *Out at Work*, and they presented us with a choice. We could program the original film on Cinemax, their arts channel, which reaches approximately seven million households. Or, we could produce a new piece for the HBO series *America Undercover*, which had a potential audience of forty million households. That was HBO's preference.

Kelly and I had spent years trying to fund the *Out at Work* project with the hope of airing it on public television, a venue we believed in and felt was most committed to open public discussion. We had never thought that our message would be carried and promoted through a commercial enterprise. Ironically, however, public television found itself in a defensive position, where it had to practice self-censorship in order to protect itself from a reactionary political agenda that wanted to eliminate public television—much as it wanted to eliminate public housing, public education, and public health care. So, Kelly and I considered our HBO options carefully and finally decided that we wanted to reach the widest possible audience, even if it meant producing a new documentary for the cable network.

Out at Work, II

HBO wanted the new film to have a national perspective and perhaps make an impact on public policy. At the time—1997—it was still legal to fire homosexual employees in forty-one states, and that was the issue HBO wanted us to address. With that as our focus, the film in effect would be a plea for the passage of the proposed federal Employment Non-Discrimination Act (ENDA), which would ban discrimination against lesbian and gay workers. In 1996, the U.S. Senate had failed by one vote to pass ENDA, and we thought the film could help reinvigorate the campaign for this bill.

A story of successful union activism, the example of Nat Keitt was not particularly germane in this context, and HBO asked us to make a substitute for Nat. Dropping him from the film was not an easy decision. Nat had become a national spokesperson for the film. More importantly, he was the only person of color among the three main characters. On that basis, it was troubling to consider omitting him, and we knew we would face some criticism if we did.

Although Nat was upset by our decision, he ultimately understood the logic in finding a new story for this film. In the end, we chose to feature Mark Anderson, a trainee at the Los Angeles branch of Cantor Fitzgerald, a large securities trading firm. Anderson had not come out on the job, but rumors spread he was gay. He was the butt of degrading pranks and slurs, instigated not only by his coworkers, but also by top executives in the branch office. Ultimately, he was fired.

The HBO film required a narrator, and we chose retired Army Colonel Margarethe Cammermeyer, herself a victim of workplace homophobia. In 1992, after a long and distinguished military career, Cammermeyer was fired for telling the truth about her sexual orientation during a routine security check. In addition, we updated the stories of Ron and Cheryl. After the UAW dropped its demand for gay rights in negotiations with Chrysler in 1996, Ron became depressed. During this period, Cheryl had also become depressed, which took a toll on her relationship with Sandy, and they separated temporarily. The film ends with Cheryl and Sandy reconciled, looking at a photograph of the two of them at their recent commitment ceremony.

Out at Work: America Undercover premiered on HBO on January 6, 1999. HBO organized several events around the country to promote it. One of these was scheduled for the Four Seasons hotel in Washington, D.C. Representative Barney Frank, a cosponsor of ENDA, would emcee the event. The RSVP list was over three hundred, and there was a rumor that Senator Edward Kennedy might make an appearance.

At the time, none of us involved in the event knew there was a longstanding labor dispute at the hotel. A member of Pride at Work informed me of the situation when I called to invite the organization to participate. He told me that the workers at Four Seasons had been trying to organize for twelve years; that the hotel was notorious for its union-busting tactics; and that the union had pickets out front on special occasions. As in many hotels, a large number of Four Season employees were gay. Ironically, the intersection of class and sexual identity—the intellectual core of our films—was there on the picket line, in flesh and blood. And we were caught on the horns of a dilemma. Not wishing to separate issues of class and sexual identity, we nevertheless found ourselves trying to establish our priorities. What was more important—honoring a picket line or promoting the cause of gay and lesbian rights? For Pride at Work, the answer was clear. They would not cross a picket line in any circumstance, but certainly not when the rights of gay workers were at stake. Someone from Pride at Work left me a phone message: "Hi, Tami. Well, we'll see you in D.C., only we'll be on the outside of the hotel with picket signs."

I called back and pleaded with them. HBO, after all, had not intentionally scheduled this event at a nonunion hotel. At that moment, I honestly believed it would be better for the cause of gay rights if Pride at Work went along with the event and struggled with HBO afterward. I tried to explain that HBO, to its credit, had taken a risk with this film; that it was a big step forward for gays and lesbians; and that this was a moment for compromise.

I then tried to get HBO to call the Hotel and Restaurant Employees union and work things out. A senior producer assured me that everything would be fine. Without anything more specific, this promise was not very encouraging. By Monday morning, as Kelly and I were preparing to leave for the airport, we learned that things had escalated. A picket line was planned for 5:30 that evening. Barney Frank wouldn't cross. After a long, soul-searching discussion, Kelly and I concluded that our place was outside the hotel. We couldn't cross the line, either.

In the hopes something might be worked out, we boarded the plane to Washington, determined to turn back if the picket line was up. While we were en route, HBO was galvanized into action. The public relations director spoke to the local union president. Explaining that she had been ignorant of the labor dispute at Four Seasons, she agreed to be more vigilant in the future. From that point on, she said, HBO would schedule Washington events only in unionized hotels. She also agreed to try and arrange meetings between the hotel management and the union. In return, the union called off its picket for the day. Barney Frank arrived, as did three hundred well-dressed guests.

While Kelly and I had hoped our films could contribute to social change in some way, we never imagined the most tangible bit of progress would be made through this encounter between a commercial TV organization and a labor union. In his opening remarks at the hotel reception, Barney Frank put it well: "Out of this evening will come not just this reaffirmation . . . in the powerful form of rights for many of us to be free from discrimination based on our sexual orientation . . . but also, a good working relationship between HBO and the hotel workers' union in advancing the rights of people to bargain collectively. This [event] has become a very important demonstration of the meaning of workplace rights in all of its regards."

"The Rights of All People"

In 1992, in the course of gathering material for the first version of Out at Work, Kelly and I interviewed Carolyn Forest, a UAW vice president. She had read about Ron Woods and Cracker Barrel in Solidarity magazine.

"Quite frankly, I was shocked that that kind of thing would happen in today's world," she told us. However, she was uncertain about the politics of coming out. "The question of whether or not [gays and lesbians] should come out on the job is one that I can't answer. I don't think, in my opinion, that people have to announce. Of course, I don't have to announce that I'm a woman, you can tell when I walk in a room."

Regardless of her ambivalence on this question, Forest was unambiguous about injustice and about where she stands when the question is called. "I don't think you can be a little bit discriminatory. Either you believe in the rights of all people, or you really don't believe in the rights of anyone, unless it's someone just like you. I don't eat at Cracker Barrel because of their anti-gay policy, and I loved the Cracker Barrel food. I loved to eat there because I'm from the South, and they have all of my food. But I've never been in there since. I don't expect to be there until they've changed their policy publicly."

I have thought about Forest's comments many times since we spoke. For me, her words capture the essence of what is best about the labor movement. I say that though I know very well unions are not perfect. In the last several years, for example, D.C. 37 (the parent union of LAGIC) has been struggling to overcome the disgrace of corrupt leadership practices. Some unions have problems dealing with homophobia and other issues of identity. But when unions work the way they are supposed to, they are about fairness and equal rights for all workers.

Not all workers are members of unions, of course. Cheryl Summerville was not in a union; nor was Mark Anderson. Laws that inhibit the right to organize are one reason that the struggle for gay rights in the workplace is not yet complete. I recently was elected to the executive committee of the Professional Staff Congress, which represents staff, faculty, and administrators at CUNY. So I am an out lesbian and a voting member of the delegate assembly. Colleagues occasionally ask me why a professional artist with a decent income would want to be active in a union. I tell them I do it because there is no other institution that has the same potential to bring about progressive social change. In plain English, I believe that unions provide a way to struggle that can't be beat.

Notes

1. The D.C. 37 Executive Board approved LAGIC's formation in April 1990. The regional conference that we attended was titled "Pride at Work." In 1994, LAGIC sponsored a second conference, "Pride at Work—Stonewall 25," also held at D.C. 37 headquarters. That conference laid the groundwork for the formation of the national Pride at Work organization, which was established as an official AFL-CIO constituency group in 1998.
2. Eleven states now prohibit workplace discrimination on the basis of sexual orientation.
3. Unfortunately, Woods was no longer at Chrysler in September 1999, when contract renewal talks established protections for gay and lesbian workers. Health benefits for same-sex domestic partners were added to the contract in June 2000.

"Top-Down" or "Bottom-Up"?: Sexual Identity and Workers' Rights in a Municipal Union

Tamara L. Jones

The windowless room in the basement of the multistory building near the World Trade Center is packed with people passionately discussing an upcoming workshop to examine the details and terms of their job contracts. Although I do not share their employer, I share their excitement. Sitting in the room are a police dispatcher, a construction worker, an architect, secretaries and clerical workers, administrative assistants, safety and health inspectors, and a Board of Education administrator. They are men and women, Black, Latino/a, White, Native American, and Asian, and come from widely varying educational, cultural, and economic backgrounds. Despite these differences, they hold common commitments as members of the Lesbian and Gay Issues Committee (LAGIC) in District Council 37 (D.C. 37, the union of New York City employees). I have been talking with LAGIC members for over a year in order to document the history of their organizing efforts. Since 1988, LAGIC has been fighting for changes in both union and municipal policies to address the specific needs of lesbian and gay workers. These include full domestic-partner benefits; HIV/AIDS education and services; equal employment opportunity protections; state and local anti-bias legislation; and workplace protections. Above all, by strengthening the voices of lesbian and gay workers, LAGIC aims to transform their union's culture.

What expressions of lesbian and gay identities and what forms of lesbian and gay participation are supported within union environments? This essay explores the effects of one kind of institutional environment—bureaucracy—on the ability of lesbian and gay workers to engage in collectivist, member-driven organizing within unions. How do activists negotiate the tensions inherent in trying to organize lesbian and gay workers to exercise power within heavily regulated bureaucratic unions? The question is key because the rule-driven and formalistic features of bureaucratic organizations would appear to conflict with the decentralized decision making and power sharing often associated with an organizing model of politics. As such, I will pay particular attention to how the rules, procedures, organizational structures, and culture of unions can shape both the process and outcomes of lesbian and gay workers' activism.

LAGIC has emerged as a powerful force both within its parent union, D.C. 37, and in New York City. D.C. 37 is an affiliate of the American Federation of State, County, and Municipal Employees (AFSCME) and is one of the largest and most established unions in the city. LAGIC's history within D.C. 37 demonstrates that while unions offer some of the most fertile ground for developing progressive lesbian and gay politics, entrenched union structures can also limit democratic political practice and the ability of (lesbian and gay) union members to radically redefine workers' rights. This latter aspect of union bureaucracy is difficult to acknowledge but crucial to face if we are to build unions and a labor movement that can successfully represent lesbian and gay workers.

At the same time that the D.C. 37 bureaucracy provided opportunities for member-driven organizing and the pursuit of lesbian and gay workplace issues, it also constrained democratic participation by, and representation of, LAGIC members by privileging some expressions of sexual identity and some forms of member participation over others. However, at crucial moments LAGIC effectively harnessed D.C. 37's "top-down" bureaucratic structure to support more inclusive "bottom-up" political practice and to place lesbian and gay concerns on the union's agenda. LAGIC's experiences point to the strengths and weaknesses inherent in attempting to build radically inclusive and democratic lesbian and gay organizations within strong bureaucratic environments.

The evidence provided in this essay demonstrates that D.C. 37's bureaucracy wielded enormous influence on LAGIC's organizational structure, goals, and programming. Indeed, LAGIC's emergence and existence was largely dependent on its ability to conform to the union's institutional demands. While this "institutional isomorphism" produced many tangible benefits for LAGIC—access to money, physical space, and other necessary union resources—it also caused LAGIC to adopt and reflect many of the less democratic elements that had become part of the everyday union culture and practices over time.[1] These included appointment of the committee's chairpersons by the union executive council rather than through membership elections and ad hoc budgets that promoted gate keeping by union officials. Union bureaucracy would pose a greater challenge to lesbian and gay workers' organizing than homophobia within the union.

District Council 37: A Brief Overview

District Council 37 is widely seen as "the richest, the largest, and the most politically generous union" in New York City.[2] AFSCME chartered the union in November 1944. At the time, its membership consisted of a few hundred members in hospitals, parks, city finance offices, and other agencies. Today, D.C. 37 represents over 120,000 men and women in fifty-six local unions that are further divided into six divisions: Professional (38,000 members in twenty locals); Clerical Administrative (26,000 members in Local 1549); Schools (20,000 members in Local 372); White Collar (15,000 members in fourteen locals); Hospitals (11,000 members in Local 420); and Blue Collar (10,000 members in nineteen locals). As city employees, members have passed rigorous qualifying civil service exams. The union collects $88 million in annual membership dues from members, who averaged an annual salary of $26,500 in 1998, with full-timers paying approximately $18 in monthly dues. D.C. 37 officials' salaries were among some of the highest in the labor movement. Stanley Hill, D.C. 37's Executive Director from 1987 until he was forced to resign in 1998, enjoyed an annual salary exceeding that of the governor of New York State.

Although D.C. 37 does not collect information on its members' racial, ethnic, gender, or sexual identities, a union brochure notes "[o]ur union reflects the ethnic mix of our city. No one group is in the 'majority.'" However, anecdotal evidence suggests that women and people of color constitute the majority of the membership.

In its first few decades, D.C. 37 developed a reputation as a progressive union with strong collectivist organizing practices. For example, members of the New York State legislature had come to know and fear the busloads of workers that would arrive in Albany to lobby for issues important to the union. Against this collectivist-organizing past, the current relative weakness of D.C. 37's organizing efforts is even starker. For example, buses to Albany were no longer commonplace under the Hill administration. During this time, both the service provision and the bureaucratic functions of the union intensified. This link seems more than coincidental and appears to have been a key factor contributing to the union's later political and fiscal difficulties.

At this point it is perhaps necessary to remark on the corruption scandal that embroiled D.C. 37 starting in 1998. The scandal is significant because it points to the organizational environment in which LAGIC emerged and operated, and suggests some of the challenges to democratic practice within D.C. 37. In 1997, members of Local 983 (city drivers and boiler tenders) pleaded for Stanley Hill to intervene in the fiscal mismanagement of their local. The members claimed that their local was close to financial ruin. Hill's failure to investigate the charges formally prompted the desperate members to request an investigation of their local by Manhattan district attorney Robert Morgenthau. Soon after, investigators from both the federal government and

AFSCME began independent probes. The mounting investigations revealed widespread corruption and larceny within D.C. 37, including allegations of embezzlement by top union officials, mob kickbacks, job selling, extravagant fees for lunches and services, election rigging, and even death threats to the challenger in the election for one local's presidency. In one widely cited incident, a local was found to have spent $92,000 for 250 holiday turkeys distributed to members. Most disturbing of all were allegations of ballot tampering in a crucial vote on a 1996 city contract in which D.C. 37 negotiators accepted a two-year wage freeze. Many workers opposed the contract and some saw it as evidence of D.C. 37's curious cronyism with the conservative, antilabor Rudolph Giuliani.[3]

In less than a year, several locals witnessed their presidents and executive councils placed under suspension, forced to resign, and even indicted for criminal offenses. An audit of D.C. 37's finances led AFSCME to place the union under trusteeship in November 1998. Stanley Hill was removed from office, and Lee Saunders, from AFSCME's Washington, D.C., office, was appointed to pilot the union through necessary reforms.

How could things have gone so wrong in D.C. 37? How could well-meaning union staff and activists not see the growing evidence of D.C. 37's undemocratic and corrupt practices, or fail to challenge such practices? Undoubtedly, many of the staff and union members simply did not have personal knowledge of the illegal acts performed by individuals within the organization. This was certainly Stanley Hill's personal defense. But there are other explanations. D.C. 37 had developed an organizational culture that emphasized obedience to the rules and superiors, which lessened opportunities to critically interrogate and assess the actions of union officials. In addition, the division of labor within the union made it harder to know exactly what union officials were doing. The union's bureaucratic culture also promoted a concentration of power and control, and decision making and actions carried out in private, away from members' scrutiny. All of these factors helped to weaken the mechanisms for accountability within D.C. 37 and increased the efforts and costs necessary to correct deviations. In this environment, it was easy for good people to support bad processes and bad outcomes as they followed "normal operating procedures" within the union.

This effect becomes important to keep in mind as we examine lesbian and gay organizing in the union. It helps to explain both the intransigence of union officials who were perceived as personally supportive of lesbians and gays, and the less-than-democratic practices that emerged within LAGIC itself.

However, one must not suppose that LAGIC was entirely at the mercy of its institutional environment. While union rules and procedures mandated particular organizational forms and actions, LAGIC both challenged and coopted specific union practices in order to better meet the needs of lesbian and gay workers within D.C. 37. LAGIC's accomplishment in this regard can be found in its ability to balance members' commitment to supporting and strengthening their union against the need to challenge and broaden the union's institutional structure and practices in order to better represent lesbian and gay workers.

Linking Organizational Structure and Political Action

How well do the bureaucratic structures of unions support a collectivist model of union organizing in which groups of workers participate directly in everything from decision making to planning and attending union activities? The organizing model of politics can productively be associated with collectivist types of organizations whose values, goals, and structures are often presented as polar opposites of bureaucracies.[4] How then can unions hope to reconcile these two models of union politics: bureaucratic and collectivist? The question goes right to the heart of the labor movement's current efforts to organize groups of workers who historically have been excluded or underrepresented in the movement because of their sexual identity, race, citizenship, or other identity status. What effect will unions' organizational environment have on how such groups voice and pursue their interests? Before I consider the specific case of LAGIC and D.C. 37, let me briefly review some of the main characteristics of ideal-type bureaucratic and collectivist organizing unions.[5]

Bureaucratic versus Collectivist Union Model

Bureaucratic organizations are a central feature of modern states and advanced capitalist economies. The logic and form of bureaucracy have become so pervasive that it can be found even among social movement organizations—where efficiency goals, resource dependency, and plain old familiarity often explain its adoption. But pure collectivist organizations are scarce on the organizational landscape. Nonetheless, the values of collectivist organizations, if not their wholesale practice, continue to inform much of our understanding of effective organizing.

First and foremost, bureaucracies share a heavy emphasis on organizational rules as guides for members' behavior. These rules are often formalized but they can also include unwritten rules that help to define acceptable behavior within the organization. The rules are universally applied and usually not easily amended. Thus the appropriate behavior can often be predicted by reference to the appropriate set of (written and unwritten) rules. One common criticism of union bureaucracies is that this heavy reliance often seems to shift the role of rules in the organization such that they function as ends-in-themselves, rather than as means-to-an-end. In other words, workers themselves can seem like an afterthought. As my discussion of D.C. 37 will demonstrate, union members are most legitimated when they conform to the established rules and procedures; violators risk punishment or nonresponsiveness. In contrast, substantive values and commitments that in turn determine which rules are adopted and how they are used drive a collectivist-organizing model of action. As one union activist put it, "Our goal is to build an organization where workers exercise power on their jobs, in their union, and in their communities; an organization which fights for the rights of the working class, *union or not* (emphasis mine)."[6] With this approach, there must be ample room for creativity and ad hoc decision making, qualities that decry rigid rule-conformity above all else.

Second, the term *bureaucracy* has become synonymous with rigid hierarchies that dictate appropriate behaviors for individuals at each level of the organization. Power imbalances are accepted as necessary for the proper functioning of the organization, and the structural hierarchy itself justifies the internal inequalities. Collectivist-organizing groups are suspicious of hierarchies and the concentration of power they represent. A key goal of organizers is a wider distribution of power in order to increase both the number and kinds of voices and interests that are represented within the organization. Consequently, collectivist unions would tend to decentralize key governance and programmatic structures in order to spread power widely among members and to encourage members' participation at every level.

Third, bureaucratic organizations are networks of highly differentiated tasks and roles that produce and rely on specialists (lawyers, contract negotiators, and so forth). However, the presence of specialists alone is hardly evidence of an entrenched bureaucracy in a union. Rather, the appropriate measure is the degree of ease with which rank-and-file members can participate in the processes and shape the outcomes of such efforts. In the collectivist union model, workers would have ample opportunities for such interventions because there would be minimal division of labor. The collectivist approach places a high value on building community in which there are few if any constraints on the types of relationships that can be formed among members.

These three characteristics—rules as guides to action, the relationship of power to organizational hierarchy, and division of labor—describe not only two particular organizational forms, but also two organizational *logics*, or ways of acting. Unions, like many other social justice organizations, reflect both logics. The challenge lies in developing a strong collectivist-organizing culture with minimal bureaucratic practice. My argument is not that unions should eschew all bureaucratic practice and instead follow the collectivist model. Rather, by examining some of the key elements in the logic and practice of both bureaucracies and collectivist-type organization, I hope to draw attention to some of the ways unions embody both models. I also hope to delineate the gains and challenges that this implies for lesbian and gay union activists.

Maintaining a proper balance between the two has proven difficult for D.C. 37 and LAGIC. For example, as part of an agency shop, all city employees receive the benefits of a negotiated contract, and all must pay dues. They can opt not to join the union, but then they lose the right to vote in union elections. Not surprisingly, almost everyone chooses to join. As an agency shop, D.C. 37 has little incentive to pay attention to organizing new members or to strengthening collectivist-organizing strategies as a recruiting tool. As one lesbian staff member at D.C. 37 put it, "[D.C. 37] is a service organization. We don't organize. We're not the classic trade union. Because we have an agency shop, we don't have to be an organizing model" (Interview, October 8, 1998).[7] Another lesbian member noted that it was easy to do general educational workshops in the union, "but to go beyond that, to turn it into any kind of activist kind of thing, that's truly difficult. Or even to turn it into a [member] support kind of thing is very difficult" (Interview, June 14, 1999).

Both collectivist and bureaucratic politics do coexist in D.C. 37, but over time, D.C. 37's practice of collectivist-organizing politics failed to keep pace with the rapid growth of the union's bureaucracy. For example, under Victor Gottbaum's leadership as executive director from 1965 to 1985, D.C. 37 was noted for organizing busloads of workers who directly petitioned lawmakers in Albany; under Stanley Hill's watch, this organizing strategy was largely abandoned in favor of increased union staff lobbying and professional negotiations. As a D.C. 37 committee, LAGIC both confronted and reflected this seeming contradiction within the union, i.e., a bureaucratic structure that weakens members' participation tied to an organizing mission that encourages members' full participation and empowerment.

This fact raises some key questions for union activists in general and for LAGIC members in particular: What forms of organizing are supported in unions with strong bureaucracies? When is direct member involvement encouraged and when is it discouraged in such unions? How does the bureaucratic "culture" of unions shape members' expectations, their sense of what can be accomplished within the organization, and the meanings attributed to particular actions? How do specific institutional features of unions impact organizing efforts by workers?

Twenty-four in-depth interviews conducted between January 1998 and June 1999, roughly evenly split between union staff and LAGIC members,[8] provided data for this study. They also included conversations with three individuals not affiliated with the union but who worked closely with LAGIC activists on various campaigns and events. Those interviewed roughly reflect the diversity of D.C. 37 and of LAGIC: 38 percent (9) Black; 13 percent (3) Latino/a; 45 percent (11) White; and 4 percent (1) Asian Indian. Fifty-eight percent (14) identified as lesbian, 29 percent (7) as gay, and 13 percent (3) as heterosexual. Of the 18 union members and staff who identified as gay or lesbian, 83 percent (15) were out on the job and 17 percent (3) were not. Some of those quoted in this essay remain anonymous at their request. Additional data is provided by D.C. 37 and LAGIC documents, articles in the union newspaper, and by my participation in and observation of both LAGIC and general union events. My primary aim is to offer an analysis of how the union's bureaucracy provided both opportunities and constraints for collectivist organizing by lesbian and gay workers.

Conditions on the Job and in the Union for Lesbian and Gay Workers

The overall climate for gay and lesbian workers in D.C. 37 has been a mixed one. In 1982, AFSCME added a sexual orientation clause to its constitution, sending a powerful message of support for lesbian and gay workers and their issues. In the early eighties, no other union had enacted such a clause. However a policy statement by the International was a long way from enactment at the local level. Several years after AFSCME's historic vote, D.C. 37, like the majority of unions across the country, was still not formally addressing lesbian and gay workplace issues. In 1989, there were still no explicit protections for lesbian and gay workers either in D.C. 37's contract language or in the union's constitution. Lesbian and gay union members were not granted bereavement leaves if their partners died, nor did their partners receive health coverage and other benefits comparable to their straight union brothers and sisters.

The sheer size and diversity of jobs and locals within D.C. 37 produced widely varying experiences for gays and lesbians in the workplace. The responses of coworkers and bosses to those who were out on the job ranged from full acceptance and active support to blatant acts of discrimination. Some workers described quite supportive job environments in which they felt safe expressing their sexual identity. As one gay man who works as a library supervisor tells it, "I'm a gay man at work. Everybody knows it. When my partner calls and my coworkers say, 'Oh, [your partner's] on the phone,' I'll say 'Oh God, it's the husband again?'" (Interview, May 27, 1999).

No one interviewed could recall a single incident of physical violence directed against lesbians and gays on the job. However, many did identify verbal and psychological harassment as common in the workplace. Lee Clarke, former LAGIC chair, noted that she had gotten "plenty of reports of people being harassed at work, being called *dykes* and being called *sissies*" (Lee Clarke, September 28, 1998). More commonly, lesbian and gay workers reported a general feeling of not being supported and fears of invisible discrimination by their bosses, colleagues, and even by union staff.

> I feel the union as a whole is antigay. I don't think honestly there's a lot of harassment, but there's a lot of talking behind people's backs. Also we've got a local president and even though he has a lot of gay people in his local, he won't even acknowledge them with a little room to have a meeting. (Interview, October 28, 1998)

> Superficially, everyone said that there was no discrimination and no problem. A lot of people felt that way. But a lot of discrimination that I have experienced as a lesbian has been very subtle. It has to do more with perception than with things that were actually done to me. I don't think the union would automatically fight for lesbians or gay men to have bereavement leave or maternity leave because they didn't perceive lesbians and gays like that. I think if the union had perceived lesbians and gays in a different way, they would have fought for those issues long before LAGIC brought them to light. (Interview, October 29, 1998)

The Struggle for Recognition

In 1988, a letter appeared in the *Public Employee Press* (PEP), D.C. 37's newspaper, pointing to the need for equitable benefits for lesbian and gay union members.[9] The letter had a sole signatory: Angela Christofedes, a Human Rights Commission (HRC) worker and a member of Local 154. As a member of HRC's staff, it was her job to battle discrimination cases. This experience, coupled with her own lesbian identity, no doubt motivated Christofedes to action.[10] Local presidents soon received a letter from Christofedes asking them to announce a meeting for lesbian and gay workers in D.C. 37. Julie Schwartzberg, another former LAGIC chair, recalls,

> My local president read this [letter] at our local meeting. Now, trust me, most local presidents did not read this letter. And so she announced this meeting and a date and a time and I went. It was in March of 1989. And there were about ten people there from maybe four or five different locals whose presidents had read this letter, and that was the beginning of it. (Julie Schwartzberg, May 18, 1999)

From the beginning, D.C. 37's lesbian and gay workers had to bypass bureaucratic obstacles to their organizing. Because D.C. 37's rules restricted use of its buildings to officially recognized union groups, lesbian and gay members convened at the city's Lesbian and Gay Community Services Center. A similar rule governed submissions to PEP, the union newspaper. "They wouldn't put any of our articles in the union newspaper. We asked them 'Would you please announce this in the union newspaper?' and they said 'No'" (Julie Schwartzberg, May 18, 1999). Therefore LAGIC submitted their announcement as a letter to the editor, knowing that members' letters were not subject to such restrictions, and thus succeeded in having it printed.

The constraints and barriers that these rules imposed, coupled with an expectation of little support from union officials, spurred some lesbian and gay union members to argue at that first meeting that the new group should constitute itself *outside* of the union. Those who made this argument had been long-time activists in D.C. 37. As such, their experiences within the union had led them to believe that "the union would try to control the lesbian and gay group, set the agenda, and try to control what the issues were" (Interview, May 18, 1999). They feared that D.C. 37's top-down politics would undermine the organizing efforts of the new group.

But such voices were a minority within the group. After some debate, the majority voted to remain and to fight for recognition within the union. Their reasons for doing so reflected both a desire to access the union's resources and an empowerment philosophy that required the participation of lesbian and gay workers on the job and at work.

> I think the majority of us felt that we were going to get the union to address our issues and we would not let the union control what we do, and that it's very important that we have a presence in a huge organization like that. If you have a labor organization, to me it doesn't make sense to meet outside of that organization and to have our group be autonomous [outside the union]

when one of the goals is to make us feel comfortable where we are, in our labor union and in our workplace. The other thing is D.C. 37 has a lot of resources, and we wanted our share. We felt that they should use our dues to address our issues. (Julie Schwartzberg, May 18, 1999)

Even before formal recognition of LAGIC by D.C. 37 had been granted, this group of lesbian and gay workers engaged in an impressive array of political, educational, and social activities that demonstrated a strong collectivist-organizing orientation. They formed subcommittees on topics identified by the workers themselves and that defined the group's primary issues. These included domestic partner benefits, HIV/AIDS, legislative and political action by the union on lesbian and gay issues, and outreach within the union.

In addition, the group established a volunteer steering committee that was responsible for overall coordination and leadership of the group's activities. The steering committee structure increased the opportunity for participation and leadership by a greater number of the group's members, and consciously avoided a concentration of power in a single group leader. It is significant that the steering committee continued to function several years after recognition had been granted to LAGIC and alongside the formal committee chairs.

Winning recognition by the union was, of course, a high priority. But instead of submitting a formal request for the creation of LAGIC and awaiting the decision of union leaders, these lesbian and gay union activists used collectivist-organizing strategies to mobilize support within the union. First, they organized a petition drive among the general union membership to win widespread support for the idea of a lesbian and gay committee. The petition functioned as a powerful organizing tool, with individual LAGIC members circulating visibly in their locals, talking to and educating fellow members, and collecting signatures in support of LAGIC's formation. The petition drive was highly successful, with members collecting hundreds of signatures from workers all across the union. The petitions were also important in convincing the executive council that the committee would be serving a real need in the union.

Second, the group targeted influential union leaders to support their campaign. They convinced presidents of several locals and members of the executive council to sign letters of support and to lobby the executive council to the committee. Third, the group sought the support of local presidents by sending them letters about the campaign signed by members of their local. The letters asked the presidents to support both the official establishment of LAGIC and the appointment of a D.C. 37 representative to the AFSCME Gay and Lesbian Rights Committee of the International. The letters closed with a request for LAGIC representatives to meet and discuss the proposals with each president.

Fourth, LAGIC organizers circumvented established procedure and took the unprecedented step of initiating a meeting with members of D.C. 37's executive council to discuss the needs of lesbian and gay workers and to press for recognition.

> How it usually works is that the executive director perceives a need for a particular committee so he appoints a committee, then he appoints a head of the committee. That's how it's usually done. But we wrote to him, and the executive council arranged a meeting with some of us who were in the group. Now, the executive council was surprised. They were somewhat leery but they were very cooperative. They didn't understand why we wanted to do this. They were concerned that we were asking for 'special privileges.' (Interview, October 29, 1998)

Despite an initial wariness and misunderstanding of LAGIC's objectives by some members of the Executive Council, LAGIC organizers discovered that the Council would become quite open to the idea of a lesbian and gay committee. In particular, Stanley Hill won praise for his willingness to support and listen to lesbian and gay workers.

> Stanley Hill and some of the other folks that work with him really and truly believed that this was a civil rights issue, a human rights issue. So on that level we had support and we could work with people [on the Executive Council]. (Interview, May 18, 1999)

Fifth, the early group of activists believed that acting as if they had formal recognition as a union committee would help them win such recognition. It was important to conform to the union's expectations of 'proper' union activity. These organizational expectations were closely tied to the union's bureaucratic environment, in which both written and unwritten rules of conduct helped to define legitimacy. The group therefore organized social and educational activities that paralleled those offered by other constituency groups in the union.

One of its earliest successes was a lesbian and gay dinner dance. Dinner dances are a popular part of union culture, often serving an educational function. In addition, the dances help reward those who have served the group, and they are just plain fun. LAGIC's first dinner dance, held at the Lesbian and Gay Community Services Center, provided an opportunity to organize both rank-and-file union members and the union leadership. Again, it is significant that these lesbian and gay workers seized on this opportunity to increase participation of union members in everything from the administrative tasks inherent in organizing a dance to the hard work of organizing union members and staff to attend this decidedly 'queer' public event. At the same time, lesbian and gay workers recognized that their formal recognition also depended on their ability to conform to the union's organizational expectations.

Recognition and Formalization

On March 14, 1990, LAGIC was formally approved by D.C. 37's executive council.[11] Formal recognition brought both rewards and difficulties. As a recognized constituency group, the committee now had access to the union's wide resources, such as meeting rooms, money, mailings, printing and publication resources, the union newspaper, lobbyists, lawyers, researchers, and general staff. However, LAGIC would discover that the union's bureaucratic structure would also play a significant role in the committee's ability to organize workers. That structure would both facilitate and pose obstacles to the integration, representation, and empowerment of lesbian and gay workers in the union. Specifically, LAGIC's history demonstrates tension between a top-down institution and a more participatory, collectivist approach to unionism. This tension was sometimes productive, yielding favorable outcomes for the group. But at other times, D.C. 37's bureaucracy sought to limit and weaken involvement by lesbian and gay workers.

One instance of this tension can be clearly seen in the process through which LAGIC's leadership was established. As a new constituency group within the union, one of the first orders of business was the choice of a chairperson. D.C. 37's constitution did not specify requirements for committee chairs. Rather, the executive council appointed presidents and vice presidents of locals—individuals with a proven record of activism and who had attained formal positions of power within the union through democratic elections in their locals—to head these committees. Schwartzberg recalls her reaction when she learned of this process. "I was shocked when I joined D.C. 37 and discovered that so many of the appointments were top-down and not elected. Of course they should be elected" (Julie Schwartzberg, June 16, 1999).

Thus it was that LAGIC's first appointed chair was a female president of a local who was not publicly identified as a lesbian. LAGIC members' practice of a more collectivist-democratic form of union involvement soon clashed with the more bureaucratized forms of committee work that D.C.

37 officials had come to expect. LAGIC's first chair was apparently quite taken aback by the aggressive involvement of LAGIC members:

> We were following the normal procedure. And so Stanley Hill appointed this woman as chair. I think that she just thought of it as a nominal appointment. But we weren't that kind of a committee [laughs]. Some D.C. 37 committees are like that, where the person that's in charge just tells you what's going to be done and you go ahead and do it and that's it. She was like, "*You're* calling *me* to tell me there's a meeting? I didn't call no meeting [laughs]." (Regina Shavers, October 29, 1998)

After the first chair's speedy resignation, Hill had some difficulty locating a willing replacement chair from his list of potential appointees. This created a window of opportunity for LAGIC members, who wanted cochairs— one male, one female—to reflect the gender diversity and equality that some had grown accustomed to seeing in nonunion gay organizations. However, when no gay men volunteered, the group proposed two women, one black and one white, this time with an eye to having the committee's leadership reflect the racial diversity of gay and lesbian workers in the union.

However, this proposal encountered some initial resistance from Hill and the Executive Council. Committee cochairs were unheard of in D.C. 37, and one of the proposed chairs, Regina Shavers, was only a rank-and-file member and not an officer in her local. No doubt prompted by the fact that no one else was stepping forward for the job, and perhaps partly assuaged by the fact that the other proposed cochair, Julie Schwartzberg, was a vice president in her local, the executive council finally approved the appointments. LAGIC had successfully overcome its first bureaucratic challenge as a committee.

The victory was more than symbolic. As Shavers notes, her presence as cochair was also intended to be a recruiting tool for Black lesbians and gays in the union.

> I felt that if other people saw me they would feel more comfortable. You know, African people—African American lesbians and gays—ain't about all of that. I'm telling you from my experience, my age, my generation, working people are not about going down to the union and being in no lesbian and gay issues committee.

The steering committee that had formed before recognition continued to play an active role in LAGIC alongside the chairs. LAGIC's newsletters indicate that the steering committee met frequently, alternating monthly meetings with those of LAGIC's general membership. Members of LAGIC's steering committee were largely volunteers who were approved by a vote of the committee's members.

Over the next eight years, LAGIC activists engaged in a wide array of activities, most facilitated by D.C. 37's existing organizational procedures and practices. LAGIC chairs, like other D.C. 37 committee chairs, routinely reported on their committee's events and issues before the union's delegates meetings. Members of LAGIC's legislative committee coordinated the adoption of five of the committee's resolutions by D.C. 37's legislative conference, organized busloads of workers for a general union march on the state capitol, and worked with D.C. 37's lobbyists to promote legislation friendly to lesbian and gay workers. LAGIC members organized numerous workshops and conferences on topics as wide-ranging as dealing with HIV/AIDS to understanding employees' contracts. As cochairs, Julie Schwartzberg and Regina Shavers sat on union boards, including their appointment by Stanley Hill to AFSCME's Lesbian and Gay Advisory Board, in which capacity they met with AFSCME's president, Gerald McEntee.

Whenever possible, LAGIC made use of opportunities provided by the union to broaden the committee's agenda and outreach. For example, the LAGIC-sponsored performance by the lesbian and gay gospel choir, Lavender Light, for Black Heritage month attracted a large audience of both gay and straight workers from all across the union. LAGIC also won the right to curate an exhibition in the lobby of the union building in the same way that the Hispanic and Black committees decorated the lobby for each of their heritage months. In 1992, LAGIC again drew on organizational precedent to use the D.C. 37 float as part of the committee's contingent in the Lesbian and Gay Pride Parade in Manhattan. Cultural events such as these were standard fare in the union, but they had added importance for lesbian and gay organizing in D.C. 37. They were powerful recruiting tools and mobilized many lesbian and gay workers who may not have otherwise participated in union events. For example, as the D.C. 37/LAGIC float moved down Fifth Avenue, workers would stream from the sidewalks shouting, "That's my union! That's my union! I'm D.C. 37!" One worker remembers,

> By the time the float got to the end, it was just packed with people. Because people didn't know that their union had a lesbian and gay committee, but they saw that float and our banner and our T-shirts and they were flying! That's how we got people to come to the meetings, too! (Interview, October 1, 1998)

Gay Pride Day, New York City. Members stream from the sidewalk. "That's my union! That's my union!" Photograph courtesy of Cheryl Minor, LAGIC cochair. Reprinted with permission.

LAGIC was a primary sponsor of the historic June 1992 "Pride at Work" (PAW) East Coast Lesbian and Gay Labor Conference, hosted at D.C. 37's headquarters. The one-day conference aimed to educate participants about the rights of lesbian and gay workers with workshops on topics ranging from the legal rights of workers with HIV or AIDS, to building union support for lesbian and gay political action. Among the two hundred participants were Stanley Hill, several presidents of D.C. 37's local unions, a representative from the AFSCME research department, members of the New York city council, and the director of the Governor's Office of Lesbian and Gay Concerns.

Although the primary aim of the conference was to educate, it also produced some tangible outcomes. The enthusiasm of this first conference spurred a national PAW conference in 1994 (again hosted by LAGIC at the D.C. 37 union hall), and eventually led to the formation of a national PAW organization, with rapidly growing chapters all across the country. The AFL-CIO passed a resolution in September 1997 that led to PAW's eventual establishment as an official constituency group. The 1992 conference also helped to strengthen the relationship between LAGIC and top D.C. 37 officials and served to spur the union to take greater action in support of the rights of lesbian and gay workers, especially with regard to domestic-partner benefits.

LAGIC's Domestic-Partner Benefits Campaign:
Bureaucratic and Collectivist Politics in Action

LAGIC's campaign for domestic-partner benefits provides many examples of how the committee used bureaucratic structures to further collectivist-organizing goals. LAGIC members worked with union negotiators to push for these benefits at the collective bargaining table, and with union lawyers to pursue broad-based antidiscrimination legislation. In 1989, the union first won domestic-partner benefits in workers' contracts in the form of bereavement leave. In November 1992, five months after the first PAW conference, LAGIC members Julie Schwartzberg, Regina Shavers, and Michele Valdespee watched proudly as Brenda White, assistant to D.C. 37's executive director, testified at a city council hearing in support of a strong and wide-reaching antidiscrimination bill. In 1993, D.C. 37 strongly supported Mayor David Dinkins's Executive Orders 48 and 49, which established the city's domestic partnership registry, recognized the rights of succession to public housing, and granted visitation rights in prisons and hospitals. In 1994, the city extended health benefits to domestic partners of city employees and retirees, including lesbian, gay, and unmarried heterosexual couples. This agreement was negotiated with representatives from the Municipal Labor Committee (MLC), a coalition of New York City unions chaired by Stanley Hill. In addition, the specific domestic-partner provisions were negotiated by the MLC's subcommittee on health insurance issues, which was headed by three key D.C. 37 officials.[12] Thus, by educating and building strong relationships with union leaders, negotiators, and lobbyists, LAGIC harnessed the power of the union's hierarchy and differentiated areas of expertise. This was especially crucial on those occasions when union officials had access to policy-shaping and policy-making venues from which rank-and-file LAGIC members were barred.

LAGIC also used collectivist-organizing tactics to build important power coalitions within the union, effectively increasing both the volume and diversity of union voices demanding domestic-partner benefits. For example, LAGIC had consistently defined domestic partners to include unmarried heterosexual couples.[13] By doing so, the group was able to link the specific needs of lesbian and gay workers to those of another category of unprotected workers, moving beyond rigid identity politics. LAGIC chairs and members contacted other union committees, made presentations, and talked to workers in one-on-one encounters in their effort to build broad-based support for domestic-partner benefits. They were thus able to mobilize and win the support of other key D.C. 37 constituency groups, like the Retirees Association and the Committee on Disabilities, by showing how an expansive domestic-partnership policy would benefit their members as well, regardless of sexual orientation. It should be noted that D.C. 37's organizational structure facilitated these coalitions and collectivist interventions, both by making it easier to identify other constituencies in the union that might have an interest in domestic-partner benefits, and by promoting the delegation and coordination of resources and activities.

LAGIC had a choice. The committee could have sought the support of only committee chairs, local presidents, and other key power-holders within the union. Instead, LAGIC used the bureaucratic features of D.C. 37 to facilitate "bottom-up" organizing of workers, thereby (re)defining domestic-partner benefits as a general union issue, and increasing the pressure on union officials to respond to the demands of mobilized members. LAGIC urged members to write letters and speak out in support of domestic-partner benefits at meetings in their locals and chapters, noting in one mailer that "it is important to make these demands and to let the union leaders know that there are many different types of 'family.'" LAGIC thus used the opportunities provided by the union's governance structure and procedures to mobilize gay and lesbian workers and to attempt to place the issue of equitable benefits for lesbian and gay workers on the union's agenda.

In building support for domestic-partner benefits for city employees, LAGIC employed a dual-pronged strategy. The committee used the bureaucratic strengths and services of the union, such as lobbying, D.C. 37's bully pulpit, union press releases, and representation at the bargaining table. But LAGIC also engaged in powerful collectivist-organizing efforts, such as educating union leaders and members, building coalitions with nongay union groups, direct action by members at union meetings, and a letter writing campaign to union officials. LAGIC used an organized membership to push the bureaucratic mechanism of D.C. 37 further than it might have gone on its own, and conversely, used the union's bureaucracy to strengthen the committee's efforts to organize lesbian and gay workers.

Sexual Identity and Ideological Gatekeeping

D.C. 37's bureaucracy exerted a tidal pull on those within the organization. It required sustained deliberation by LAGIC activists to determine when and how best to swim against the current. D.C. 37's strong bureaucratic structure placed pressures on LAGIC to conform to long-established union practices. This conformity conferred benefits, as we have seen. But it also brought liabilities. Over time, LAGIC became more vulnerable to bureaucratic influences that weakened its practice of collectivist democratic politics. An especially significant bureaucratic effect on LAGIC was the gatekeeping function of the union's leadership structure. Fiscal oversight and general management strategies presented the greatest opportunities for gatekeeping and the exercise of bureaucratic control. LAGIC's budget was ad hoc, with committee chairs submitting budget requests for activities as needed. The lack of an appeal process encouraged committee chairs to submit only budget requests that were likely to be approved, which were often activities that had clear union precedent. LAGIC successfully relied on precedent to get D.C. 37 to support activities such as LAGIC's annual dinner dances, a gay body-building exhibition at the union hall, gay and lesbian pride exhibits in the union lobby, and the use of D.C. 37's official float for the city's Lesbian and Gay Pride Parade. These were tremendous accomplishments and went a long way toward normalizing lesbians and gays in union culture.

However, there were occasions when appeals to precedent were not enough to overcome bureaucratic decision making that worked against LAGIC's collectivist organizing. For example, in 1995 committee members found themselves embroiled in a struggle with Brenda White, LAGIC's liaison to the executive council. LAGIC's routine application for a Gay Pride exhibit in the lobby of the union hall was contested by White, who objected to the nudity depicted in some of the work submitted by gay artists. In a highly contentious meeting with White, LAGIC representatives pointed to previously approved lobby exhibits sponsored by other nongay union committees that had included nude subjects. The decision to ban nude subjects in LAGIC's exhibit thus seemed arbitrary and unfair. The argument proved unsuccessful. In protest, LAGIC left one of the exhibit walls blank, and in his remarks city councilmember Tom Duane, who was a featured speaker at the reception, denounced the union's failure to fully support the exhibit. Paradoxically, the very bureaucratic procedure—precedent—that LAGIC had successfully used on previous occasions to radically mobilize lesbian and gay workers in D.C. 37 was now being used to limit the ways in which they could publicly express sexual identity in the union.

Hierarchical decision making and gatekeeping also raised challenges to diversity within LAGIC itself. Although they mobilized around their common identities as gays and lesbians and as workers, LAGIC members came from many different backgrounds and had many different ways of understanding and expressing their sexual identity. Some members were publicly out, while others were closeted; some behaved flamboyantly, while others were conservative; some believed that their sexual identity played a significant role in their life experiences, others believed that its effect was negligible. Yet conversations within LAGIC seemed to have rarely addressed these differences and the possible implications for how the committee would represent lesbian and gay workers in D.C. 37. The radical inclusivity that had been a highlight of the early LAGIC was increasingly challenged by a union structure that comfortably supported less equitable representation and participation. Further, the ideological and political tensions that were latent in some of these differences surfaced in response to shifts in power within the committee.

As LAGIC matured within the union and behaved more traditionally, it seemed also to lose some of its ability to represent members and interests that were themselves less mainstream. Members and activities that could be seen as transgressive became less visible in the committee over the years. For example, cross-dressing members and union drag queens had attended LAGIC's early dinner dances and were frequently recalled in later conversations with committee members. Julie Schwartzberg still sounds incredulous years later when she recounts how a drag queen walked up to the executive director of the union and sat in his lap!

However, by 1998 not only were cross-dressers and drag queens noticeably absent from LAGIC's annual dinner dance, but the committee no longer even participated in the city's Pride Parade. These changes are partly explained by the many AIDS deaths among LAGIC members in the early nineties, but they also reflected a change in leadership within the committee. LAGIC's new chair, Lee Clarke, brought a very different outlook to the committee. Clarke considered the sexual energy of the Manhattan Pride Parade to be at odds with the "family values" of the union.

> It was something you can't bring your kids to. So the committee members wanted a float and wanted to go to that and I said, "No, you can't bring your kids." We ended up doing the Brooklyn Pride Parade thing. I wouldn't go to the executive committee to ask for money to hold an event where it's not a family-type affair or something where you're not comfortable with a young person being there. . . . That's my personal philosophy and the prerogative of the chair. (Lee Clarke, September 28, 1998)

To her credit, Clarke did support members who chose to march without the float in the Manhattan parade, and she personally led LAGIC contingents in pride parades in other parts of the city.

Clarke's decision was rooted in a personal ideology that was also shaped by her many years of union activism, as evidenced by her repeated assertion, "We're workers first! We are workers who just happen to be gay." In Clarke's view, the promise of lesbian and gay union organizing lay in recognizing the primacy of their identification as workers over sexual identity: "You have to be respected as a worker, you have to be respected as a person, [but] you don't have to be respected because you're lesbian. We have more rights as workers than we have as lesbians and gays" (Lee Clarke, September 28, 1998). She believed LAGIC's goals would be best achieved if they fit within the union's existing model of workers' rights. Clarke did believe in increasing union visibility at other, smaller pride parades, but failed to see how the Manhattan parade, with its "half naked men," was "worker oriented."

What was clearly missing in LAGIC were public conversations about what it meant to be a worker in relationship to lesbian and gay identities. At least three competing understandings of that relationship were evident in my conversations with committee members. Some believed that their identities as workers trumped their identities as lesbians and gays. Others believed that both identities were inextricably linked, and that paying attention to sexual identity in the union would broaden the union's understanding of what it meant to be a worker and what constituted workers' issues and appropriate union activities. A small minority saw little or no relationship at all between their identities as workers and as gays. Interestingly, although individual members were comfortable expressing some disagreement and discomfort with Clarke's decision in private conversations, none had raised formal objections in the meetings or to Clarke directly. As one lesbian worker put it, "It wouldn't change anything." The opportunity for these much-needed discussions lessened when LAGIC's committee structure became even more bureaucratized.

The strength of Clarke's personality and growing power in the union, the effective demise of LAGIC's steering committee, and the de facto veto power of the committee chair all combined to foster the perception among some members that LAGIC had grown less tolerant of some of the differences among members. Pointing to declining turnout at committee meetings and events, Clarke and other LAGIC activists explained this growing demobilization as the flight of members who had become accustomed to the "social" focus of the committee's earlier activities, and who were uncomfortable with the committee's refashioned "political" agenda. However, it is difficult to reconcile this explanation with the extensive organizing and political accomplishments of the committee in the years leading up to Clarke's appointment as chairperson. The lack of a clear objective after the 1994 domestic-partner benefits victory offers a partial explanation of lowered turnout. But additionally, there was a growing sense of alienation among some members who no longer felt that they had a voice in the committee: "I couldn't take the crap that goes on. It's the same people that come to the event, to the committee, and it's the same people's views that get looked at. . . . " Although LAGIC members continued to have many opportunities to define and shape the committee's agenda and activities under Clarke's leadership, power imbalances between the chair and members proved significant when there were contested issues, such as the Manhattan Pride Parade. The gatekeeping and consequent narrowing of discursive space within the committee was not the result of malicious intent by Clarke or others. Rather, it can be understood as the inevitable outcome of the growing bureaucratic logic and practice that displaced the collectivist-organizing orientation and emphasis of the early committee.

Conclusion

The case of LAGIC and D.C. 37 suggests that both labor scholars and activists need to consider the ways in which organizational structures and institutional environments affect unions' ability to organize workers. Specifically, union bureaucracy has been shown here to function both as a catalyst for and as a constraint to the empowerment of lesbian and gay workers. One of the most considerable features of D.C. 37's bureaucracy was its gatekeeping function, which served to filter some of LAGIC's more direct challenges to the union. When D.C. 37 workers began to organize around both their sexual and class identities, they turned the spotlight on a hidden ideological war within labor unions. LAGIC began to unmask heteronormative assumptions and values embedded in D.C. 37. While homophobia is a very real problem in unions, it is itself only a symptom of the deeper malady of heterosexism that devalues not only lesbians and gays, but also heterosexual men and women who fail to conform to dominant standards of gender and sexuality. Prior to LAGIC's formation and its domestic-partner benefits campaign, the seemingly objective category of "worker" presumed a heterosexual worker. In addition, it presumed the worker had the ability and the desire to enter into family configurations that were legitimized by the state through the institution of marriage. Thus, there existed an unstated validation of marriage to the exclusion of many other forms of family. The relationship between the worker and the employer, as evidenced by demands for benefits and protections, was partially mediated through a normative relationship between the worker and the ideological apparatuses of the state. In other words, certain job benefits and protections were only granted to those who matched traditional gender and sexual roles. LAGIC challenged and reshaped those relationships, both by trying to change the state's normative standards through legislative reform and by negotiating benefits at the collective bargaining table.

However, even after LAGIC's successes, these ideological battles continued to be fought not only between LAGIC and union officials, but also within LAGIC itself. The discomfort that some committee members felt about the Manhattan Pride Parade says something about what lesbians and gay activists themselves consider to be acceptable expressions of gender and sexual identity. This internal ideological contestation becomes even more pronounced in organizational settings characterized by uneven distribution of power. It is significant that LAGIC both challenged and reified traditional gender and sexual values at different points in the committee's history. The key lesson here is that the existence of a lesbian and gay union caucus does not automatically pose a radical challenge to the status quo, nor is it inherently conservative. Rather we have to look deeper at the specific conditions, institutional settings, and issues being addressed, as well as their relationship to the interlocking ideologies of class, gender, and sexuality.

Activists do not always have the freedom to determine the environment in which they work. Often, mobilization and organizing occur within organizational fields and institutional settings that were not designed to support transformative or collectivist politics. LAGIC activists had to confront a bureaucracy that alternately impeded and promoted nonnormative ideologies and collectivist-organizing politics. LAGIC's history in this regard suggests that lesbian and gay union activists must give sustained consideration to the ideologies and values that inform their organizing if they wish to counteract the conservatizing and paralyzing effects of union bureaucracies.

Notes

My research was assisted by a fellowship from the Sexuality Research Fellowship Program of the Social Science Research Council, with funds provided by the Ford Foundation. I am also grateful to Jae Chung, Cathy Cohen, Miriam Frank, Desma Holcomb, Lynne Huffer, Joy James, Alethia Jones, Shannon Leonard, Elizabeth Long, and Kris Peterson for their careful readings and comments. As always, that which is found wanting remains the sole responsibility of the author.

1. "Institutional isomorphism" refers to the tendency of organizations to mirror the blueprint and behavior of others in their particular institutional environment. See John W. Meyer and Brian Rowan, "Institutionalized Organizations: Formal Structure as Myth and Ceremony," in *The New Institutionalism in Organizational Analysis*, ed. Walter W. Powell and Paul J. DiMaggio (Chicago: University of Chicago Press, 1991), 41–62.
2. "The Storm at D.C. 37," *Village Voice*, September 15, 1998, 49.

3. Like other union constituency committees, LAGIC did not take an official position on the "zero-zero" contract.

4. Joyce Rothschild, "The Collectivist Organization: An Alternative to Rational-Bureaucratic Models," in *Critical Studies in Organization and Bureaucracy*, ed. Frank Fischer and Carmen Sirianni (Philadelphia: Temple University Press, 1994), 448–74.

5. On bureaucracies, see Max Weber, "Bureaucracy," in *Economy and Society*, ed. Guenther Roth and Claus Wittich (Berkeley and Los Angeles: University of California Press, 1978), 956–1003; Karl Marx, "The Spirit of Bureaucracy," in *Writings of the Young Marx on Philosophy and Society*, ed. Lloyd Easton and Kurt Guddat (New York: Doubleday, 1967), 185–87. On collectivist organizations, see Joyce Rothschild, "The Collectivist Organization"; Jane Mansbridge, "Feminism and the Forms of Freedom," in Fischer and Sirianni, *Critical Studies*, 544–53. See also Monica Russo, "This World Called Miami: ACTWU Approaches Union-Building in a Multicultural Framework," in *Labor Research Review* 20 (1993): 37–49.

6. Monica Russo, "This World Called Miami," 38.

7. Some of the quotations used in this essay have been edited for clarity. Specifically, conversational fillers have been excised, and indirect references have been made explicit.

8. Nonstaff jobs represented in the sample include secretary, library supervisor, library trucker, architect, emergency services dispatcher, emergency services supervisor, and administrative assistant. Staff positions include union lobbyist, reporter for the union newspaper, Health and Safety Unit program coordinators and supervisor, shop steward trainer, assistant to D.C. 37's executive director, and assistant director of D.C. 37's research and negotiations department.

9. For additional history of LAGIC, see Miriam Frank, "Lesbian and Gay Caucuses in the American Labor Movement," in *Laboring for Rights: Unions and Sexual Diversity across Nations*, ed. Gerald Hunt (Philadelphia: Temple University Press, 1999), 87–102.

10. Angela Christofedes was not available to be interviewed, having left the union before the start of this research. Those who knew her personally or who had worked with her described motives for her actions.

11. "Set Gay Rights Panel," *Public Employee Press* 31, no. 6 (April 6, 1990): 4.

12. Zita Allen, "Health Benefits Won," in *Public Employee Press* 34, no. 19 (November 12, 1993).

13. Union activists have consistently pressed for a more inclusive standard for recipients of domestic-partner benefits. See Desma Holcomb, "Domestic Partner Health Benefits: The Corporate Model vs. the Union Model," in Hunt, *Laboring for Rights*, 103–20.

Homophobia, Labor's Last Frontier?
A Discussion with Labor Leaders William Fletcher Jr., Yvette Herrera, Gloria Johnson, and Van Alan Sheets

Kitty Krupat and Patrick McCreery

William Fletcher Jr., Assistant to the President, AFL-CIO

Yvette Herrera, Assistant to the Executive Vice President, Communication Workers of America (CWA)

Gloria Johnson, Director of Social Action, International Union of Electrical Workers (IUE); President, Coalition of Labor Union Women (CLUW); Vice President and Member, AFL-CIO Executive Council

Van Alan Sheets, Assistant Director of Political Action, American Federation of State, County, and Municipal Employees (AFSCME); Officer, Pride at Work (PAW)

YVETTE HERRERA: Kitty and Pat asked us how widespread homophobia is in the workplace and is it receding. The way I would answer is that homophobia is very widespread. But to answer the second part of the question is trickier. Is it receding in the workplace? I think it's gotten better, and I think the primary reason is because more gay people are coming out. That allows someone to get to know a gay coworker and realize, of course, that they like this person and that these are regular folks. For some people, it alters their judgment. So, I would say that it's gotten better. But I would hasten to say that it's really bad. I run workshops and roundtable discussions on this topic at CWA, and I am often shocked and hurt and offended by what goes on. This is the last frontier in the workplace where people can be intolerant and often get away with it.

Many of us, and many of our progressive movements, have made it inappropriate in the workplace—in public areas, in mixed company—to make racial jokes or remarks or sexual jokes or remarks. Workers may still do that with their buddies on break or in the bathroom, but in the cafeteria or in the hall or in a business meeting, it's just no longer appropriate. Certainly I don't run into it very much. But gay-bashing is still okay. So, this is our next project.

As progressives, the labor movement has to play a major role in this, even at that minimal level of what is acceptable in public. Our membership

196

is a microcosm of society. We have our bigots, we have everything. In some places we have terrific leaders who are really leading. They're in front of the membership—more liberal than the membership—and are trying to do something about this. But there is a huge amount of education to be done.

I run diversity workshops and sexual harassment workshops, and they're all emotional and tough. But none are as difficult as workshops we do on gay rights, because the prejudices people bring are so vast. I was born in Cuba, I'm Hispanic, right. So I sit in a room with other Hispanics and African Americans and Asian Americans, and we are the worst on this topic, it seems to me. Now this is anecdotal . . .

GLORIA JOHNSON: I've run into that, too. You're absolutely right. Some of the worst offenders I have come across in my union—in the labor movement, in the workplace—have been minorities. The issue is raised over and over again. It's almost like, "It's going to rub off if I'm not careful." But, Yvette, I want to go back to a point you made with which I don't agree. I tended to believe, as you did, for a long time, that discrimination against women and minorities was disappearing, and people were not going to make attacks on women and minorities any longer. Yvette, it's coming back full force—in any setting, at any time of the day. I have seen it in the workplace and I've seen it in the union. What is most tragic to me is seeing people just accepting it passively. So when we get to the issue of gay-bashing, of course, people are continuing to do it. And there's some very subtle ways of doing it. You don't have to bash somebody out loud, you can do it through actions or lack of actions.

I wonder if coming out is the answer. I tend to believe the reverse is true. If the labor movement is fully committed—and we've got to see to it that it is—a lot has to be initiated at the top rather than expecting it to come from the rank and file. I'm talking not only about the development of programs for members, but about how unions treat their own employees, as a starting point. How many have created domestic-partner benefits for staff? What happens at a union's executive level tends to establish the image, the climate, for the rest of the union.

KITTY KRUPAT: Yvette, why did CWA start to do programs specifically on gay rights? Where did it come from—the bottom or the top? Could you elaborate a little on the awful things that happen in these trainings?

YH: The reason we started doing the trainings is because the leadership of CWA took a stand on this issue. A number of years ago, we wanted to add sexual orientation to the antidiscrimination clause in our union constitution.

It created a big deal on our convention floor—people getting up, not wanting it. It turns out that we didn't do it the first time. The second time we tried to do it, there was less hoopla, but enough to prevent us from getting it in there. The third time, we got it done.

More recently, we negotiated domestic-partnership language in our contracts with some of our major employers. We get E-mails and letters from members saying, "This is immoral. What are you doing? This is special treatment." A whole series of things like this have happened that made it quite clear that . . . we really had to focus more on gay workers—gay members—and all that they're going through and how they're treated. That's what drove us to do more of this. I must say that I did not think it would be as bad as it is out there.

Also I think people—some unionists, certainly—talk out of both sides of their mouth. For example, maybe three or four years ago, I was doing a roundtable discussion on this topic. This African American woman—a wonderful person, very religious, she's an organizer for us and has been a union officer—says, "This is against my religion. This is immoral. I cannot tolerate this." Then a little bit later in the conversation, she says, "Gays are all pedophiles; they do this and that to children." Then, late in that discussion—she was sort of hearing what I was saying—she brings up a grievance she had handled for a gay man who had HIV and was fired. As she's telling the story, she gets incensed about it. She describes how she'd gone in there and told management that they were treating him differently, that it was not right. She had fought this big battle for him, but she had sat there for forty-five minutes saying all this other stuff. So I said, "How do you reconcile these two things?" And she just said, "That's different. I'm a chief steward and I represent my members and he's one of my members." So somehow she carries these two things around in her head. Things like this are why we continue to do the training. I heard what Gloria said about racism and sexism, but I would say that in the workplace—even in corporate business meetings, where they're all minding their P's and Q's—the homophobia is unbelievable. Any time we negotiate anything in this area, we get letters from members; we get members tearing up their union cards.

PATRICK MCCREERY: Are there other issues where you get those same kinds of responses, or is this one the most inflammatory?

YH: Oh, sure. The same thing happened in the '60s when we were instituting affirmative action policies. Lots of guys wrote even *more* letters, nasty letters, to the union: "What are you doing? I was bypassed for promotion in favor of a woman." You know, all that malarkey. "I'm tearing up my union card." There were a lot of bad feelings about that. We negotiated child care, so members said that instead of negotiating family leaves (this was before the Family Medical Leave Act) and child-care programs, we should put the money into wages—in other words, if we didn't have all these women working, they could get bigger raises. So, the answer to your question is, "Yes." Which is why I used my language of the "last frontier," because we've been through this before.

PM: Getting back to a point both of you have made, it's interesting that the oppressive group seems to be different now. From what you're saying, it's no longer solely or even primarily white males.

YH: What I find most frightening about homophobia is that it's a unifying issue. I don't want to be so depressing here: we have lots of great people who understand the injustice and are fine on the issue. But, on the other hand, in a workplace, homophobia can be the one thing many people agree on.

KK: Do you think workers prioritize claims of identity? For example, do they say that issues of race and gender are more important than sexual identity? When it comes to collective bargaining, how important are questions of sexual identity, relative to race and gender?

VAN ALAN SHEETS: Where you have a larger number of females or a larger number of racial minorities, the union sees a greater need to address their issues. In Pride at Work, our position is gay people are everywhere, not just in AFSCME and the service employees union, or in the teachers union or CWA. Pride at Work has members in the machinists union and the Teamsters and some other unions. But for the most part, those who are out come from unions that also have a large number of minorities or a large number of women. In AFSCME, we're over 50 percent women.

Gays and lesbians are not immediately identifiable. It's the issue of the closet. There's a whole lot of us out there who—I hate to use the term—pass for straight. And I hate that, but that's one of the things that goes on. They might be in a good union on this issue, but they don't know it. Or their particular local or the atmosphere in their workplace is not particularly good, and it's easier for them to leave that part of their life behind them when they walk in the workplace door. So, that's one of the issues Pride at Work is dealing with. Most African Americans, Asian Americans, and women are identifiable as such. But not all gays and lesbians are identifiable. Visibility is a continuing struggle.

WILLIAM FLETCHER JR.: I don't subscribe to identity politics. And it might just be a semantic thing. To me, politics is not just about who you are and how you choose to identify. It has to do with how you look at strategy, history, and things like that. The issue of ranking of oppressions is always a hot-button issue, and the way I would look at it is this: If you look at the history of U.S. capitalism, race and gender are much more central than anything else as the mortar for keeping the system together. Race particularly is the continual landmark of every major social movement this country has ever seen. That may not be a very popular statement, but I hold by it. That does not mean, in my mind, that sexual orientation is less important an issue or that people have some excuse for not dealing with it. But it does mean that in the way I look at history, social movements, and strategy, it does not play the same role as race or gender in the way that the working class exists, the way that capitalism functions, or the way that political unity has been blocked.

KK: In a sense, I don't subscribe to identity politics either. I'm beginning to think that social identities are components of class and, in that sense, factors in class struggle. When gay rights comes to the shop floor, then, isn't it a class issue?

YH: I think my problem with that is I don't understand what you're saying about this issue of gay rights being a class issue. The reality of the situation is whether you're a gay lawyer or a gay doctor or a gay nurse—it doesn't matter what you are—you have the same problems as a gay mechanic. There are forty states where you can be fired for being gay, and that's true for all gay people.[1]

KK: That's my point. Gay workers whose jobs are in jeopardy because they are gay share a common class interest—and it's a bottom-line economic interest. In the auto industry, protection for gay workers was put on the bargaining table in the 1996 Chrysler negotiations. Ultimately, it was withdrawn in exchange for concessions from management that the UAW felt were more generally important.[2] Given the pressures to prioritize workers' rights, what should have happened at the time?*

YH: Well, I think Gloria hit it on the head. And that is you have to lead. Gay rights is an issue that is not going to come from the bottom. This is an issue that's going to come from the top. You can't stand for the principles of union-

---

*Editors' note: Inadvertently, this question was based on misinformation. After this interview was completed and published in *Social Text*, Krupat learned that the UAW had dropped the demand, not as a concession, but because it didn't believe the issue could be the basis of a national strike. While the conclusions reached in discussion of this question might have been the same, it is possible they would have been expressed somewhat differently.

ism and not stand up for gay rights in the workplace. You just cannot possibly do that.

VS: Yvette, I think the woman that you were describing earlier as having almost two contradictory views on the issue was standing up for those issues in the workplace. She was saying this member was being discriminated against. When the issue is framed around discrimination in the workplace, I think it's much easier to say, "That's wrong." Now if you take it outside of work— "I don't know any gays and lesbians" or "My religion says it's a sin"—that's a different matter. But when you bring it to the workplace, trade unionists can place it there as an important issue.

WF: See, I don't think the UAW example you gave, Kitty, is an example of prioritization or of privileging certain oppressions. I think it's an example of opportunism. So I think that this is a question of democracy—a question of whether or not as trade unionists we take the lead in fighting all forms of oppression or whether we turn a blind eye to certain ones.

GJ: I'm glad to hear you say that this was a case of opportunism, Bill. We're dealing here with folks—whether they're gay, straight, man, woman—who are looking to maximize their benefits in the workplace, as selfish as it might seem.

YH: Do you mean "equalize"?

GJ: No, each group wants to maximize—not equalize.
   You have this bargaining unit negotiating a contract. If the skilled trades is a part of this bargaining unit, you'd better believe that they're going to push hard for extra benefits for that skilled trades group, even it means making a choice and eliminating, say, child care. We have to start by recognizing that. Our goal is to maximize for all of the groups without making it a competition. The question is, how do we do that when we know that even within a single bargaining unit we have people whose responsibilities are almost at odds with their own personal feelings: "I can't stand this woman. She's a lesbian." But let something happen to this woman on the job that might establish a precedent so that it could happen to others, you'd better believe self-interest comes into the picture and, even beyond that, the feeling of doing the right thing. So I see the labor movement obligated to address this issue to the fullest.
   If you say, as we have, that you've been fighting discrimination all these years, and if you say you believe in this fight, then it ought to come easy. It should be a continuation of earlier struggles. When you hear an antigay joke,

respond—stand up and say something. When you see gay people left out, stand up and say that they should be part of the structure. And obviously there's several ways of dealing with all of this in unions—policies, resolutions, changing constitutions.

KK: There are thousands of union members who may not have been on the front lines of earlier battles for social justice but who have suffered discrimination. What I've heard you say is that experiencing one form of discrimination doesn't necessarily make someone more sensitive to discrimination in other forms. For example, you have said homophobia seems to be more prevalent among people of color.

WF: I don't know whether that's accurate. I know absolutely that there is homophobia in the black community but it's also extremely complicated. First of all, in terms of why would oppressed people be homophobic it seems to me there's all kinds of reasons—many factors to take into account, including competition, religion, and notions of gender roles. Particularly among the oppressed, people are brought up with what it means to be a man and what it means to be a woman. Whether homophobia's more or less virulent among minorities, I don't know. It's a complicated question.

In a way, it's related to a discussion Kitty and I had earlier about the black character in the film *Out at Work*.[3] This effeminate gay man was stereotypical of what many blacks think of as gay. There's a kind of role that exists for that character within the black community. It's as if, within certain parameters, that role is accepted. It gets much more complicated when someone is not openly gay. So I'm just saying for the record that I'm not prepared to make that statement—that minority group members tend to be especially homophobic.

YH: I want to get back to unions and what unions can do about all of this. I think what we have to realize is that the strength of unions is that they're democratic, and they provide a voice, and so even a minority group in a bargaining unit can get something out of contract negotiations. But they have to be vocal, and they have to be visible, and they have to be somewhat organized . . .

GJ: . . . and have support of others in the bargaining unit . . .

YH: . . . right. So, for example, if the majority of a bargaining unit are older people, all they might care about is pensions. They couldn't care less about the other things we're bargaining for—just improve the pensions. But there can be a smallish percentage of young people, and as long as they come to membership meetings and make a fuss, we end up getting something for them, too. It's a Catch-22, though, with gay workers. A lot of them, for a lot of very good reasons, don't come out—certainly not in a union meeting or in the workplace—because they get discriminated against. And so, in the context of how a union functions it becomes problematic, because they aren't a vocal bloc. They are invisible in a way. I can go to a meeting and say 20 percent of your membership is gay, but, on its own, a statement like that doesn't work in the context of how a union functions. What you're left with is leadership from the top without strong support at the base, which you've seen in my union and in other unions.

PM: We've been talking about the civil rights movement and the feminist movement. These were not top-down movements, and I don't think they would have been as effective, by any stretch of the imagination, if they had been. I understand the point that unions have to foster an atmosphere where gay and lesbian workers can organize around their particular issues, but I wonder how effective a top-down approach can be.

GJ: Pat, I did not mean to suggest that there are not other strategies that will involve the rank and file. But I still maintain, again based on experiences handling other issues of discrimination, that the greatest progress made in many unions was by having folks at the top, on executive boards or whatever, take strong positions. That doesn't eliminate or detract from the need to deal with what I see as the other part of this issue. I think there's a real division in dealing with this. There are some innate feelings that folks have. They've inherited them.

I'm looking now at the labor movement. On one side of the coin you have the challenge of union responsibility. If you are a shop steward you have a job to do; if you are a union president, you have a job to do. But on the other side of the coin, you have those personal homophobic feelings. I think among minorities there's some fear that what would be mine or might be mine is now being divided or claimed by others. Of course, religion is a much bigger issue than I realized. The sad thing here is that a lot of young people are invoking religion. Some of these young people have no experience in fighting discrimination, and when you raise this issue, they say, "It's against my religion."

My point here is that forums for discussion—like this one—are extremely important. Classes on this subject are very important. If we could get to the point where we could have small-group discussions, that would be very helpful.

KK: Let's talk about Pride at Work and other activist caucuses in the labor movement. What's going on? What does the labor movement need to do in quite practical terms?

VS: Come out, come out, wherever you are. [Laughter.]

That's easy to say, but that's really what it comes to. I'll give you a personal experience. Twelve years ago my partner was dying of AIDS. I was working at AFSCME long enough that most people knew me. Statistics and studies show that if a straight person knows a gay or lesbian, they're less likely to be homophobic. A lot of people knew me. I did the trade unionist's job, and they respected that. I wasn't a one-issue person. They saw me struggling to take care of my partner. Before he died, AFSCME employees were in collective bargaining. We put bereavement benefits for gay workers on the table, and it came off the table. So when my partner died, my union contract did not have bereavement benefits for same-sex partners. I don't blame anyone for that. We, the progressives in the union, had not done our homework. We had not gotten out there to explain why it was important. The first time it was there on the table, it was an easy one for the bargaining committee to let slide. By the second time it was on the table, my partner had died, and everyone realized I had not gotten official bereavement leave. And they said, "This is wrong!" And they stuck to it.

But it's a slow process. We have some wonderful leadership within the AFL-CIO and within several unions. But we also have some terribly homophobic folks. I was just at AFSCME's convention in Hawaii. An antigay resolution almost came to the floor for debate. The resolution took issue with AFSCME's support of Pride at Work. I was dumbfounded when I heard that this was going to be an issue. I like to think the best of all of my sisters and brothers. In the end, leadership talked to the sponsors of this resolution and it never was introduced, so it did not become an issue. But this is a feeling those folks had.

There's still other issues that the gay and lesbian movement is working for, such as marriage, that we're a ways off from. Once we've addressed issues in the workplace—bereavement leave, nondiscrimination, health-care benefits—an issue like gay marriage gets almost outside the workplace. That's where you start hitting up against the person who says, "It's against my religion" or "It's against my upbringing. It's not right. I'm uncomfortable with it."

I look at what has happened and continues to happen with racial minorities and issues of gender and we're still not where we need to be. But what has been made clear to most folks is that if you go into a union meeting, it is inappropriate to make a racial slur. As Yvette said, in a lot of union meetings it is not yet inappropriate to make an antigay or lesbian slur. That is slow in coming. We're changing what's acceptable in public, because I also know that some of those folks in the union meetings are racist and sexist, but they know better than to bring it up.

YH: Right. When we talk about transformation, that takes a long time. The very last thing you accomplish is for individuals to internalize the change. But the union can change other things. It can take steps—such as those Van is talking about—to make it clear that *publicly* it's inappropriate to say that stuff, that *on the job* we guarantee that everyone is treated the same and has the same rights. So there are all kinds of things we can do short of changing the individual—like providing domestic-partner benefits and health coverage for HIV. Increasingly, as I talk to people, these things are important to them.

GJ: Pride at Work passed a resolution in 1996 asking to become a constituency group of the AFL-CIO. I was extremely pleased that I was asked to serve on the committee that came up with the recommendation, but I can say to you very candidly that I don't know how everybody else felt. That wasn't the issue, however, and that's my point. Some people are not happy about the affiliation of Pride at Work, about going full force behind it. But who cares, because there were folks there, including John Sweeney and Linda Chavez-Thompson, who knew that this was the right thing to do, and "To hell with what *you* think or *you* think, *we're* going to move ahead." That's what I mean when I talk about taking leadership.

WF: There are people in the leadership who take a position against homophobia. But I look at most of them as being where they are on that question largely because of the women's movement. A lot of people underwent a transformation in the way they looked at things because of prior movements, particularly the women's movement. So, I think we should qualify it when we talk about leadership. Leadership is definitely important, and we need leaders to lead, as opposed to abdicating their responsibilities, but their awareness comes from a lot of grassroots activism that happened over the past thirty years.

PM: I want to go back to the issue of HIV and AIDS in the workplace. How did the emergence of AIDS galvanize workers and unions? I assume that for a lot of workers—gay workers especially—domestic-partner benefits were not such a pressing issue before the epidemic. I also assume AIDS brought a lot of people out of the closet, either as people with AIDS or as activists.

YH: I just have anecdotal information, which is that at the beginning of the AIDS epidemic, we actually saw gay workers going further into the closet.

In the beginning, remember, there was this hysteria in the workplace and people were getting fired if they were gay. For the first five years or so, gays really went undercover because the discrimination from coworkers and from the employer was really intense. That was fueled by this hysteria about getting HIV.

VS: A lot of this is about education. I tested positive in 1985. About a year later, I was at a gay and lesbian fund-raiser where one of the speakers said, "I would like everyone in the room who has tested positive for HIV to raise their hands." I knew I was HIV-positive and a few close friends knew, but even among the supposedly progressive lesbian and gay people attending this event, I was *not* going to raise my hand, and I did not raise my hand. There was discrimination within the lesbian and gay movement, particularly among males. That's something that I've seen really change over the years.

That so many of my coworkers were around me when I took care of my partner was wonderful to me—the support they gave me—but I think it was also wonderful to them to learn more about what was going on. Now we're finding folks in our workplaces who have a sister or another nongay relative who has the disease. It is no longer a gay, white male disease. It's still in many ways the "C" word—the cancer of thirty years ago. If you had cancer you didn't admit it; if you had AIDS you didn't admit it. But that's slowly changing as people find out what causes it, how widespread it is, how it affects people's lives, or how it does *not* affect people's lives. I know there was someone in my own union building—this is about ten years ago—who, if I took a piece of paper and delivered it to that person's desk, they would not touch that piece of paper until the next day because they did not want to come into contact with the germs that cause HIV. We all know that's foolish, but that was a real fear for that individual.

KK: Did that person ever change?

VS: Slowly, yes.

YH: There are all kinds of things that we can do and that unions have done, like health-care coverage for HIV and domestic-partnership benefits. Increasingly, as I talk to people, those things are important to them.

I'll tell one story that began unhappily but ended very well. Several years ago, CWA as an employer offered its clerical staff domestic-partnership benefits for gay and lesbian employees. This was not during negotiations, this was in-between. It was just, "Here, take this. We think this is the right thing to do. We're negotiating this for our members; we think our employees

An AIDS vigil in Washington, D.C., November 1996. Photograph by Ray Crowell/Page One Photography; reprinted with permission.

should have this as well." I have to tell you, it created a firestorm and was very divisive.

GJ: . . . and in a progressive union . . .

YH: . . . The clerical workers decided to put it to a vote and the membership turned it down. People were not speaking to each other afterward, because it was so divisive. We had gay clerical staff who were in the closet who came out during this and gave very emotional speeches and who were hurt by their coworkers giving this back.

But here's the important part: In 1997 CWA made the offer again, but this time as a benefit for *both* gay and straight domestic partners. It passed overwhelmingly, and now the clerical workers have domestic-partner benefits in their contract with the union.

KK: Before we end, I'd be interested to know what role you think gay caucuses—particularly Pride at Work—can play in the labor movement. Along with that, what are the possibilities for coalitions between caucuses in unions and other gay and lesbian activist organizations?

VS: When we first started discussing forming a national umbrella group, which eventually became Pride at Work, we had to ask, "Why are we forming it?" There had been local groups in San Francisco, Boston, and New York, many of them union-based but some of them not. For instance, in San Francisco the lesbian and gay union group there was responsible for getting the Coors boycott onto Castro Street, and I understand that to this day you cannot buy Coors beer on Castro Street.

Anyway, as we started to come together and talk about why we needed the umbrella group, we arrived at two primary reasons: one was to better educate our own membership and leadership. I've had people come up to me in tears and thank me for being so out. I've got to tell you, that really gets to you. Or people come up to me and say, "I can't come out yet, but tell me how I get there." So that's very important, and that was one of the issues we addressed.

The other primary reason was organizing. Here in Washington, D.C., the local chapter worked with Whitman-Walker Clinic employees and then with Human Rights Campaign employees as they were organizing, bringing the message of trade unionism to the lesbian and gay community. We think we are an integral part of the union movement. We think we can be a huge help when organizing the "stereotypical" lesbian and gay occupations—waiters, bartenders, hairdressers, or what have you. But by the same token, we can help to organize in any industry. One of our cochairs is a CWA rank-and-file member up on the telephone pole. We have a number of members of Pride at Work working for Chrysler on the line. Those are not "typical" gay and lesbian jobs. When labor goes into an unorganized workplace—anywhere—we can be a resource, sometimes sensitizing them to certain issues. I think we can educate the lesbian and gay community, and we can educate the labor community.

WF: On this issue of education, a couple of things: one is that I think the role of union education is very important, particularly because there are whole parts of our society that are turning a blind eye to issues around gays or lesbians or AIDS. One of the things I was thinking about when the question of AIDS was raised earlier was how in the black community large sections of the black church refuse to deal with AIDS. We have to do something to penetrate and rip this veil off and get a discussion going. And I think the union movement can play a very important role in that.

The AFL-CIO is trying to develop a social justice curriculum dealing with issues of homophobia and heterosexism. One thing we have to figure out is ways of being proactive, because all too often you get called upon when there's an explosion or when a chain reaction has started. You're called in and treated like Merlin the Magician, like somehow you can wave a wand and resolve a crisis.

That leads me to my last point, which is that a lot of these issues are not going to be resolved through education, regardless of how good we are. First of all, it would be suicidal to begin a campaign against religion and against the way all this plays out in religion. Some people are going to change their minds, and they will figure out ways to reconcile their religious beliefs and their beliefs in democracy. And I think we should encourage that. And some of that will occur through struggle. No one wants to look at this as a very protracted fight. But engaging people in struggle can change their minds. It needs to be linked with education, but I don't think we should ever assume that simply by educating people in the absence of practice that their views will fundamentally change.

GJ: When Kitty called and asked if the Coalition of Labor Union Women would take part in this roundtable discussion, several of the CLUW officers began to talk about it. We have a policy of support for gay rights that goes back quite some time, and we thought this would be a wonderful time to find out exactly what the labor movement has done or is doing to address this issue. We sent out a survey to every union in the AFL-CIO. Of those unions that responded, there was a bottom-line issue that they all agreed on. The issue was lack of education on gay people and their status in the workplace.

However, I couldn't agree with you all more that even with education and visibility you are not going to change everybody's minds. I don't see that as our goal. I think the more important goal at this point is to gain equity, to do the right thing.

Not to belabor this, but many years ago, in 1946 when I was preparing to get married, I was a senior at Howard University looking for a job for the summer. And for the first and only time in my entire life, I passed for white. I worked down on Constitution Avenue making paper boxes at thirty-five dollars a week. Here's what happened there: I didn't realize how many myths and stereotypes were out there about "Negroes." To sit there and work around this stinking glue making these paper boxes for the first few weeks was the most tortuous experience of my life, because I had to weigh keeping the job—and I needed the money—or speaking out. After a couple of weeks it became very clear to me that I was going to speak out, but without identifying myself as an African American. So I became the spokesperson for the rights of "Negroes." I sort of see now the need for all of us to speak out now about homophobia in the workplace, regardless of our sexual orientation.

YH: I would just say that unions can make a difference on this. We haven't done enough, but increasingly we're doing more. I think we've already made a difference. For example, early on in the HIV crisis workers in union settings had more protections than workers who were not unionized. I think generally in union settings there was more HIV training earlier. But I think we certainly have a long way to go. As I said earlier, homophobia is the last frontier for public intolerance. I think what makes this unique and more difficult for unions is the whole issue of gays not coming out. That's understandable, but nonetheless it is very hard to have a grassroots movement when people are afraid of coming out. The union needs to step up and do more, but we also need to have visible constituency groups out there.

Notes

This roundtable discussion took place on September 25, 1998, in the Education Department of AFL-CIO headquarters in Washington, D.C.

1. Since this discussion took place, an additional state—Nevada—has provided protection for gay and lesbian workers.
2. In 1999 contract talks with the Big Three Auto manufacturers, the UAW won protections against discrimination for gay and lesbian workers. As a result of continuing talks, same-sex domestic-partner health benefits were added to the contract in June 2000.
3. *Out at Work: Lesbians and Gay Men on the Job* (ANDERSONGOLD Films, 1997). Fletcher is referring to Nat Keitt, a librarian at the New York Public Library. Keitt did not appear in a later version of this documentary, *Out at Work: America Undercover* (HBO, 1999).

Kingdom Come: Gay Days at Disney World

Jeff Truesdell

Walt Disney might have been horrified. Self-appointed guardians of the "family values" label *definitely* would have been horrified. But there was no fear—or even a hint of irony—on the part of the video crew stationed in the forecourt of Cinderella's Castle in the Magic Kingdom, their camera trained on a well-toned man wearing a goatee, cut-off shorts, a red T-shirt and, dangling from his neck, rainbow-colored beads. "So," said the interviewer, reporting for a tourism show to be broadcast on German TV, "Tell us: What kind of man do you like?"

On that Saturday in June 1999, the question turned few heads among the passing swarms also garbed in red—the official uniform of the unofficial Gay Day at Walt Disney World in Orlando, Florida. But the occasion that filled Disney's parks that weekend with an estimated 80,000 gays and lesbians did not go unchallenged: as the crew zoomed in on the man's T-shirt (which said on the front, "If you like what you see" and on the back, "E-mail me"), a chartered plane floated a banner overhead for a ministry that vowed

Photograph by Michael McElroy; reprinted with permission.

it could turn gays straight. "Freedom from homosexuality: Jesus Christ," it read.

The camera crew's assigned escort, one of the troops who famously police Disney's public image, didn't seem to notice.

Gay Daze at Disney

Walt Disney's enduring impact on popular culture justifies portrayals of him as a visionary. But he was not an enlightened visionary. The man whose name has no match as a stamp for wholesome family fare also "remained to the far right on the political spectrum, suspicious of foreigners, and unwilling to hire Jews or blacks in his company," writes Stefan Kanfer in *Serious Business: The Art and Commerce of Animation in America from Betty Boop to Toy Story*. "More than once he announced his preference for animals over people, and called his time 'the century of the Communist cutthroat, the fag and the whore.'"[1] Over time Disney also took a hard line against his workers—an animosity rooted in a strike against him for which he blamed Communist agitators. He created his Southern California amusement utopia, Disneyland, in part to keep undesirable carny elements at a distance.

Disneyland was just eleven years old when Walt died in 1966. Florida's Walt Disney World, designed to improve upon the lessons of Disneyland and today the planet's most popular vacation resort, would not open until 1971. But so indelible was Walt's imprint that the loss of his creative vision caused the company to stagnate for almost two decades after his death. Not until 1984 did new management, led by CEO Michael Eisner, start to shake The Walt Disney Company back to life. Yet the family-friendly franchise that Walt created left the company shackled with restraints. Although its earnings and consumer base had shriveled, the image endured of a company as virginal and clean-scrubbed as Annette Funicello in Mickey Mouse ears. Tampering with tradition and Disney's long-established mainstream, Middle-American appeal might backfire. Could the new team redefine Disney without losing their core audience? Would they?

Eisner gave them no choice, saying that without radical change Disney could not compete in the entertainment industry. In the years that followed, Eisner set out to fortify the foundation. He launched Disney's own cable television network, opened a retail chain, built new resorts and theme parks in Orlando and Paris, and revived Walt's signature Sunday night television show with himself as host—all moves that furthered the franchise. But Eisner also broke the mold. When the former movie executive jump-started Disney's film division, he initially ordered up slick, urban fairy tales for adults;

the first of the Eisner era, *Down and Out in Beverly Hills*, deliberately sought Disney's first "R" rating. He pushed Disney into television sitcom production, rock-music releases, and urban redevelopment, making over a famously seedy stretch of New York City's Times Square with a retail monolith, a restored Broadway theater, and a time-share hotel tower. Under Eisner, Disney acquired ABC—which debuted the bare butt on network TV with the drama series *NYPD Blue*, and which featured the first series about an openly gay woman, *Ellen*. In short, Eisner diversified the company with subsidiaries whose output was everything the Disney brand was not: gritty, sexy, and controversial.

And yet the Disney name itself was still something to safeguard. Divisions such as Touchstone Television or Miramax Films or Mammoth Records, whose products might have been a blemish on the franchise, were given or remained affixed with non-Disney labels. It was less a conspiracy to defraud the public than an admission that certain lines were not to be crossed. As America's most calculating purveyor of family values, the new Disney placed image above everything but profit. Which is why, in the early 1990s, as some of its gay and lesbian employees began urging Disney to extend health-care benefits to their same-sex partners, the company once again seemed paralyzed. Like most large corporations, Disney was loathe to empower any group of workers, no matter their sexuality. In workforce clout, Disney in 1998 became the nation's largest single-site employer, 55,000 workers at the hotels, theme parks, and attractions of Walt Disney World alone. Same-sex domestic-partner benefits would impact potentially thousands of workers and be big news. Eisner's successful forays into sophisticated, adult-oriented entertainment had not harmed the Disney brand in the public eye. Could Disney risk also being perceived as progay?

In 1995, after a three-year internal review process, Disney finally decided to make domestic-partner benefits available to its gay and lesbian workers. The move infuriated conservative religious and right-wing lobbies, who unleashed what would grow into the largest prolonged attack on Disney in the company's history. But the origins of that attack lay elsewhere—in the Gay Day celebrations at the Orlando theme parks, a grassroots annual event, begun four years earlier, over which Disney's heavy-handed corporate management actually had little control.

In 1991, subscribers to an Orlando computer bulletin-board service picked a Saturday in June for a group outing in a Disney World theme park. They spread the word locally with fliers in bars, advising all who showed up to wear red so they would stand out and be seen. That first Gay and Lesbian Day at the Magic Kingdom attracted a few hundred people. By 1995—the year that Disney announced it would offer domestic-partner benefits—the annual Gay Day in Orlando was drawing an estimated 32,000 people. Opponents took note. A growing backlash brought national media attention. Alarmed and fearful when Gay Day began, Disney initially tried to keep its head low, saying only that anyone had the right to buy a ticket to its theme parks. But as the event grew over the next few years, the company had to confront reality. Even before the benefits debate, Disney was made to deal with Gay Day. And it did so in a way that finally embraced the gay and lesbian communities with which Disney already had a winking alliance.

Gay Day led Disney to stand up to its conservative critics. Gay Day showed Disney that opponents, even when mobilized, couldn't tarnish the brand—or, more significantly, affect the bottom line. Gay Day made it easier for Disney itself to come out of the closet.

From *Dumbo* to Domestic-Partner Benefits

Disney's "family values" are nothing new, according to Rick Foglesong, a political science professor at Rollins College in Winter Park, Florida, who tracks Disney's activity in the state:

> Walt Disney built Disneyland because there were not amusement parks that were appropriate for families. As a grandfather and as a parent, he lamented that he could not take his kids to an amusement park—or didn't feel comfortable doing it—because of the carny types who were employed there. In fact, he gave instructions to his people not to hire people who had worked at boardwalk-type theme parks, because he wanted to keep that boardwalk element out.[2]

That determination to police disruptive influences was obvious again with the announcement, ten years after Disneyland's opening, that the company would build Walt Disney World outside of Orlando. The new, 27,000-acre site was deliberately vast and distanced from anything nearby to avoid a repeat of the clutter that had swiftly surrounded Disneyland. When plans for the Florida park were announced in 1966, Walt offered this none-too-prophetic assurance: "When [patrons] come into this world, we will take the blame for what goes on."

Tattooed workers were not the only workers shut out. As Richard V. Francaviglia pointed out in a 1981 essay, the Main Street U.S.A. of Disney's theme parks—a scaled-down version of an idealized small town, dotted with flower vendors, ice-cream parlors, and barbershop quartets—represents a turn-of-the-century Anglo vision, absent blacks and immigrants.³ Yet those groups were represented elsewhere in the original park. "Frontierland in the '50s was, ironically, a much more ethnically and racially diverse place than it is today—populated, like the real frontier, with multitudinous Indians and Mexicans, and even some black people," wrote Jon Weiner, a historian at the University of California at Irvine.⁴ In a 1958 article in *True West* magazine, Walt himself wrote of Frontierland's "Indian Villages." One of them, he wrote, contained a "forest of teepees, built exactly as the redskins made them, plus a tribe of Indians. They're friendly, though, and will perform their tribal dances." Old Disneyland maps also show a Casa de Fritos restaurant and Aunt Jemima's Pancake House, at which "Aunt Jemima" herself signed autographs.

In the 1960s, attacks on racial stereotypes of this sort accelerated their end. By the early 1970s, Disneyland's Indian Village had been remade into Bear Country, its entertainers converted to audio-animatronic robots. Tony Baxter, senior vice president of creative development at Walt Disney Imagineering (WDI), told Weiner the Indians' demise began when "the Indians got unionized—the dancers joined the . . . International Alliance of Theatrical Stage Employees (IATSE)."⁵ According to Baxter, the switch to Bear Country required "five shows a day minimum." Robots didn't complain or demand pay increases, and they performed on cue. By then, union affiliation also had doomed the Indian guides on the people-powered "Indian war canoes" (later renamed "Davey Crockett canoes"). The guides' mistake had been to join the Teamsters union. John Hench, the senior vice president of WDI, told Weiner: "They complained that the white people didn't know how to paddle. They said the work was too hard. They wanted motors put on the canoes." They were soon let go.⁶

Though these changes took place after Walt's death, they perpetuated his aversion to organized worker movements. A prolonged labor strike at the Disney studio in 1941 had been a huge turning point in Walt's relations with his employees. "Up to that time, the studio in Walt Disney's view was sort of a workers utopia—almost a kind of school for artists," says Steven Watts, author of *The Magic Kingdom: Walt Disney and the American Way of Life*.⁷ "The problem with the labor strike is that he was very old-fashioned in that populist way, and he believed in individualism." That outlook served him well in his studio's early days. But as the studio grew, a burgeoning bureaucracy developed that distanced Walt from his creative team, and wages grew uneven. The unfolding war in Europe and an overextension of the studio's efforts at the time added further economic pressures. When a group of animators, cartoonists, and staff people came together to seek union representation, "Walt Disney reacted very, very badly," says Watts. "He saw it as a sort of betrayal."

A walkout dragged on for months. Confrontations and fistfights erupted on picket lines outside the studio gates. About 40 percent of the workforce backed the protest. In anger, Walt walked out on settlement talks, leaving his brother Roy—who shared Walt's anti-union sentiment but balanced it with a practical business side—to work with government negotiators. Meanwhile, the episode started Walt on a slide in which his temperament "became darker and defensive and reactionary," says Watts. "This was a very embittering experience for Walt Disney, and it was one of the things that helped push him in a more conservative direction in the '40s and '50s."

An eventual agreement to allow union representation corrected inequities in the company by establishing a seniority system and pay rates across the board. "But I think it also made the Disney studio, according to much evidence I saw, a much more hard-nosed kind of place," says Watts, who summarized Walt's subsequent resolve: "If they want unions and they don't want the old way of doing things, by god we'll have unions, but we'll only sort of do what the unions demand we do and not do anything more."

Decades later, steely control remained a characteristic of corporate management. But that control was challenged by the company's growth. No longer simply a caretaker of Walt's cartoon characters and theme-park legacy, Eisner's Disney had diversified long before its 1996 merger with Capital Cities/ABC formed a then-unrivaled giant in entertainment production and distribution. At the time that diversity created contradictions aplenty. The animated features *The Little Mermaid, Pocahontas,* and *Beauty and the Beast* (both the film and the Broadway musical) had restored Disney's status as the dominant producer of family-friendly fare. But its book division also had released titles ranging from Ross Perot's anti-NAFTA screed, *The Dollar Crisis,* to *Growing Up Gay,* a humorous collection of coming-of-age tales by the comedy trio, Funny Gay Males. Meanwhile, on film, its Miramax division had released the gay-cleric film *Priest* and the unsettling *Kids,* an unrated (to avoid the equivalent of X) docudrama about aimless youth in the age of AIDS. Rapid expansion also meant some things slipped through the cracks: just before the 1995 release of *Powder*—a feature film about a boy with pale skin and mysterious powers—Disney presumably was surprised to learn the film's director had served jail time as a convicted child-sex offender. (Two years later, in 1997, Disney's Hollywood Records label would recall an album by an obscure rap act, Insane Clown Posse, on the same day of its release after red-faced executives learned too late of its obscenity-laced lyrics.) Starting not long after Eisner's arrival, advocates of traditional morality already had accused the company of abandoning standards set by Walt Disney. By the mid-1990s the opportunities for those voices to focus their attacks were starting to multiply.

Only one exception interrupted the company's progress: In 1994, Disney announced plans to build a historical theme park, Disney's America, outside of Washington, D.C. The howls over this plan caused an unprecedented retreat. But in all other matters of business and creative direction, the complaints were scattered, and Disney could easily ignore them. Besides, the company was charting its own course. As long as quarterly earnings continued to climb, Disney didn't need to answer to anyone.

Gay Day became the lightning rod critics needed to challenge that corporate strategy. Never mind that the event was imposed on Disney rather than initiated by it; by refusing to discourage the gathering, argued those critics, Disney condoned it. The irony is that Gay Day caused Disney to align itself with organizers whose smirking ambition—if they thought about the company at all—was to rub Disney the wrong way.

Its beginnings—as a mere social outing, organized by an Orlando computer-users group—couldn't have been more humble. "I don't think at the time we had any anticipation of [Gay Day] doing anything of this scale, or that it would have any influence on Disney making any decisions to benefit their own employees, or would influence the way they deal with outside groups trying to influence what they do," says Doug Swallow, who is credited as Gay Day's founder.

> Back in 1991 when we started it, it was truly [just] . . . why not tell everybody else about it at the bars and see who would show up? I'm sure there was a little bit of, you know, it'll be fun to see how Disney reacts to this. But it wasn't meant to be in-your-face—"Hey look at us, we're going to make a mess in your park." It was meant to be, "We're going to go out and have fun like everybody else." That was how it began.[8]

Disney's history with gay and lesbian communities is long and complex. Sean Griffin examined that relationship in *Tinker Belles and Evil Queens: The Walt Disney Company from the Inside Out*. Starting with the 1930s use of Mickey Mouse as a code phrase for gay, Griffin says, gay culture has affectionately embraced much of Disney's output, whether in animation, live-action films, TV series, theme parks, or merchandise.[9] The appeal, according to both Griffin and cultural analyst Jamie O'Boyle, lies in Disney's storytelling themes of inclusion. (This, says O'Boyle, despite the fact that, "When Walt first started, Mickey Mouse was the little irreverent guy kicking authority

Photograph by Michael McElroy; reprinted with permission.

figures in the butt. Walt's biggest supporters at the time were the political-theorist leftists."[10]) "Disney's core message for the past fifty years is that the underdog outsider always has something of value to offer," says O'Boyle, who studies Disney and has worked for the company as a consultant.

> People who refuse to recognize this are either fools or evil. When you are gay and have to come to terms with yourself, your family, and society in general, this message resonates with you. In fact, it's the core theme of all of our hero stories. Disney is not the only company that tells the story, but it's the only one that tells the story exclusively. Add that to the association with childhood, when sexuality was not an issue, and it's not surprising that all of show business has a strong attraction for gays . . . I'm not sure if I would call Disney "pro-gay." It's more like they are pro-values, and those values center around inclusion.

Although in the 1930s Walt is said to have stood by an animator who was arrested on a charge of homosexuality, any compassion vanished when the company's public image was at stake. In 1963, Tommy Kirk—a child actor in such live-action Disney films as *Old Yeller, The Shaggy Dog*, and *Swiss Family Robinson*—had his contract suspended "because of growing awareness of his homosexual orientation," says Griffin, whose book relates the story, based upon Kirk's published comments. "Supposedly [Kirk] got too frisky with a boyfriend at a public pool in Los Angeles, and the other boy's mother found out about it and went to Disney," he says. "They called Tommy in and fired him."

Not until 1978 did a gay group first attempt a large-scale event inside a Disney theme park. That year a group of West Hollywood bar owners, organized as the innocuous-sounding Los Angeles Bar and Restaurant Association, picked a date and secured a block of discounted tickets to be used during Disneyland's regular operating hours. The sponsors succeeded in keeping Disney in the dark about the nature of the gathering. "Disney didn't realize until a week before, and freaked," says Griffin.

According to his interviews with participants, the company "sort of made preparations for the worst. Live music was canceled at the last second so that there would be no encouragement for same-sex dancing. They beefed up security. They told people who were working that day, or at least for that night, that courtesy was optional." When as many as 10,000 people showed up, "it really became a major sort of war zone," says Griffin. "Not that it got violent or anything. But the people who attended that night—and it was mostly gay men who attended—were very aware of the fact that they were not welcome there." Some had something further to prove; groping, and more, broke out on rides, in bathrooms, behind bushes. "Things really got sort of out of hand in general between people, to the point where a number of gays and lesbians who worked at the park themselves were sort of shocked and appalled at what the visitors were doing," says Griffin.

Fooled once, Disney would not be fooled a second time. "It was not until the '80s, and very specific AIDS charity events, that you had anything going on like that [at Disneyland] again," he says, "and I'm sure there was much more careful surveying of who was asking for various things."

Even in the interim Disney took a high-profile stand against open homosexuality in its parks. To be sure, those parks had—and still have—unposted policies for conduct and appearance. For example, bare chests are not permitted, and park hosts have replaced shirts on guests whose clothing bore offending words or images; at Gay Day in 1998, a man whose drag outfit featured a purple gown was politely but firmly steered into a store on Main Street U.S.A. to pick out other apparel, at Disney's expense. Those policies also forbid overt and inappropriate sexual behavior by any guest, homosexual or not. As one gay supervisor at Disney World put it, "Anything that you wouldn't do in a mall, you shouldn't do here."[11] More than two decades after the opening of Disneyland, however, "inappropriate" for homosexuals still meant dancing together.

"We knew that Disney had a policy against same-sex dancing, and we knew that we were going to challenge it," says Crusader, the mono-named Palm Springs activist who carried out the challenge on September 13, 1980.[12] At an end-of-summer event called Date Night, Crusader—then nineteen and known as Andrew Exler—took to the dance floor of Disneyland's Tomorrowland Terrace with a male friend. Told by a security guard that they would have to find female partners, the two refused. Five guards escorted the pair to security, where they were separated, lectured on the policy, and told they could return to the park if they agreed not to dance; when they refused again, their hands were stamped with an "X." Says Crusader: "We were ejected and branded and tossed out of the park as though we had committed some sort of crime."

Four years later an Orange County, California, jury finally found Disney guilty of civil rights discrimination. Disney appealed, but in 1985 quietly dropped both the appeal and the policy and agreed to pay $25,000 for Crusader's legal fees. It was thus a surprise when, a year later, a similar squeeze was put on members of a gay student group from the University of California at Los Angeles who danced with same-sex partners in a Disneyland disco. The men later contacted Crusader, who joined them in a meeting with Disney representatives, along with an attorney for the American Civil Liberties Union. The resulting lawsuit was settled out of court. "I don't think there's been any problem since then," says Crusader.

That same year, 1986, Disney for the first time lent its name, as well as Disneyland, to a glittering "A-list," after-hours fund-raiser for AIDS Project Los Angeles. The company even pledged to match the money raised by ticket sales with an equal donation. Subsequently, "AIDS charity" became code language for a series of annual after-hours "gay nights" at Disneyland that continued without Disney sponsorship. Marketed to a gay and lesbian audience, the private events were organized by travel agencies that rented out the park, with proceeds to benefit AIDS service organizations. In the mid-1990s, however, a promoter came under attack for not sharing enough of its profit with the intended beneficiary, resulting one year in a boycott campaign. By 1997 such "gay nights" had run their course. The next year, Disney scaled back the number of private parties for which the park would be closed, and "gay night" was no more.

By contrast, Orlando's Gay Day had no activist or fund-raising agenda. Nor, despite its June timing, was it tied to that month's Gay Pride events. "All month long you're bombarded with 'give me money for this, give me money for that, donate here, donate there, fight for our rights.' It gets to be a bit much," says Doug Swallow. "I was just wanting to see something done for fun."

A computer software designer, Swallow was a subscriber to Compu-Who?, an Orlando-based computer bulletin-board service that linked local gays and lesbians, some of them Disney workers. Online members also met up with each other through regular group outings. In February 1991, Swallow was chatting about possible events with others online when "the idea just came: Why don't we go to Disney?" he says. In the theme-park culture of Orlando, a day at a Disney park is on par with a trip to the beach or an afternoon at the mall; many people buy annual park passes, and others get in for free through friends or family members who work there, making it just another place to hang out, even for off-duty employees. And so the activity was tacked onto the social calendar for early June, when a tourism lull also prompts Disney World to sell discount tickets to Florida residents.

But Swallow knew the potential impact. Working with the Orlando gay and lesbian community center, he had previously promoted an unofficial gay and lesbian day at the Central Florida Fair, with attendees encouraged to dress in red so they'd stand out. The goal there, he recalls, was nothing more subversive than to let straight people see gay people openly enjoying themselves in a shared public setting. The day at Disney simply offered the same thing on a bigger stage. A week before the event, Swallow tipped a columnist for the *Orlando Sentinel*. The result was a two-hundred-word item, beginning, "Should be a colorful crowd at Disney World this weekend. Central Florida homosexuals are being urged to turn out in force at the theme park and wear bright red to take part in The First Annual Official Unofficial Gay & Lesbian Day at the Magic Kingdom."[13] The item sparked debate on local radio and bought the free publicity that organizers would come to rely upon in subsequent years. Between five hundred and one thousand people showed up.

That first gathering caught Disney off guard, but was otherwise uneventful. To mark the second gathering, organizers printed their first red T-shirts, and sold all two hundred. It was again a mostly word-of-mouth event, says Swallow, although word now reached well beyond Orlando's gay community. With the memory of the 1978 episode at Disneyland not forgotten, Disney steeled itself for a repeat. Conversation overheard inside the park about a mass gathering—some of it in clandestine tones—fed suspicions that a protest was in the works. "I remember hearing people say, 'We need to make sure there's security around the Castle at three o'clock because something big's going to happen,'" recalls one gay Disney manager. "Well, the big thing that happened was that people got together at three to watch the parade. The company couldn't believe it. It was almost like the two groups had such little awareness of each other that it created this huge space of fear."[14]

Photograph by Michael McElroy; reprinted with permission.

Among the estimated five thousand who attended that year were a minority who saw it as a defiant political act. As at Disneyland fourteen years earlier, the chip-on-the-shoulder attitude didn't sit well with all who went or worked there. In response, about a dozen gay "cast members"—the title Disney gives to its theme-park employees—took it upon themselves the third year to embark on some image control of their own. Groups that showed up wearing red were welcomed outside the park and given the rules: Keep your shirts on. Avoid overt sexual comments and conduct. "To walk hand-in-hand is great; to French kiss in the middle of the street is inappropriate—not for Disney, but for us as a community," advised one greeter. Inside the park those greeters later acted as "queer police," stepping ahead of security to ensure that parade lines were not blocked and playfully obscene chants were redirected. "It was done tongue-in-cheek, but there was no question that this team of people was there to facilitate this event," recalls one gay Disney supervisor, who was among the volunteers. "And the crowd accepted it. It really was one of those epiphanies for me. People behaved." The greeters were never identified as Disney employees, and their hours were unpaid. Magic Kingdom management never endorsed their presence. "But I communicated with [management] regularly," says the supervisor, "and they never told me to stop."

Evidence of Disney's unease was everywhere. The company lined up shuttles to other theme parks for guests who complained, or gave them passes to return another day; in some instances, straight guests embarrassed to be caught wearing red shirts were given white ones. Most glaring were the sandwich-board signs placed that year at the Magic Kingdom's entrance, alerting guests that there was a large gathering of gays and lesbians inside. Homosexuals weren't the only ones offended; many heterosexuals also objected to what was, in effect, a warning. But participants from Orlando who were accustomed to the Disney culture saw history in the making: It was the first time Disney featured the words "gay" and "lesbian" so prominently. Antigay activists, meanwhile, interpreted the signs as proof of the company's collusion.

Disney struggled to keep its distance. But it grew more difficult as the focus on Gay Day widened—and as Swallow garnered advance headlines by mailing more than 125 news releases to gay and mainstream media. That third event, in 1993, drew coverage that included a day of mentions on CNN. When advance publicity reached a small group of parents at an eastern Florida middle school, the parents protested a field trip that coincided with Gay Day. But the kids wouldn't buy it. At a hastily arranged meeting at the school, student after student took the podium and told their parents to "grow up, there's room at Disney for everybody." And yet the bigger surprise followed: When the parents demanded a refund on their tickets, the company—whose policy of swiftly soothing its guests' concerns is legend—said no.

Disney, says Swallow, had started to develop a backbone.

Photograph by Michael McElroy; reprinted with permission.

It's Off to Work We Go . . .

Two years earlier, Sass Nielsen—then a technical writer at the Disney Studios in Burbank, California—asked to place a free notice in *Newsreel*, the company newsletter, advertising a meeting to gauge interest in a new employees group. The newsletter already carried notices for groups formed around hobbies and social activities. Disney even had an unofficial policy of kicking in two hundred dollars to help such groups get started. Nielsen wanted to launch a group for gays and lesbians. "She had a couple problems with them sort of coming up with various excuses not to run the ad," says Griffin, who pieced together his account from interviews with other participants. "And so eventually she just wrote a letter to Michael Eisner directly, saying, 'What's the deal here?'" Eisner intervened, and the meeting notice ran. By the end of its first gathering, in August 1992, the new group had a name: Lesbian and Gay United Employees (LEAGUE).

Nielsen's advocacy grew out of Hollywood Supports, a nonprofit group promoting awareness of AIDS and gay issues, and whose members included a few Disney employees. They thought a similar group might serve a purpose within their own company. At the time, Disney already had a year-old, company-wide written policy that protected employees from discrimination based on sexual orientation. This policy had emerged from negotiations with a local of the Hotel Employees and Restaurant Employees Union that represented 1,200 food service workers at Disneyland. LEAGUE began a push to extend health and medical benefits to same-sex partners of Disney employees. Or at least Nielsen herself pushed. "Sass was very much trying to make [LEAGUE] more of an activist, in-the-front-lines type of thing, which turned off both the bigwigs at the studio and a number of the people who were possible members of the group," says Griffin.

Disney's skittishness was obvious. A memo in the wake of LEAGUE's launch specifically forbade employee groups from advancing a "political agenda," says Griffin. "Disney was really worried about that possibility, since LEAGUE came out of Hollywood Supports, which came out of ACT-UP and Queer Nation and that whole early '90s activism." To the company, a social club was the only acceptable purpose for LEAGUE, and that's how LEAGUE primarily defined itself. Image-conscious corporate suits also objected when, just months after LEAGUE's founding, its members created a banner for pride events that displayed a pink triangle and the words, "Part of the Family at the Walt Disney Company." As LEAGUE members readied for the April 25, 1993, national gay rights march in Washington, D.C., Griffin says, "the company told them they couldn't use the Disney name on their banner." The group quickly doctored the wording so it read, "Part of the Family at THAT Company." But the marchers' Mickey Mouse ears and Mickey Mouse balloons erased any doubts. (Disney relaxed its opposition the next year, and the group has marched with the original banner in every Los Angeles gay pride parade since 1994.)

LEAGUE established Disney as the first film and television studio with a gay employees group. But that pioneering effort did not make change come any faster than the company could handle it. Among major Hollywood studios, Disney was one of the last holdouts when, in October 1995, its decision to offer health benefits to partners of gays and lesbians finally was announced—quietly—in an employee newsletter. Before making that decision, top management had spent three years mulling over its impact; debate focused less on the bottom line than on public perception.

Incremental steps taken up to that point had been mostly outside the public eye, including such symbolic gestures as extending to same-sex partners the theme park passes that were a standard perk for spouses of straight employees. Even the nondiscrimination clause seemed to be more like an update than a groundbreaking addition. But the determination of conservative political and religious groups to debate morality guaranteed a firestorm over any public embrace of gay workers. And in the corporate arena, nothing was more public than rewriting an insurance policy to add same-sex partners.

Meanwhile, as airlines, beer companies, and national gay magazines began to sign on as sponsors to the event and the spillover activities that were starting to take root, Gay Day's momentum grew. And the media—always eager to poke at Disney's virginal veneer—kept the controversy alive. In Florida each June, spokesmen for the Christian Coalition and the American Family Association encountered a press eager to disseminate their views. Calls from religious conservatives for Disney to halt Gay Day mounted. Escalating complaints aimed at the company were sometimes as goofy as the one by the American Life League, an obscure group whose members claimed to see S-E-X spelled out in a cloud of dust in *The Lion King* and who insisted that a line of dialogue in Aladdin whispered, "Good teenagers, take off your clothes."[15] (In January 1999, the company did recall 3.4 million videos of *The Rescuers* after finding that animators inserted a split-second frame of a naked woman.) But the prolonged pull through the mud only served to toughen the target of the attacks.

Finally, Disney and Eisner would take no more. For both Disney and its opponents, the last straw was the launch of domestic-partner benefits. A subsequent letter to Eisner from fifteen Florida lawmakers condemned the policy as "anti-family" and added, "We strongly disapprove of your inclusion and endorsement of a life-style that is unhealthy, unnatural and unworthy of special treatment."[16] The Florida Baptist Convention—citing Gay Day, partner benefits, and the company's ties to cruise ships that offer alcohol and gambling—urged members to stop patronizing Disney. The Assemblies of God urged its 2.5 million members to boycott "until Disney returns to its former stance of producing products of high family and moral values." When Ellen DeGeneres came out, both in real life and as a fictional TV character, leaders of the fifteen-million-member Southern Baptist Convention—America's largest Protestant denomination—followed the lead of their Florida delegates and imposed their own boycott, citing Disney's "Christian-bashing, family-bashing, pro-homosexual agenda."[17]

Wall Street scoffed—five months after the Southern Baptist vote, Disney's stock was up roughly 10 percent. So did Disney, which at last rose out of its bunker. The statement that followed would have been considered tame coming from any other source, but in Disney's corporate culture it was jaw-dropping. "We find it curious that a group that claims to espouse family values would vote to boycott the world's largest producer of wholesome family entertainment," it said. In other words: Go ahead. Abandon Disney. Where else can you turn?

"It concerns me that they're ignoring the facts," spat corporate spokesman John Dreyer in December 1995, following the Florida Baptists' resolution. "This year we produced more family-values entertainment of every kind than we have in any other year of our seventy-plus-year history. Our Disney brand of entertainment makes us the world's leading producer of entertainment for every family."[18]

Manning the front lines, Eisner himself sat down for an interview with *60 Minutes*. Of Gay Day, he said:

> The homosexual organizations arrange that day themselves. We do not put up signs that say, "No Blacks Allowed," "No Jews Allowed," "No Homosexuals Allowed." As long as they are discreet and handle themselves properly, are dressed properly, they're welcome in our doors, and I think it would be a travesty in this country to exclude anybody.[19]

Of critics, he said: "We're large, and when somebody attacks us, it gets their agenda in the news." As for the peaking attacks on Disney's content, he added: "[W]hen somebody says Pocahontas is anti-Christian, or anti-Jewish, or anti-black, or anti-Native American, I say, inside, deep down—they're nuts, they really are."

Says Doug Swallow: "It was amazing to finally see [expressed in words] what I think everybody at Disney thought."

Gay Patrons Bring Gay Dollars

A month after the third Gay Day—at which gay Disney employees acted on their own to police the crowd's behavior—management asked one of the volunteers to return a phone call to an angry guest. The visitor was gay, and livid about the signs he'd seen at the entrance. When the employee also identified himself as gay, the guest called him an Uncle Tom; the sympathetic employee could only reply that progress was incremental, and told him to come back the next year to see how the signs evolved. "As an activist, I knew where he was coming from," says the employee, a seventeen-year Disney World worker. "But I also knew he had no concept of what it takes to move a corporation this size."

Indeed, Disney's ever-expanding corporate embrace means that the company may be doing the right thing in one area but not in another. And for many progressives, Disney presents a real political dilemma. It has won plaudits for its stance on rights for gay employees—still a rare occurrence, given that only 2,900 employers in 1999 offered domestic-partner benefits (and 2,100 of those were directly linked to a San Francisco city ordinance), according to a report from the Human Rights Campaign (HRC).[20] And yet Disney also has been a target of the anti-sweatshop movement, condemned by consumers, religious leaders, and such human rights groups as the National Labor Committee—the same NLC that charged Kathie Lee Gifford with enabling the exploitation of teenagers and women garment workers in Central America. Shareholders repeatedly have been rebuffed in their efforts to require better wages for Third World workers who produce toys and clothing such as Pocahontas pajamas and Lion King T-shirts for pennies a day in the apparel sweatshops of Haiti, Burma, and Indonesia.[21] Moreover, the company continues to strong-arm its unions: about two thousand camera and equipment operators were locked out of their jobs at Disney's ABC unit for seventy-four days in 1998, and when a few costumed performers called in sick one day that same year during a protracted union negotiation in Orlando, they were suspected of strike activity and fired.

There is an obvious connection between Disney's benevolence toward gay patrons and its mean-spirited attitude toward workers in general: money. After all, the decision to finally offer domestic-partner benefits was made not because it was the right thing to do, but because it was necessary to keep benefits competitive with others in the film and TV industry. But does the profit motive wash out any contribution that Disney has made to the advancement of gay rights? For identity-conscious activists, the answer to that question may not be so obvious.

"Gay Day put [company executives'] feet to the flame," says a gay middle manager at Disney World:

> It was a time when the company had to put up or shut up on the issue. They didn't do well initially. But because it's recurring, they keep learning from their mistakes, to the point where they now recognize what a positive financial impact Gay Day has. There's always people who want to use it as a hook for their own negative, bigoted experience. But the company has prepared themselves to deal with that piece of it.

And the posted signs did evolve. With their second appearance, in 1994, the alarmist tone was softened, replaced with language that said "members of the gay community have chosen to visit the Magic Kingdom today in their recognition of Gay and Lesbian Pride Month" and that Disney "does not discriminate against anyone's right to visit the Magic Kingdom." After a brief display in 1995, the signs were removed for good. (Perhaps not coincidentally, park management was shuffled that same year, and two long-time, pre-Eisner-era Disney World executives were forced into retirement.)

Photograph by Michael McElroy; reprinted with permission.

The next year, 1996, Disney welcomed a film crew from Gay Entertainment Television, which produced a thirty-minute documentary-style video on Gay Day for its syndicated programming. Then, in 1997, Disney played host to two gay-targeted events as bookends to the traditional first-Saturday-in-June gathering. An Orlando gay newspaper, *Watermark*, rented a Disney World water park for a Friday night event and sold 2,500 tickets, and Los Angeles–based circuit party promoter Jeffrey Sanker secured the Disney–MGM Studios theme park for a post–Gay Day dance that drew similar numbers. Both events have since established themselves as private, annual, after-hours affairs that compete with Gay Day's founding vision to mix gay and straight crowds in a setting open to all. But Disney's willingness to work with the private promoters shows how the company has come to recognize the bottom-line benefits of a weekend it initially feared.

Minimal membership in an Orlando chapter of LEAGUE suggests no passion to organize; openly gay and lesbian workers at Disney World portray a work environment where they are free to be themselves, where gays and lesbians in management positions are proof that no one is discriminated against because of sexual orientation, and where the coming-out process at all ages is eased by coworkers who already have gone through it. "In the areas where I've been working, there's an atmosphere not just of tolerance but of acceptance," says one gay manager at the theme parks. "The heterosexuals who work with us are part of our family, just as we are part of theirs."

Ten years into its existence, that simple truth still filters through Orlando's Gay Day as well, says organizer Doug Swallow. There's even an equivalent these days on the West Coast; absent "gay nights," the California contingent launched an annual Gay Day at Disneyland in 1998. "The effect it's had on the corporate culture of Disney has been a positive one, because it lets people stop wasting energy on hiding and start spending their energy on company business. And anything that can do that is certainly good for the company," says Swallow. "And, I don't know if this would be a long-term trend, but if you can stop bowing down to interest groups every time they want to fuck you in the ass, then maybe that's a good thing, too."

And yet Disney still has ground to make up; its message remains a mixed one. In 1998, for example, Disney staffed an employee recruitment booth at Orlando's gay pride parade, marking the company's first official participation in the event. The appearance was even more significant because it coincided with civic hand-wringing over a rainbow flag display that made national news when televangelist Pat Robertson warned the city of Orlando, which permitted the display, to brace for divine wrath in the form of "earthquakes, tornadoes and possibly a meteor." But while Disney World management that year also designated Gay Pride Month for the first time on its in-house calendar, there was a noticeable absence of events to mark it. Executives who championed diversity among employees—with a response that otherwise included such events as panel discussion and special guest performers—still seemed fearful of antagonizing potential opponents, even within their own ranks.

Thus, it was again groundbreaking when, the next year, 1999, employee diversity teams that advise individual units of the Disney World resort sponsored a "family picnic" for Pride Month and arranged for the Orlando Gay Chorus to be hired for a separate, behind-the-scenes concert for Disney workers. Such small steps represent progress in the opinions of gay workers and outside advocates, who observed how Gay Day evolved for the company from a potentially paralyzing event to one that brings both patrons and profits, and who see reason to cheer the future. As one Gay Chorus member—who is also an activist and a Disney employee—said at the time, "When they see that the theater doesn't burn down, maybe next year they'll let the chorus perform in front of guests."

Notes

1. Stefan Kanfer, *Serious Business: The Art and Commerce of Animation in America from Betty Boop to Toy Story* (Scribner, 1997), 51–52.
2. Rick Foglesong, "Does Disney Care?" *Orlando Weekly*, December 14–20, 1995, p. 11. Unless otherwise noted, other quotes from Foglesong in this essay come from interviews with the author, December 1995.
3. Richard V. Francaviglia, "Main Street USA: A Comparison/Contrast of Streetscapes in Disneyland and Walt Disney World," *Journal of Popular Culture* 15.1 (summer 1981).
4. As reported by Jon Weiner, "Tall Tales and True," *The Nation*, January 31, 1994, 133.
5. Ibid.
6. Ibid.
7. This and all following quotes from Steven Watts come from an interview with the author, June 30, 1999.
8. This and all following quotes from Doug Swallow come from an interview with the author, June 5, 1999.
9. Quotes and observations from Sean Griffin come from an interview with the author, June 21, 1999.
10. Quotes from Jamie O'Boyle come from an interview with the author, August 5, 1999.
11. This quote from the Disney World supervisor comes from an interview with the author, August 15, 1999. Because midlevel managers in the theme parks are told that only designated spokespersons are allowed to speak to the media, the supervisor consented to an interview only with the promise of anonymity.
12. Quotes from Crusader (née Andrew Exler) come from an interview with the author, August 5, 1999.

13. Bob Morris, "Gays and Lesbians Plan Day at Disney World," *The Orlando Sentinel*, June 3, 1991.
14. Disney's theme-park workers—especially those who have risen above the ranks of hourly employees to become department managers or supervisors—live in fear of being fired for their outspokenness. These and all quotes obtained from employees during interviews with the author were given only with the promise of anonymity.
15. Foglesong, "Does Disney Care?" 10.
16. Don Lee, "Disney's Health Benefits for Gays Draws Protest," *Los Angeles Times*, October 19, 1995, p. D-1.
17. Foglesong, "Does Disney Care?" 10.
18. Quotes from Walt Disney Company spokesman John Deyer come from an interview with the author, December 1995.
19. Transcript from *60 Minutes* segment titled "Taking on Disney," broadcast November 23, 1997.
20. For more on HRC's "State of the Workplace" report, see: http://www.hrc.org/feature1/stwork.html.
21. Andrew Ross, *The Celebration Chronicles: Life, Liberty and the Pursuit of Property Values in Disney's New Town* (New York: Ballantine Books: 1999), 296–97.

Imagining the Gay–Labor Alliance: A Forum

To conclude this volume, the editors have asked four activists from different backgrounds and professional sectors to reflect upon a single question: What is the practical potential for a gay–labor alliance? We have asked them to answer that question from the perspective of their own personal history and professional experience. Responding to this question are Urvashi Vaid, director of the Policy Institute of the National Gay and Lesbian Task Force (NGLTF); Kent Wong, director of the Center for Labor Research and Education at the University of California, Los Angeles; Desma Holcomb, director of research for UNITE (Union of Needletrades, Industrial and Technical Employees); and U.S. Representative Barney Frank (D.-Mass.).

Getting There Means Mapping Here: Challenges to Collaboration between a Workers' Rights Movement and Today's LGBT Movement

Urvashi Vaid

The possibility of radical collaboration between organized labor and the lesbian, gay, bisexual, and transgender (LGBT) movement requires consideration of several sets of threshold challenges: the challenge of developing an economic analysis inside the LGBT movement; the realities of how economic, gender, racial, and educational class differences operate in American society and inside the LGBT movement; and the challenge of constructing a real, pragmatic, multi-identity, progressive movement. I do not think such a partnership is possible without discussion of these challenges, and the future depends on how we choose to approach them. Frankly, a broad partnership may never be possible because there is real disagreement among us about these issues.

What's the Frequency, Kenneth?

To a large extent, the lack of a shared political and economic analysis to ground the work of the LGBT movement is a problem we share with a wide range of social justice movements.[1] The civil rights movements of our times have been primarily directed toward the goal(s) of achieving equality. Such goals are distinct from the goals of movements for economic rights. Indeed, one can draw a distinction between movements for civil rights, with their focus on equality, and movements for human rights, which have as their focus justice (including economic justice).[2] As a movement launched by a people who are still very far away from achieving full civil equality, the LGBT movement has not spent a great deal of time dealing with the social justice values that ground its work.

Progressives have run away from discussions of sexuality, gender roles, family structure, individual, and institutional racism—issues arising from the conflict between religious doctrine and public policy. These are so-called cultural issues. The right has brilliantly (if inaccurately) addressed the anxieties inherent in these issues and has come up with answers to address these anxieties. Strategically, they have created a backlash analysis for—and a movement against—every contemporary progressive social justice movement, from feminism to civil rights to gay rights to environmentalism.

The right has also articulated a clear and strong economic perspective: libertarian economic values (which argue for privatization of public services and unfettered markets) have replaced traditional conservative economic principles (which favor limited government) as the dominant approach to the economy. Indeed, the right has grown because it married its long-standing corporate-elite driven economic agenda (free markets are best) with a clear cultural agenda (traditional values are functional values for American society).

To this combination of backlash, nostalgia, and strategic action, the left and the liberal middle have, on one hand, responded with a scapegoating of identity politics, posing it as the reason why the left is disempowered; and, on the other hand, an appeasement of the right, an acquiescence to and endorsement of conservative ideas in the politics of centrism. The ruling premise in contemporary progressive discourse is the liturgy of '60s New Left patriarchs, who argue that identity politics derailed a preexisting, universal, class-based social change movement. The fact that the old movement could not be broadly successful because of its racial, gender, and class composition is ignored. In this flawed analysis the only hope for progressive renewal lies in the cessation of the politics of difference and the resumption of a politics of deference to the old universals. Mythologizing the old days (in the form perfected by right-wing nostalgics), the patriarchs of the left ignore the value, energy, exciting ideas, and pragmatism found in the identity-based movements. They fail to realize what the newly revived labor movement today is showing to be true: by paying attention to gender, race, sexual orientation, and other kinds of "identities," and by incorporating critiques that gave rise to identity-based movements, movements for workers' rights and for a fairer economy can find new strength.

In response to the right, many good people working within identity-based movements have called for more single-issue politics, not less; more focus on narrow agendas, rather than a focus on broader objectives of social justice. Inside the LGBT movements, for example, gay progressives are not the dominant voices. Gay moderates and conservatives for the most part urge our people to focus solely on LGBT issues—defined quite narrowly as issues pertaining to sexual orientation, as if it can in all instances be severed from other human characteristics, like gender, economic privilege, race, ethnicity, or even religion. We are urged not to "dilute" our movement with involvement in broader debates. Parallels to this argument can be found inside other identity-based movements, such as in black politics today, where calls for nationalism and particularism are also on the rise.

There is another view. And that is the view of those of us who are inside these identity-based groups, inside the single-issue organizations—those who respect the value and strength we have gained from working here; who are committed to ending homophobia or racism or sexism; who also see the connections between these systems of exclusion and prejudice; and who long for a movement that moves "through" identity, not somehow "beyond" it. We want a movement that is not either-or, but both. We believe that a renewed progressive movement of the new century ought to approach social problems holistically. It ought to reconstruct and reimagine the economic and social systems under which we live so that it does not structurally reproduce inequality, heterosexism, homophobia, racism, poverty, and human misery.

The LGBT Economic Analysis?

To the extent that we have an economic agenda in our movement, it is an agenda developed by middle-class and upper-middle-class people, who are the most active constituents and constructors of the movement we currently have. To date, very few analyses and no studies have been done examining the possible differences in priorities, policy goals, and political aspirations between LGBT people of different classes.[3] To start with an admission of class bias is not to put down the amazing leaders, funders, and workers who have built a wonderful and thriving movement for LGBT equality in the past five decades. Rather it is to enable us to examine, with clear eyes, what the underlying economic assumptions of our political movement are. I think it is fair to say that the economic assumptions that underlie our movement are uncritically promarket, procorporate, and probusiness far more than they are prolabor. This is logical and historically based: each of these forces—the market, corporate America, business, and capitalism in general—have been central to the emergence of gay identities and to the expansion of equality for LGBT people. Historian John D'Emilio, for example, makes the argument that the postwar economy's creation of a mobile labor pool, large numbers of single workers living away from families of origin in urban centers, and economic security gave rise to new possibilities of sexual experience and community.[4]

Within the LGBT movement, there has been a fairly uncritical acceptance of the policy implications of the new libertarianism. So, for example, at the very instant that our people's needs require more government funding, more resources for social services of all kinds (youth programs, senior programs, counseling, crisis intervention, hate-crime victim programs, health clinics, prevention programs, and so forth), we are part of a larger electorate that is increasingly supporting candidates and parties that argue for cutbacks in social services and in the taxes that pay for these programs.[5] Ironically, calls for less government and cutbacks in social services appeal to many of us at the same instant that our service organizations make arguments for more government funding.

Another example of the lack of coherence in the LGBT movement's economic analysis is the movement's silence on broad policy debates that have clear ramifications for people in our communities who are poor or working class. Despite the fact that the welfare reform act of 1996 clearly targeted single mothers and fathers, had in it outrageous notions of what were "socially sanctioned" relationships and what were not, and specifically and adversely impacted LGBT parents, hardly any LGBT voices nationally were raised in the policy debates. The majority of gay activists still do not see the welfare reform act as having anything to do with their gay and lesbian lives and their desires for family creation. And the impact of these policies on the lives of poor gay men, lesbians, bi and trans people (of all colors) has, to this date, been undocumented. Similarly, Medicaid reform is not a central gay and lesbian issue for the national movement, despite the fact that over one half of all gay and bisexual men with HIV receive their health care as a result of this poverty program.

It is important to note that a thoughtful critique of the reliance on markets and corporate support has emerged within the LGBT movement. Writers like Michael Bronski, Sarah Schulman, Amy Gluckman, and Betsy Reed, among others, have been raising this issue for the past decade. Questions are being debated. For example, is it possible to accept corporate underwriting for conferences and organizations and mount a fair critique of those companies' practices as well? Is it possible for LGBT publications to promote the results of their readership surveys to advertisers while being careful not to represent these data as representative of the entire LGBT population?[6] Is it possible for LGBT employee associations in corporate contexts to be champions of workers' rights in a broader way, to work to insure that the corporations' policies are socially responsible as well as profitable? This blending of goals—of social responsibility as an economically beneficial goal—is possible and needed.

Labor and LGBT People: Ideas for Collaboration

There are at least three promising sites for collaboration between a labor movement interested in social justice that includes LGBT people and an LGBT movement interested in a fairer economy. The first arena is in elections. The second is in campus organizing. And the third is in workplace organizing. There are other possibilities for collaboration, but I am going to focus on these three.

The potential for joint electoral work is real and untapped. The LGB vote nationally (data do not exist on the transgender vote) has ranged from 5 percent of the electorate in the presidential election of 1996 to 4.2 percent in the lower-turnout, midterm election of 1998. This is a sizable percentage of a national electorate. Studies of the LGB vote done by Rutgers University political scientist Robert Bailey reveal that the LGB vote generally identifies as more liberal than the general electorate, is more heavily Democrat (about two-thirds in the last election and even greater in earlier national elections), and votes in ways that are similar to union households.[7] The potential for an electoral coalition between a prolabor vote and LGBT voters is very real, but it requires investment by unions in grassroots voter identification, voter mobilization initiatives, and voter education efforts. To date, the tremendous electoral campaigns mounted by the AFL-CIO in 1996 and 1998, and the money invested by labor in political elections has not targeted LGBT voters.

The first step in a labor and gay movement collaboration must be the funding of systematic voter identification of progay, pro-union voters on a state-by-state basis. Voter identification can be done in a variety of ways: through phone bank campaigns to voter lists, through direct mail or through grassroots precinct—walking and door-knocking campaigns, the strategy promoted by NGLTF Policy Institute Training Initiative coordinator, Dave Fleischer. It bears stating that very little such work is presently being done systematically around the country. In states like Oregon that have done voter identification, collaboration with labor unions and women's organizations have paid for the organizing and outreach efforts. As a result, the statewide gay group in Oregon boasts a voter mailing list of over 150,000 progay, prounion, prochoice voters. Such a database is invaluable in organizing for progressive candidates and organizing against antigay, antiworker referenda. So, for example, in Florida's Dade County, we anticipate that an antigay referendum will be placed on the ballot by the Christian Coalition in 2000. The anticipated referendum will try to repeal a duly passed human rights ordinance in the county. In organizing the Save Dade coalition, which has been formed to defend the ordinance, NGLTF has promoted grassroots voter outreach and voter identification strategies. As a result, the Save Dade organization has systematically identified over fifteen thousand voters who are supportive of the ordinance (an increase in their database from the zero voters they started out with!). Labor funding and involvement in this kind of project would be invaluable in many sites where communities anticipate ballot measure attacks. The voter databases that are built through these strategies are resources that can be used again and again.

Another kind of electoral collaboration is possible around candidates. Unions can lend their weight to the gay movement by insisting that one of the criteria candidates meet to earn union support is support for LGBT civil rights measures. Reciprocally, gay political action committees (when they are progressive and nonpartisan) could also require a pro-union screen in their candidate endorsement process. Finally, an innovative and practical collaboration could also take place on voter education materials, requiring union literature to include sexual orientation and LGBT literature to address workers' rights.

The campus movement provides another site for cross-movement work. Today we are witnessing the emergence of a new, economically based, proworker student movement. This exciting development is the result of several factors. For one, it has been fostered by the thoughtful efforts of union leaders and the good work of the AFL-CIO Organizing Institute (OI). Through its Union Summer Program, the OI has systematically reached out to train student and youth activists to become labor organizers. For another, the contradictions of the global economy are hard to evade for anyone committed to workers' rights and fairness. Disparities in wages between managers and workers, the exploitation of labor internationally through the relocation of factories and paying of substandard wages, the loss of jobs to U.S. workers through downsizing have all been noticed and are deeply unpopular among large sectors of the American publics.

To date, the existing student movement for LGBT equality and rights has not overtly supported the new student movement against sweatshop labor. These student movements provide a wonderful testing ground for collaboration and for the arguments and strategies that we need in the broader effort to forge a connection between labor and progressive queers. Again, we must remember that not all LGBT people will ever agree with the idea that a gay student movement ought to have a progressive economic analysis—that political diversity is something we must respect. But in fact many LGBT student activists are involved in United Students against Sweatshops, and the practical connections they are trying to make between sexuality and economics have a lot to teach activists in the broader progressive LGBT movement.

The final arena for greater collaboration exists in the pro-LGBT workplace movement. The existence of a growing number of LGBT employee associations is a wonderful development for gay workers in many contexts. These workplace groups have pushed for internal reforms and policy changes that have materially improved the lives of gay employees in major companies and in unions. I think a strategy that strives to educate employee associations about the goals and priorities of the gay union movement and about why and how the union movement has helped LGBT workers would be a great beginning point. In this arena (as in others) there is a tremendous need for data—for more studies of workplace discrimination, for testing different theories of why discrimination takes place in the workplace and what can be done to eliminate it. Collaborations between union activists and LGBT workplace organizers to secure such data and to fund such research would be enormously helpful.

Thinking Even More Broadly

For those who want to build a renewed progressive movement that strives to coalesce the existing streams of progressive social justice movements into one powerful river, there are several parallel tasks to be undertaken. Indeed, what is required is nothing less than a multifaceted attempt to reconfigure a progressive movement out of the progressive wings of identity-based and economic-justice movements. Among those advocating such a renewal of the left are activists and scholars associated with a small working group in New York City called the Center for Progressive Renewal (CPR), a project supported by the NGLTF Policy Institute. CPR attempts to build relationships among progressives working in different sectors of the left in New York City, and develops strategy on how a left could be revived.

Creating progressive renewal will require the development of multi-issue organizations dedicated to movement building, collaboration, and information exchange; the development of a broad progressive political platform to articulate what we are fighting for; and lots more discussion and strategy development among the leaders of presently autonomous, single-issue movements so that we might come together in a new, powerful consensus. I am not talking about coalitions (which evaporate when the common goal is achieved or lost) or alliances (which imply a tactical expediency), but an organizing strategy that aims to build a common movement. I am speaking of a movement born out of the understandings of intersectionality—connections between issues, the private and the public, the racial and the gendered. Movements for race, gender, and sexual liberation have contributed these understandings to the previously straight, white, male-dominated left.

This strategy for progressive renewal rests on several assumptions about the current landscape of progressive movements and leadership:

- that an economic agenda must be linked to a cultural vision;
- that a critical core of progressive activists exists today who are willing to work across single-issue identities to create some new common theoretical and organizing ground;
- that relationships between leaders and activists at the local level hold the key to the progressive future;
- that the policy work already done by single-issue think tanks and academic scholars needs to be distributed and debated more widely so that we can arrive at a progressive platform;
- and that the visibility of a democratic progressive movement needs to be increased in this country.

While greater collaborations between an LGBT progressive movement and organized labor are possible without the construction of a movement that can hold both, the chances of success in achieving the goals of economic justice are greater if we aim to create a common movement.

Notes

For the good ideas contained in this essay, I thank Radhika Balakrishnan, Luke Harris, Laura Flanders, Kimberlé Crenshaw, and Rachel Timoner especially, as well as the scores of people who have given comments and reactions to the Center for Progressive Renewal ("CPR, because the left needs it!" is our motto), of which I am part.

1. This section is indebted to the discussions among a network of academics and organizers in the Center for Progressive Renewal, based in New York City.

2. For help in clarifying the distinction between civil rights and human rights, I am indebted to Loretta Ross from the Center for Human Rights Education. CHRE works to promote the International Declaration of Human Rights and the frameworks of the international human rights movement as a vehicle for U.S. movements to break through identity-based limitations. This is also the argument I made in *Virtual Equality: The Mainstreaming of Gay and Lesbian Liberation* (New York: Anchor Books, 1996).

3. The National Gay and Lesbian Task Force Policy Institute, which I run, has launched a Racial and Economic Justice Initiative. Its goal, in part, is to examine systematically some of these issues, and to gather and present data on the political priorities, life-realities, and goals of different economic sectors of our broad LGBT communities. One excellent resource for people interested in reading more on economics and LGBT politics is Amy Gluckman and Betsy Reed, eds., *Homo-Economics: Capitalism, Community, and Lesbian and Gay Life* (New York and London: Routledge, 1997).

4. See John D'Emilio, "Capitalism and Gay Identity," in *Powers of Desire: The Politics of Sexuality*, ed. Ann Snitow, Christine Stansell, and Sharon Thompson (New York: Monthly Review Press, 1983), 100–13; Julie Matthaei, "The Sexual Division of Labor, Sexuality and the Lesbian/Gay Liberation," in *Review of Radical Political Economics 7*, no. 2 (fall 1998): 1–37; M. V. Lee Badgett, "A Queer Marketplace: Books on Lesbian and Gay Consumers, Workers and Investors," *Feminist Studies* 23, no. 3 (fall 1997): 607–32.

5. Studies of the LGB vote in national elections from 1990–98 show that a growing number of self-identified LGB voters have favored Republican candidates. This has occurred in an era in which the GOP is most strongly identified with a curtailment of government expenditures to help solve social problems. So, in 1998, the LGB vote in the national congressional election formed 4.2 percent of the electorate, and over a third of that vote went to Republican candidates. See Robert Bailey, *Out and Voting: The GLB Vote in Congressional House Elections 1990–1998*, NGLTF Policy Institute, 1999. See also the 1998 version of that same report.

6. For an analysis of the difference between market research income data and other kinds of data to develop a true picture of GLB income, see M.V. Lee Badgett, *Income Inflation: The Myth of Affluence among GLB People* (New York and Northampton, Mass.: National Gay and Lesbian Task Force Policy Institute and the Institute for Gay and Lesbian Strategic Studies, 1998).

7. Ibid. See also, Robert Bailey, *Gay Politics, Urban Politics* (New York: Columbia University Press, 1999).

Toward a Gay–Labor Alliance

Kent Wong

Within the past thirty years, several AFL-CIO constituency groups that represent the interests of people of color and women within the labor movement have been established. The two most recent constituency groups have been the Asian Pacific American Labor Alliance (APALA) founded in 1992 and Pride at Work (PAW) in 1998. For the first time in history, the AFL-CIO has recognized the importance and role of lesbians and gays within the labor movement. The AFL-CIO has committed funds to Pride at Work, opened a national office, and hired an executive director. APALA celebrates the selection of Kipukai Kuali'i, an APALA member and Pacific Islander gay man, as Executive Director of Pride at Work.

Under the new leadership of John Sweeney and his administration, the AFL-CIO has allocated more resources to sustaining labor and community alliances, reaching out to women, people of color, immigrants, and now to lesbians and gays. The recognition and support of Pride at Work and the conscious inclusion of gay and lesbian issues within labor's agenda mark a radical departure from years past, when gays and lesbians were ignored and disregarded by the leadership of the American labor movement. This change provides new opportunities for lesbian/gay/bisexual/transgender activists within the labor movement to build a strong gay–labor alliance, forged around concrete activities and common struggle.

Fundamentally, this new alliance should strive to create a movement that organizes for economic justice, civil and human rights, and political action. This movement must ensure that civil rights and human rights are not marginalized but are embraced as an integral part of workers' rights.

While unions have generally responded favorably to legislation that calls for an end to discrimination based on sexual orientation, there are other, more specific issues of gender identity and HIV status that also need to be addressed. Unions must speak out against all forms of harassment in the workplace, beyond the employer-employee relationship. This includes actively opposing employee-to-employee harassment based on sexual orientation as well as gender, race, national origin, or immigration status. Labor unions should be at the forefront of demanding full domestic-partnership rights. The challenge to lesbian and gay–labor unionists is to educate the rest of the labor movement about the particular issues that impact their community.

I am excited about the emergence of a gay–labor alliance and, as a member of APALA, I look forward to greater collaboration between APALA and Pride at Work. Hopefully, the selection of someone knowledgeable about communities of color to lead the national Pride at Work will encourage greater collaboration between Pride at Work, other AFL-CIO constituency groups, and other movements for social justice, inside and outside the labor movement. Collaboration between the Asian Pacific labor community and gay rights groups is significantly advanced by the leadership of someone who is familiar with both the Asian Pacific community and the gay and lesbian community.

Those of us who have worked to build the Asian Pacific American Labor

241

Alliance are familiar with the challenge of building a national organization and recruiting a core of union activists from across the country who must meet locally as well as nationally. We know the difficulties of developing and advancing an agenda that has impact and meaning for the diverse members of our community. Fundamentally, however, our interests are to build a more inclusive movement for social and economic justice.

Lessons from APALA

I served as Founding President of the Asian Pacific American Labor Alliance from 1992 to 1997, and I would like to share some of our experiences in the hope they may be of some use to our sisters and brothers in the lesbian/gay/bisexual/transgender community. The Founding Convention of the Asian Pacific American Labor Alliance was held in May 1992. APALA provided a forum for Asian Pacific American labor activists to gather together. For the first time, we were not alone: the only Asian labor activist in a local, the only Asian face at a conference or convention. Prior to the formation of APALA, Asian Pacific American workers were virtually invisible within the labor movement.

Within the U.S. labor movement, there has been a long history of racism and exclusion toward people of color, including Asian Americans. The American labor movement was at the forefront of the racist Chinese Exclusion Act of 1882. Samuel Gompers, the first president of the American Federation of Labor, was a lifelong opponent of Chinese immigration, and also actively prevented efforts to bring Asians into American trade unions.

Even in recent decades, anti-Asian sentiment has surfaced within American unions. During the "Buy American" campaigns, we witnessed American unions encouraging workers to vent their frustrations by smashing Japanese cars. Much of the campaign literature contained racist caricatures of Asian faces. In 1982, Vincent Chin, a Chinese American in Detroit, Michigan, was killed by two unemployed white autoworkers who accused him of taking American jobs. Chin's killers were given probation and a small fine, which sparked a nationwide outcry from the Asian Pacific American community.

In spite of union policies of exclusion, Asian workers have a proud history of organizing independent unions, and in working with unions that have opened their doors to Asian workers, including the Industrial Workers of the World and later the Congress of Industrial Organizations. From Hawaiian plantation workers who built unions against tremendous obstacles, to Filipino workers who launched the historic Delano Grape Strike, to Chinese garment workers in New York City who have organized massive street demonstrations to demand their rights, Asians have contributed to a chapter of labor history that has largely been ignored.

The history of conscious exclusion was followed by a long period of benign neglect. But with the repeal of racially exclusive immigration laws in the mid 1960s, the Asian Pacific American community has grown exponentially. The 2000 census will reflect that Asian Pacific Americans number over ten million, and are no longer a community that can be ignored. Since the founding of APALA, for the first time in history there has been a conscious national focus to target Asian Pacific American workers for unionization.

The Asian Pacific Labor Alliance grew out of several local Asian labor committees in New York, San Francisco, and Los Angeles. The core leadership was largely composed of activists from the movements of the 1960s and 1970s who consciously entered the labor movement to strengthen working class solidarity.

When we first held national meetings at the AFL-CIO headquarters, it was the first time many of us had ever set foot into the building. An AFL-CIO staff person who saw us wandering in the halls inquired, "What country are they from?" The only groups of Asian visitors to the AFL-CIO headquarters had previously been labor delegations from other countries, so it was inconceivable that we were U.S. trade unionists.

APALA provided a forum for us to talk openly and honestly about problems within the U.S. labor movement and the barriers preventing Asian Americans from joining unions and moving into positions of leadership. We talked about some of the conservative leadership and policies that had kept unions out of touch with workers, and that had kept our labor movement from moving forward.

But it wasn't enough for APALA to talk about what was wrong with the labor movement. We needed to take action and move an agenda for change. At the Founding Convention of APALA, we pledged to recruit and train a new generation of Asian American union organizers, and began the task of reaching out to the millions of unorganized Asian American workers who need and want unions. APALA has recruited young Asian American activists into the labor movement. Among this dynamic network of young activists, union organizing has become popularized, and many have taken it upon themselves to reach out into their own networks and actively recruit others.

Struggles involving Asian immigrant workers and sweatshops, including the Jessica McClintock campaign and the Thai slave labor case in El Monte, California, helped to raise consciousness among Asian student activists nationally. Worker and union issues are now included on the agenda of Asian student conferences, and Asian student activists have been recruited by unions from campuses across the country. At the time of APALA's founding convention, there were only a dozen Asian American union organizers nationally. Today, thanks to a joint program with the AFL-CIO Organizing Institute, there are more than one hundred, and the numbers are growing.

Our hope is that Pride at Work will embark on a similar challenge to recruit and train new lesbian and gay labor activists and union organizers who could help to elevate lesbian and gay concerns within their unions. Within the lesbian and gay community, unions need to increase their visibility. It makes a difference to know that the union is reaching out to the lesbian and gay community, is embracing their issues, and has lesbian and gay organizers, staff, and leaders. In recent years Pride at Work in Los Angeles has organized a special labor contingent to participate in the annual Gay Pride parade, and they have been warmly received by the community.

APALA has actively recruited Asian immigrant workers into unions. As a breakthrough for the American labor movement, APALA conventions now routinely provide translation in Asian languages. We have brought together groups of Chinese, Korean, Pilipino, Southeast Asian, South Asian, and Pacific Islander immigrant workers that never before have gathered together within the American labor movement.

The labor movement can serve as an arena where the multiple identities of its members can be valued and affirmed. Unions can build unity between lesbians and gay men around issues of working-class solidarity. Unions can advocate for the interests of lesbian and gay workers of color, who may face discrimination on many levels. For the reality is that members of the LGBT community have multiple identities, as trade unionists, as women, as workers of color.

Since our founding, APALA has built coalitions that have never before existed between labor unions and the Asian American community around common concerns including worker rights, civil rights, immigrant rights, affirmative action, hate crimes, economic justice, and political power. APALA provides Asian Pacific American workers with a voice, and has emerged as an important progressive, social change organization within the Asian community.

In California, APALA has actively organized the Asian community to oppose the anti-immigrant Proposition 187, the anti-affirmative action Proposition 209, and the anti-union Proposition 226. APALA was involved nationally in the campaign to support Bill Lann Lee's confirmation fight as Assistant Attorney General for Civil Rights. APALA has also worked hard to coalesce Asian Pacific American community organizations and labor around a common civil rights agenda to defend immigrant rights and affirmative action. The key has been to leverage support from the labor movement within the

Asian Pacific American community and to leverage support from the Asian Pacific American community within the labor movement.

When APALA works within the Asian Pacific American community, we represent the strength and power of the American labor movement. Through the labor movement, we have access to dozens of major unions and political access in Washington, D.C. In statehouses across the country, we have access to resources that many community-based organizations do not. Within the Asian American community, most established organizations are dominated by professionals and small business interests. They generally will take progressive stands on civil rights but may not be knowledgeable about workers' rights. For example, APALA has raised consciousness within the Asian Pacific American community to encourage community-based organizations to use union hotels and union printers, and to respect union picket lines and boycotts.

On the other hand, APALA brings leverage from the Asian Pacific American community into the labor movement. Unions realize that they must reach out and recruit new workers. They must forge labor and community coalitions around a common agenda. Like other constituency organizations, APALA plays a crucial role as the bridge between the labor movement and the broader community. APALA provides a crucial link with the Asian Pacific community, with Asian Pacific elected officials, civil rights organizations, community-based organizations, religious groups, and students.

Within the labor movement as well, APALA also provides Asian Pacific American workers with a voice. We must advocate for policies of inclusion— to demand diverse staff that represents the members, and encourage affirmative action policies within unions. We need to ensure that translation is provided and that the cultural concerns of Asian workers are addressed so that Asians feel at home within their unions.

In 1995, the leadership of APALA joined with the other AFL-CIO constituency organizations to hold the first Full Participation Conference immediately before the AFL-CIO National Convention. Our agenda addressed the need for the leadership of the AFL-CIO to be more inclusive of people of color and women. The debate that began at the Full Participation Conference spilled over to the floor of the convention. As a direct consequence, more people of color and women were brought on to the AFL-CIO Executive Council than ever before.

Sumi Haru, then acting president of the Screen Actors Guild, became the first Asian American elected to the AFL-CIO Executive Council. Although Cesar Chavez, perhaps the best known labor leader of our generation, was never brought on to the Executive Council, his successor, Arturo Rodriguez, became the first United Farm Workers president to serve on this leadership body. Bill Lucy, Secretary Treasurer of the American Federation of State, County, and Municipal Employees and President of the Coalition of Black Trade Unionists, was also elected, along with several other African American trade unionists. Several more women labor leaders were also brought on to the Executive Council.

Educating the Asian Community on Gay and Lesbian Issues

Several years ago, the Japanese American Citizens League (JACL) was involved in a national debate on sexual orientation. The JACL chapter in Hawaii had endorsed a resolution to support legal rights for same-sex marriage, and fierce debate ensued at the national convention. Some chapters went so far as to threaten to leave the national organization if it supported same-sex marriage. During the heated discussion, a number of JACL activists spoke passionately about why it was so important for JACL as a civil rights organization to oppose discrimination against gays and lesbians. As a result of their efforts to educate others, the national organization ultimately took a position in defense of same-sex marriage. APALA needs to continue its own educational process on gay and lesbian rights within the Asian Pacific community.

From its inception, APALA has gone on record defending lesbian and gay rights in the workplace, and in opposition to all forms of homophobia. However, there is still significant work that we must do within the Asian community to address homophobia, sexism, and ethnocentrism. One significant factor that contributes to Asian Pacific attitudes toward diversity is that 70 percent of Asian Americans are immigrants, many with strong identifications to their countries of origin. Consequently, attitudes on gender and sexual orientation often reflect traditional perspectives from their native lands. Most Asian cultures historically are male dominated, and women have frequently been denied basic rights. Many Asian immigrants who have come to this country lack prior exposure to African Americans and Latinos, and problems of racial conflict and ethnocentrism exist. In certain Asian countries, homosexuality is still regarded as a psychological disorder. While biases exist among American-born Asians as well, the cultural and linguistic isolation of Asian newcomers contributes to a lack of knowledge about the gay and lesbian experience in this country. For many young Asian lesbians and gays to "come out" to their Asian immigrant parents is a daunting challenge. Many face being ostracized or disowned. Many stay in the closet for fear of the consequences.

As a labor organization, APALA has a responsibility to reach out and recruit new workers into the labor movement. At the same time, as a progressive organization for social change, APALA has a responsibility to promote broad-based education on issues of civil and human rights among Asian Pacific American workers. This includes embracing multicultural unity and opposing sexism, homophobia, and all forms of discrimination and intolerance.

As an example, in Los Angeles, the constituency groups have formed a new coalition, "United Labor Action," which is actively engaged in building alliances between our organizations. We sponsor the annual Martin Luther King Jr. breakfast, which has drawn as many as seven hundred people. We have collaborated on campaigns involving immigrant rights, voter registration and get-out-the-vote, and the fight against hate crimes. Through working together, we have also broken down barriers that historically have kept our organizations and our communities divided.

The initiative to build a gay-labor alliance is just beginning. But, with progressive changes in the American labor movement, opportunities exist now that have never existed before. Let us work together to organize the unorganized; to fight for civil and human rights; to beat back racism, sexism, and homophobia; and to build greater unity among all working people.

It All Begins with Coming Out

Desma Holcomb

How does a radical collaboration between the lesbian/gay movement and the labor movement begin? With lesbian and gay workers coming out at work and in their unions. Coming out is a necessary precondition for any joint work because unions can't collaborate with an abstraction—invisible lesbian and gay workers. Sometimes just coming out at work can be radical. It can mean physical danger, harassment, or firing. Coming out at work means taking direct action against the bigots and all those who assert, "there are no gays in this office or on this construction site, within the working class, or in the African American, Latino, or Asian communities." Getting a building trades or Southern textile local union to defend a worker's right to be out without being fired, harassed, or physically attacked can be a radical undertaking.

Sometimes it is relatively easy to come out (in big cities and at liberal worksites), but coming out as a gay rights activist in the union can nevertheless be a dramatic step. Organizing through the union for equal treatment and benefits from your employer can bring about harassment and ostracism.

Organizing within the union for gay rights solidarity can also provoke a backlash and put a gay union official's elected or staff position at risk. It takes work to move liberal coworkers and union leaders past *personal* acceptance and toward *political* collaboration. Getting straight coworkers and leaders to stand up to homophobic members and leaders in a fight for domestic-partner benefits or against an antigay ballot initiative can be a radical program. But straight allies will usually only take risks after lesbian and gay members and leaders have first put themselves on the line. It still begins with coming out.

I will cite some concrete examples from New York City lesbian and gay labor history, the history with which I am most familiar. But developments like these have been happening all over the country, as we learn whenever members of Pride at Work, the AFL-CIO constituency group for LGBT workers, share their stories.

Gay Teachers Confront Homophobic Campaign against Diversity Curriculum

Panic about lesbian and gay teachers "recruiting" or "abusing" children is one of the flashpoints for homophobia. As a result, gay teachers have organized support groups since the 1970s and union caucuses since the 1980s. By 1992, the children of lesbian and gay parents had become enough of a presence in NYC public schools that the Board of Education included a small section on gay families in its Rainbow Curriculum—most of which dealt with racial and ethnic diversity. A multiracial coalition of Christian fundamentalist parents surged into community school board meetings and onto the streets to protest the curriculum and to urge the banning of two children's books about gay families (*Heather Has Two Mommies* by Leslea Newman and *Daddy's Roommate* by Michael Willhoite). Most lesbian and gay parents in public schools were outnumbered and frightened. Queer Nation and the Lesbian Avengers counterprotested, but the young activists were neither parents nor educators and were easily tagged as "outsiders."

Opposition to the curriculum was the most ferocious in Queens District 24. In the midst of this firestorm, two teachers from that same district in Queens, a man from an elementary school and a woman from an intermediate school, came out as gay teachers. They did it at a press conference at the headquarters of the United Federation of Teachers (UFT) with then union president Sandra Feldman by their side, praising their courage. In a subsequent *New York Times* story, teacher Daniel Dromm said that the rejection of the curriculum "had created an atmosphere of intimidation and intolerance" in the district and that some children in his school have gay or lesbian parents and that classmates, even at an early age, show bias. In one case, he said, children taunted a girl because her mother was a lesbian. "And here I was as a gay teacher," he said, "and I felt that because my hands were tied by the district, I wasn't able to do as much as I really wanted to do for that child."[1]

On a personal note, as a lesbian parent of a child in a NYC public elementary school, I can attest that kids have teased her about her moms as early as second grade. Supportive teachers have been crucial to her sense of security and her ability to focus on learning.

When the political heat is on and unions still defend gay and lesbian elementary school teachers and lesbian and gay parents, that is a radical collaboration. The political ground shifted when these two teachers and their influential union faced down the bigots. The curriculum did not survive, but the teachers did. Later that year, a combination of gays and immigrants ousted the District 24 school board president, who was notorious for her anti-immigrant and homophobic statements.

Single-Payer Health Insurance and Unionizing the Gay Men's Health Crisis (GMHC)

In the 1980s, both trade unionists and AIDS activists were propelled by their concrete experiences with the U.S. health-care crisis to advocate a drastic change to national health insurance, similar to the "single-payer" system in Canada. As the number of uninsured Americans grew, the cost of providing health care to the uninsured rose dramatically. Both medical providers and insurers tried to pass along these costs by raising premiums for those with insurance. This placed double-digit premium hikes on almost every union bargaining table. Many unions became militant advocates of universal, national, nonprofit insurance to solve this problem for both union members and the millions of uninsured—most of whom were working families who fell in between Medicaid and union jobs.

At the same time, AIDS advocates were struggling against the homophobic and AIDS-phobic insurance industry policies, which guaranteed that most people with AIDS couldn't get insured or would lose coverage as soon as they got diagnosed. In the 1980s, the insurance industry refused to write policies for single men between the ages of twenty-five and forty-five and for employer group plans in stereotypically "gay" industries, such as theater companies and hairdresser shops. Companies required potential customers to take an HIV test and refused to cover those who tested positive. Even some employer plans that covered workers without HIV testing specifically excluded AIDS as a covered illness. Often, the only way to have coverage for AIDS was to stop working, get rid of all your assets, and go on Medicaid.

AIDS advocates came to the radical conclusion that a for-profit insurance industry that only wanted to cover healthy people deserved to be eliminated and replaced by national nonprofit government insurance, like the system in Canada. They preferred this to the insurance industry's alternative for cost control—managed care—because AIDS patients fiercely desired to pick their own doctors, given all the homophobia and AIDS-phobia in the health-care system at that time.

These parallel streams of support for national health insurance might never have actively worked together were it not for the network of lesbian and gay labor activists who had contacts in both movements. As an out lesbian labor activist in a union (ACTWU, now UNITE) that was part of the health-care reform coalition, I was able to introduce the leaders from these groups to each other. As a result, the unions endorsed and participated in an AIDS march during the 1992 NYC Democratic National Convention—designed to get AIDS and the overall health-care crisis onto candidate Bill Clinton's agenda.

It was radical for unions to demonstrate for a platform issue outside the Democratic National Convention—not just operate as an inside lobby. It was challenging for mostly straight trade unionists to march in a mostly gay/AIDS demonstration. They had to work through their anxieties about coworkers and onlookers assuming they were gay or had AIDS.

Dennis Rivera, the president of Local 1199 (Health and Human Services Employees Union, now in SEIU) was the labor speaker at the AIDS rally. I believe it was no coincidence that one year later the workers at GMHC, a large New York City AIDS service and advocacy agency, decided to unionize into Local 1199. It was also no coincidence that one of the burning issues in the campaign was the doubling of workers' out-of-pocket medical costs.[2] GMHC had grown from a tiny radical group of committed volunteers in 1982 into a $25.5 million operation with salaries ranging from $25,000 for caseworkers to $160,000 for the executive director in 1994. The annual limit on out-of-pocket medical costs had more than doubled to $1,300, and despite the wide spread in salaries, management had refused to implement a sliding scale suggested by workers.

Now it wasn't radical to be out as a gay worker at GMHC. But these angry workers might never have considered unionizing as a solution to their problems if they thought that unions didn't support gay rights and AIDS issues and if they didn't know any out lesbians or gays in unions. The workers were outraged when the executive director used hard-raised agency funds to pay a lawyer three hundred dollars per hour to resist their organizing. And the union–AIDS movement alliance came full circle when unions who had sponsored teams for the fund-raising GMHC AIDS Walk called the executive director to protest his expenditures on a union buster.

The executive director explicitly baited Dennis Rivera as homophobic because of his close bargaining relationship with then Cardinal John O'Connor (an opponent of GMHC on many AIDS policies). He tried to play on workers' allegiance to the AIDS and gay movement and posed it in opposition to unions' lack of commitment to gay rights. Fortunately, the gay–labor alliance made this tactic ineffective. But the union buster's delaying tactics, such as five months of hearings on unit questions, were demoralizing.

In this instance, the union drive was defeated; the union election was lost. But in Washington, D.C., San Francisco, and elsewhere, gay/labor collaboration has succeeded in unionizing AIDS and gay/lesbian community agencies. None of this would have been accomplished if lesbian and gay workers from the broader labor movement were not visible to lesbian and gay workers in these agencies.

Domestic-Partner Benefits: Radical Transformation of a Core Union Benefit

While some radical queers bemoan the "domestication" of the gay rights movement into issues of marriage, parenting, and domestic partnership, partner benefits are actually a radical transformation of one of the most classic core union benefits: family health insurance.[3] Once again, coming out is a necessary prerequisite to winning a struggle.

The first cochair of the Lesbian and Gay Issues Committee (LAGIC) of District Council 37 of AFSCME (American Federation of State, County, and Municipal Employees), Julie Schwartzberg, was in the closet for nine years in her city office job. When her lover's mother died, she attended the funeral, but told her boss and coworkers that it was an "aunt" who had died.[4] Until she and hundreds of other New York City municipal employees came out, it wasn't obvious that there was a need for domestic-partner family bereavement leave, much less insurance. Once again, the radical collaboration between lesbian/gay workers and the labor movement could only commence when these workers started coming out at work and in their unions.

It is also telling that domestic-partner benefits have never been achieved without at least one out gay or lesbian activist on the bargaining committee. In most cases, there has been a lesbian and gay caucus in the union, backing up that insider.[5] In 1993, by being out in large numbers, building alliances, and mobilizing their base, D.C. 37's LAGIC members were able to win domestic-partner benefits for the lesbian, gay, and straight partners of the city's 350,000 municipal workers. The city was the largest employer in the country to have such benefits at that time. Across the country, tens of thousands of lesbian and gay couples and their children have gained health insurance in an era of health benefit givebacks thanks to the power of the gay–labor alliance.

When unions adopt nondiscrimination policies, recognize Lesbian and Gay Pride month (June), and publicly acknowledge members with AIDS (as AFSCME did by adding an AFSCME section to the AIDS quilt), they are encouraging members, leaders, and staff to come out. They are making it possible to begin the work of radical collaboration.

Notes

1. Stephen Lee Myers, "Gay Teachers Say Board in Queens Is Intolerant," *New York Times*, September 26, 1992. Daniel Dromm has since been elected to that same school board and is an organizer of the Queens Lesbian and Gay Pride March.
2. Desma Holcomb, "AIDS Group Fights Union Organizing," *Labor Notes* (February 1994).
3. For more on this, see Desma Holcomb, "Domestic Partner Health Benefits: The Corporate Model vs. the Union Model," in *Laboring for Rights: Unions and Sexual Diversity across Nations*, ed. Gerald Hunt (Philadelphia: Temple University Press, 1999), 103–20.
4. Miriam Frank, "Pride at Work: Gay Labor Meeting Gets Warm Welcome from N.Y. AFSCME," *Labor Notes* (August 1992).
5. For more on this, see Miriam Frank, "Lesbian and Gay Caucuses in the U.S. Labor Movement," in Hunt, *Laboring for Rights*, 87–102.

Seeing the Links between Labor Rights and Gay Rights

Barney Frank

When I entered politics full time in the late 1960s, one of the most serious problems facing people who cared about fairness, social justice, and people's rights was the split that had developed between organized labor and many Democratic liberals. One of the most optimistic aspects of progressive politics in the 1990s is that this split has healed, and I am therefore delighted to contribute to this collection of essays about cooperation between those active in vindicating the rights of working men and women and those committed to other parts of the fairness agenda. That is, people who have opposed union-busting legislation put forward by the congressional Republicans are almost always the same members of Congress who oppose antigay riders to the District of Columbia appropriations bill; those who support raising the minimum wage overlap substantially with those who voted against a Republican effort to cancel President Clinton's executive order protecting federal workers from discrimination based on their sexual orientation.

In the current political context, and for the foreseeable future, there are very strong reasons for those fighting against homophobia to work closely with organized labor, and I am pleased that I can report that in the Congress such efforts are already a fact. When I introduced legislation in 1997 to provide domestic-partner benefits for federal employees, I worked closely with representatives of the federal employee unions and I was delighted to be able to appear at a press conference with their strong support for this concept.[1] And the large vote we received in 1996 for the Employment Non-Discrimination Act (ENDA), which outlaws job discrimination against gay men, lesbians, and bisexuals, came about in part because of the support it received from the AFL-CIO.

Conversely, the importance of showing gay, lesbian, and bisexual support for the rights of working men and women to bargain collectively and be treated fairly in the workplace was one of the motivating forces when we formed the National Stonewall Democratic Federation, linking gay, lesbian, and bisexual oriented Democratic clubs across the country into a national organization that explicitly affirms both gay rights and the broader agenda of social justice, of which the rights of working people are such an important part. In many cases, gay and lesbian union members are leaders in these Democratic clubs, and several unions have, at the request of their own gay and lesbian members, made contributions to the federation.

Indeed, the cooperation goes far deeper than these specific examples, and if one analyzes the membership of Congress today and over the past fifteen years, one sees a critical datum: there is a very high correlation between members of Congress who support the rights of labor, and those who fight against homophobia.

It is possible for people to argue, with regard to the set of issues pushed by organized labor and the issues that most concern gay, lesbian, and bisexual people, that they are different. I think they have more in common than not, but whatever one thinks about the intellectual point here, the key political fact is that the two sets of issues tend very strongly to have the same friends and the same enemies. While I have not had a chance to do the statistics, I know from my experience that there is a strong positive correlation between Congress members' AFL-CIO voting records and their voting records ranked by the Human Rights Campaign. It is certainly the case that the right wing, which has sadly become increasingly dominant within the Republican Party, regards both organized labor and gay, lesbian, and bisexual citizens as enemies, and works hard to defeat people who are supportive of the concerns of either group. And while there are corporate elements who in their sphere have been supportive of gay and lesbian rights—one of the striking aspects of the contemporary American scene is the extent to which gay, lesbian, and bisexual rights are recognized by corporations in the information technology field—when it comes to politics, most business money goes to support conservatives because they will work to weaken OSHA, undercut collective bargaining rights, oppose minimum wage increases, and push for tax cuts that disproportionately benefit the wealthy. And while homophobia may well not be the motivation for the corporate sector's selection of candidates, the result is that the overwhelming majority of those conservatives who follow their economic agenda also strongly oppose ENDA, fight domestic-partner legislation, and block hate crimes protection for gays, lesbians, bi-sexuals, and the transgendered.

A failure to recognize this important fact is one of the major differences I have with those gay rights organizations that obsess about appearing non-partisan. It is one thing to begin with a determination not to be swayed by partisan considerations and to announce one's commitment to judge solely according to what is best for the rights of gay, lesbian, and bisexual people. It is quite another—and severely mistaken—to refuse to recognize that in our current climate, there is de facto a partisan aspect to the fight against homophobia. At the national level, and in virtually every state, the Republican party leadership is increasingly conservative and hostile to gay and lesbian rights. Conversely, the national Democratic congressional leadership is strongly supportive of most of the items important to gay, lesbian, and bisexual people, and the same is true at the state level. This does not mean that gay and lesbian rights organizations ought to ignore those Republicans who are supportive. It does mean that they make a grave error when they ignore the fact that it makes an enormous difference in our ability to fight for our rights successfully whether the Democrats or the Republicans are in control. The Republicans have refused to allow ENDA to come to a vote in the House, where the leadership can tightly control the agenda. Congressman Richard Gephardt, by contrast, has promised that if he becomes speaker, he will bring it up and believes we can pass it. A similar contrast applies to a number of other issues—for example, protecting gay, lesbian, bisexual, and transgendered people against violent hate crimes—and beginning the process of addressing domestic partnership questions.

I stress that here because exactly the same considerations apply to the issues important to organized labor. Indeed, gay and lesbian organizations would do well to pay attention to the way the AFL-CIO approaches politics. The AFL-CIO is aware that the issues they care about for working people will be far better treated if the Democrats control the important leadership posts and committee chairmanships in Congress than if the Republicans do. So in general, the AFL-CIO tries to advance Democratic control of the Congress. But they also recognize that they will need Republican votes to pass much of their agenda, and therefore when individual Republicans show strong support for the rights of working men and women, the AFL-CIO supports them. This is the appropriate response to those issues that in our current climate are ideological in nature.

There are two sorts of issues in the legislative context today. One set deals with issues that are largely economic and usually relate to the fortunes of a particular industry or sector of the economy. These are in fact quite often rather nonideological and nonpartisan, and where a specific economic sector is concerned, these issues often bring together liberals and conservatives, Democrats and Republicans, labor and business. Agricultural issues, the needs of the textile and garment industries, fair treatment for American steel—these are subjects where it may make very little difference which party is in power, and where an individual's position on a particular issue will be governed far more by his or her geography than by ideology. These are the interests around which much Washington lobbying is organized—steel, real estate, corn, dairy, and so forth. The mistake some of the gay rights organizations make is to use this sort of lobbying as the model, scrupulously avoiding any indication of a preference for one party or the other. One of the things that ties both the cause of organized labor and the fight for gay and lesbian rights together is that they are both of the other type of issue—those that come as part of a general ideological mindset. It is, of course, philosophically possible for people to be opposed to discrimination based on sexual orientation and hate unions. My point is not that this is inconceivable, but that it is, in our current climate, extremely rare. In American politics today, people who support the rights of working men and women are much likelier than those who oppose those rights also to support strong action to prevent racial discrimination and legislative efforts against homophobia. While I agree that it is not intellectually required that people who believe in any one of these believe in all of them, neither do I think that it is purely random that they are so closely linked in fact. All show a willingness to support government action to promote fairness in our society. All recognize that there are unfairnesses and prejudices built into the world we live in that work to the disadvantage of various groups of people, and that absent appropriate government policies, some people will be unfairly disadvantaged, either because of their lack of ability to defend themselves in the workplace or because of inadequate incomes, racial prejudice, or homophobia.

Among the strongest links here are those that join people who have good voting records on gay and lesbian rights and those who have good voting records on the issues of primary concern to working men and women and those who represent them. Part of our job is simply to publicize this better. There are people in both groups—gays, lesbians, and bisexuals on the one hand, and union members or potential union members on the other—who do not realize how closely linked their causes are in fact in Congress; who do not realize that the champions of their particular cause are also highly likely to be champions of the others' cause as well; and who do not fully realize that those who oppose their effort to vindicate their own rights are equally committed opponents of the rights of the other group.

Not surprisingly, those who believe in a strict laissez-faire approach in which we count on an unrestrained capitalism to take care of us all have reason to oppose both minimum wage laws and ENDA. To them, the owners of capital have the right to discriminate on any grounds they wish, including sexual orientation, and also have the right to fire anyone with the temerity to seek to organize a union. On the other hand, there are those of us who support a free market system as the best way to create wealth, but understand, as Franklin Roosevelt made clear, that an unrestrained capitalism will also be an unfair one, and that it is important, if we are to vindicate the values we believe in, that government play a role in protecting people who would otherwise be victimized by private-sector forces. Of course there are times when the duty of believers in freedom and fairness is to protect people against government oppression. But there is also an important role to be played by the government in protecting individuals against unfairness that can come from concentrated power in the private sector, and it is recognition of this latter point that makes elected officials and the voters who support them likely to be advocates both of the rights of gay men and lesbians and of organized labor.

One of the questions I was asked to address is where a collaboration between these two groups might begin. As I've said, my answer is that it is well begun, and that our job is both to build on it, and to make it explicit. I do not claim that this will always be the case. Indeed, my hope is that homophobia will fade in our society—just as I have seen anti-Semitism fade as a significant factor in American society during my lifetime—and if things go as they should, the need to fight for the rights of gay men and lesbians will not be a factor decades from now. This is, of course, not true with regard to organized labor. Because there will always be a tension between employers and the employed, there will always be a need for unions to represent the workers who would otherwise individually be solely at the mercy of their employers. But as long as this society continues to be plagued by homophobia, there will be strong practical, intellectual, and moral ties between those who fight for fairness in the workplace on economic grounds, and those who fight against unfair discrimination and for fairness both in the workplace and out. That alliance already exists among elected officials, and part of our job is to publicize it, explain it, and in the process of doing these things, broaden it, deepen it, and strengthen it.

Note

1. The bill, the Domestic Partnership Benefits and Obligations Act, was H.R. 2761. Unfortunately, the Republicans controlling Congress would not even allow it to get a hearing and it died in committee. I reintroduced it in 1999; it was H.R. 2859.

Afterword

Lisa Duggan

I had a dream about the twenty-first century. Actually, it was a nightmare. In it there were two worlds; I had to choose between them. One world, called The Left, operated smoothly and efficiently, its population officially Unified around the Universal Progressive Agenda. The Agenda was posted everywhere, signed by the Universal Visionaries. I don't remember all the names, but I think I saw Richard Rorty, Todd Gitlin, Eric Alterman. There were women and people of color—even a few queers—on all the Universal Welfare Committees, but everyone had learned the error of divisiveness from the teachings of the Visionaries (who were only incidentally all straight, white, and male—I think there was a woman, too, but I couldn't find her name), so there were none of those "identity" caucuses that had destroyed the twentieth-century Left.

The other world, The Gay Movement, was also very well run, and additionally very well dressed. Having overcome the infantilism and hedonism of twentieth century LGBT/Queer Liberation, this world based its operations on personal responsibility and maturity, or more specifically on business principles. Emphasizing the central importance of Marriage and Military Service to Public Life, The Gay Movement world devoted the remainder of its political efforts to sales and marketing. Under the banners Advertising Equals Access and A Dollar Is A Vote, the Responsible Leadership addressed The Donor Base through announcements in the very democratically distributed *USA Today*. There were very few names mentioned, but occasionally I could make out Andrew Sullivan, Chandler Burr, Elizabeth Birch.

This dystopic dream went on and on. I couldn't shake it. I started thinking that wandering back and forth between one nightmare world and the other had become my life. Then I woke up, a copy of *Out at Work* in my hands. This volume had finally jolted me awake—relieved and excited to find other worlds, other visions, animating the past, present, and possible futures of progressive politics.

Out at Work offers us crucial information and sharp analyses about the relations between workplace organizing and queer politics—the collaborations, impasses, missed opportunities, and significant new horizons. But perhaps even more importantly, it provides substantial cause for sorely needed optimism. I think it's worth recapping and highlighting at least six areas in which the essays collected here show us how to see possibilities, and find where to build a multi-issue radically democratic politics:

1. History. Kitty Krupat's essay, "Out of Labor's Dark Age," counters the tale of the decline of the left since the 1960s, offered to us by legions of nostalgic New Leftists and "pragmatic" neoliberals who wish to put "identity politics" aside and themselves front and center. Krupat argues persuasively and compellingly that new social movements have kept the left alive, laying the basis for (among other things) a reinvigorated labor movement in the 1990s. Krupat is seconded by John Sweeney. In "The Growing Alliance between Gay and Union Activists," he points specifically to a series of stunning successes of union/gay movement collaborations beginning with the campaign against the Briggs initiative in California during the 1970s. This revisionist history maps a difference and makes a difference in thinking about progressive politics now.

2. Unions. Nikhil Singh and Amber Hollibaugh's call for a new social unionism for the 1990s ("Sexuality, Labor, and the New Trade Unionism") rings a loud clear bell, calling us to reimagine the union movement, not as merely a Workers' Lobby, but as a site for political transformation, for a new culture of life and labor that might encompass the wide range of issues that matter to working people today. The discussion among union activists in "Homophobia, Labor's Last Frontier?" shows that struggles over workplace cultures are happening now, and might be expanded rather than squelched as divisive by defensive or frightened union leadership. Heidi Kooy ("Trollops and Tribades: Queers Organizing in the Sex Business") and Andrew Ross ("Strike a Pose for Justice: The Barneys Union Campaign of 1996") describe the difference that queer-inflected cultures can make in organizing two widely differing workplaces. Nothing could matter more, as this volume goes to press, than whether the revitalization of workplace organizing occurring today can mobilize transformative political energies, or only recruit members to strengthen wage and hour negotiations. The inclusion of queer cultures and issues of sexuality in union discussions and actions is one kind of bellwether at this crossroads.

3. Social Movement Organizations. Cathy Cohen, in "What Is This Movement Doing to My Politics?" provocatively argues that social movement organizations representing excluded or deprived populations have too often come to represent the class politics of the most privileged members of those groups. Urvashi Vaid lays out the class tensions and specific political conflicts within the mainstream gay movement today ("Getting There Means Mapping Here"), confirming Cohen's call for new organizational forms. But wait, there's more! Cohen also reminds us that we have already begun to build alternative progressive political institutions—the Audre Lorde Project, the Black Radical Congress, the Esperanza Peace and Justice Center—that are busy imagining political realignments and organizing resource redistributions as you read this afterword.

4. Electoral and Legislative Politics. Between the probusiness conservatism of the NLRB, the widespread support for the Defense of Marriage Act, and the appearance of a Reform Party that is anything but reform-minded . . . this landscape doesn't generate optimism easily. But Pat McCreery, Kitty Krupat, and Riki Anne Wilchins offer us some hope nonetheless. In their discussions of the politics of the Employment Non-Discrimination Act ("Beyond Gay: 'Deviant' Sex and the Politics of the ENDA Workplace" and "Conversations with a GenderQueer"), they offer provocative ways of thinking about how identity-based antidiscrimination legislation works—to close down as well as open up horizons of political inclusion and cultural invention. They also emphasize that democratic process may be more important than immediate legislative success—thus challenging the top-down operations of nearly all of our progressive legislative and lobbying organizations.

5. The Cultural Front. Tami Gold's fancifully titled "Making Out At Work" offers a riveting account of what a left/queer cultural producer is up against—funding strictures, time squeezes, distribution constraints, political attacks. Ouch. But with a keen sense of humor and attunement to paradox, Gold's essay takes us through the perilous obstacle course on the road, in this case, to stunning successes. That *Out At Work* was finally aired for millions of viewers on HBO rather than PBS tells us how uneven the landscape of commercial opportunity and state/nonprofit support can be, and how necessary it is to make inroads on all cultural fronts.

6. Academic/Activist Connections. The existence of this volume, and the conference that generated it, constitute an effective intervention against the bifurcation of inaccessible, smugly elitist, left academic scholarship on the one hand, and anti-intellectual, self-righteously moralizing "community" (whatever that is) activism on the other. Another nightmare-world pairing averted! In these pages, a conversation among variously located intellectual activists proceeds productively—though not with the smooth Unity that chills rather than promotes democratic change!

What, then, do we learn as we step out of the nightmare of a well-run, top-down, efficiently pragmatic because closed-down and carefully contained progressive movement, and into the dream of a more contentious but potentially transformative politics? What do we learn specifically from the essays in *Out at Work*? I think we learn that current strategies of containment in

U.S. political culture—antidemocratic strategies across the left, right, and center of the political spectrum—mobilize arguments for the *reprivatization* of the lives and issues of huge segments of the population. There is a broad call for normative, respectable representations of constituencies and issues—*including on the left, and in gay politics*. These normative, respectable worlds of enforced Unity, Maturity, and Pragmatic Efficiency are nothing like any left or queer movement I ever imagined. They define either a faux, faintly authoritarian populism or a narrow elitism, founded on cultural conformity and exclusion; they make my nightmares. The writers in this volume reach back to other visions of the left, from 1930s social unionism to 1960s gay liberation and counterculture inclusiveness, not to posit unitary utopias, but to locate resources for a more promiscuously public, cantankerously democratic, libidinously imaginative, prolifically creative, compellingly attractive politics of freedom, equality, and justice. In other words, to define something worth living for.

Contributors

Cathy J. Cohen is associate professor of political science and African-American studies at Yale University. She is the author of *Boundaries of Blackness: AIDS and the Breakdown of Black Politics* and has been active in progressive organizing projects, including the Audre Lorde Project and the Black Radical Congress.

Teresa Conrow works on the organizing of campaigns with unions in North America, Central America, South America, Australia, and New Zealand. She is the program director of the Labor Center at Los Angeles Trade-Technical Community College and has written widely on organizing, labor education, and strategic campaigns. She was a founding cochair of Pride at Work.

Lisa Duggan is a journalist, activist, teacher, and writer. She teaches queer studies and the history of gender and sexuality in the American Studies program at New York University. She is the author of *Sapphic Slashers: Sex, Violence, and American Modernity* and the coauthor (with Nan D. Hunter) of *Sex Wars: Sexual Dissent and Political Culture*.

William Fletcher Jr. is assistant to the president of the AFL-CIO. He has held numerous leadership posts in the labor movement, including director of education for the AFL-CIO and director of education and field services for the Service Employees International Union (SEIU). He is a founding member of the Black Radical Congress.

Barney Frank is a Democrat who represents a suburb of Boston in the U.S. House of Representatives.

Tami Gold is a filmmaker whose documentaries include *Another Brother* (broadcast nationally on PBS in 1999); two versions of *Out at Work*, coproduced with Kelly Anderson (the second version, *Out at Work: America Undercover*, premiered on HBO in 1999); and *Juggling Gender: Politics, Sex, and Identity*, which premiered at the 1992 New York Film Festival. A professor of film and media studies at Hunter College, Gold is a union delegate to the CUNY Professional Staff Congress.

Yvette Herrera is the assistant to the executive vice president of the Communication Workers of America (CWA). She has also been the director of education and mobilization for CWA, with a special interest in diversity within the labor movement.

Desma Holcomb is Deputy Director of Policy and Research for Local 32B-J of the Service Employees International Union (SEIU) and a founder of the Lesbian and Gay Labor Network. She was a first national cochair of Pride at Work. With her domestic partner, Miriam Frank, she is the coauthor of the organizing handbook *Pride at Work: Organizing for Lesbian and Gay Rights in Unions.*

Amber Hollibaugh is an organizer, filmmaker, and writer. Her film about women's sexuality and AIDS, *The Heart of the Matter,* won the Sundance Freedom of Expression Award in 1994. She is the author of *My Dangerous Desires.*

Gloria Johnson is a founding member and current president of the Coalition of Labor Union Women (CLUW). She is the director of social action for the International Union of Electronic, Electrical, Salaried, Machine, and Furniture Workers (IUE) and a vice president of the AFL-CIO. She has taught at her alma mater, Howard University.

Tamara L. Jones is a Ph.D. candidate in political science at Yale University, where she was active in the graduate student union organizing campaign. She is a member of the Black Radical Congress and works with the Audre Lorde Project. She is a contributor to *Dangerous Liaisons: Blacks, Gays, and the Struggle for Equality* and *Women Transforming Politics: An Alternative Reader.*

Heidi M. Kooy holds a master's degree in social and cultural anthropology from the California Institute of Integral Studies. She has worked as a dancer during the past ten years and has been a labor activist for the Exotic Dancers Union at the Lusty Lady Theater in San Francisco for over two years.

Kitty Krupat is a doctoral candidate in the American Studies program at New York University, a union organizer, and a labor educator. She is a contributor to *No Sweat: Fashion, Free Trade, and the Rights of Garment Workers,* edited by Andrew Ross.

Patrick McCreery is a doctoral candidate in the American Studies program at New York University and a member of GSOC–UAW, NYU's graduate student union.

Andrew Ross is professor and director of the American Studies program at New York University. A frequent contributor to *The Nation, Village Voice,* and *Artforum,* he is also the author of *The Celebration Chronicles, Real Love, The Chicago Gangster Theory of Life, Strange Weather,* and *No Respect.* He is the editor of several books as well, including *No Sweat: Fashion, Free Trade, and the Rights of Garment Workers.*

Van Alan Sheets was the associate director of political action for the American Federation of State, County, and Municipal Employees (AFSCME). He was co–vice chair of Pride at Work, a national organization of lesbian, gay, bisexual, and transgender union members, affiliated with the AFL-CIO. He died in October 1999.

Nikhil Pal Singh is assistant professor of history at the University of Washington, Seattle. As a graduate student organizer at Yale University, he served on the staff of the Hotel Employees and Restaurant Employees union (HERE). He is the author of *Color and Democracy in the American Century* and the coeditor of *Rethinking Black Marxism.*

John J. Sweeney is president of the AFL-CIO and a former president of the Service Employees International Union (SEIU). He is the author of *America Needs a Raise: Fighting for Economic Security and Social Justice.*

Jeff Truesdell is editor of the alternative *Orlando Weekly* and has frequently written on Gay Day and other matters involving Disney. He previously was a reporter for *The Miami Herald* and the *Columbia (Mo.) Daily Tribune.*

Urvashi Vaid is a community organizer and attorney who serves as the director of the Policy Institute of the National Gay and Lesbian Task Force, the national LGBT think tank based in New York City. She is author of *Virtual Equality: The Mainstreaming of Gay and Lesbian Liberation* and is a frequent commentator and writer on social justice and LGBT issues.

Riki Anne Wilchins is executive director of GenderPAC, a national nonprofit organization devoted to pursuing gender, affectional, and racial equality. She is also author of *Read My Lips: Sexual Subversion and the End of Gender.*

Kent Wong is director of the UCLA Center for Labor Research and Education. He was the founding president of the AFL-CIO Asian Pacific American Labor Alliance from 1992 to 1997.

Permissions